The Garden of Love:
Mystical Symbolism in Layla Majnun & Gita Govinda

Every aspect of the culture not only expresses the ethnic genius of that human collectivity but carries the spiritual fragrance of the Revelation which is its wellspring. The work at hand deals with two twelfth century mystical poems, one Persian, one Indian: *The Story of Layla Majnun* and *The Gita Govinda* (or *Love Song of the Dark Lord*), attributed respectively to Nizami and Jayadeva.

The Garden of Love:
Mystical Symbolism in Layla Majnun & Gita Govinda

NIZAMI & JAYADEVA

by

LALITA SINHA

New Age Books

THE GARDEN OF LOVE: MYSTICAL SYMBOLISM IN LAYLA MAJNUN & GITA GOVINDA

ISBN: 978-81-7822-374-2

First Indian Edition: Delhi, 2011

P.O. Box 2682, Bloomington, IN 47402, USA
www.worldwisdom.com

Library of Congress Cataloging-in-Publication Data

Sinha, Lalita

The Garden of Love: Mystical Symbolism in Layla Majnun & Gita Govinda /by Lalita Sinha; foreword by Harry Oldmeadow.

p. cm.—(The Perennial Philosophy Series)

Includes bibliographical references and Index

ISBN 978-81-7822-374-2 (pbk.: alk. paper)

1. Nizami Ganjavi, 1140 or 41-1202 or 3. Layli van Majnun. 2. Jayadeva, 12th cent. Gitagovinda. 3. Mysticism in Literature. 4. Love in Literature. I. Title.

PK6501.L33S52 2008 808.8'03543–dc22 2008025019

Published by

NEW AGE BOOKS

A-44, Naraina Industrial Area, Phase-I
New Delhi (India)-110 028
Email: nab@vsnl.in
Website: www.newagebooksindia.com

For Sale in India and Indian Subcontinent

Printed in India
at Shri Jainendra Press
A-45 Naraina Indl. Area, Phase-I, New Delhi-110 028

To

the memory of
Shaykh Abu Bakr Siraj ad-Din
who lived the Way
&
beloved
Sri Swami Damodaranandaji Maharaj
who lights the Way

Proof that man is not of this world

CONTENTS

LIST OF FIGURES

FOREWORD

It is sometimes forgotten that the wisdom of the ages is enshrined not only in the Scriptures of the integral traditions, and in the exegetical, theological and metaphysical works of the great doctors and sages but in the variegated expressive forms of any traditional culture—music, dance, costume, poetry, painting, and architecture, to name but a few. The animating principle of any traditional civilization shines forth from a Revelation which irradiates every aspect of life of the people in question. In such a world there is no fundamental distinction between "religion" and the rest of life, and there is no cultural production which lies altogether outside the ambit of religion. Every aspect of the culture not only expresses the ethnic genius of that human collectivity but carries the spiritual fragrance of the Revelation which is its wellspring.

The work at hand deals with two twelfth century mystical poems, one Persian, one Indian: *The Story of Layla Majnun* and *The Gitagovinda* (or *Love Song of the Dark Lord*), attributed respectively to Nizami and Jayadeva. It is one of the achievements of this study that the author wells understands that such texts are *traditional* works—which is to say, works in which the "author" is not intent on some idiosyncratic self-expression but acts rather as a medium through which the tradition itself is expressed. And by "tradition" we mean something which encompasses but infinitely surpasses those continuities referred to by modern scholars in terms such "the literary tradition" or "the tradition of philosophical thought." One is here really speaking of a whole spiritual universe. Through the timeless stories of Layla and Majnun, and Radha and Krishna, *Unveiling the Garden of Love* takes us deep into the medieval worlds of Islam and Hinduism.

Frithjof Schuon has remarked that "sacred art... is made at the same time for God, for angels, and for man; profane art on the other hand exists only for man and by that fact betrays him." In any traditional culture we will find works of varying degrees of "sacredness," if one might use such an awkward formulation, but we will be hard-pressed indeed to find any art (in the full amplitude of that term) which is altogether profane—that is to say, any art entirely devoid of a vertical or spiritual dimension. And so it is with the works with which this book is concerned; on the face of it they are love stories of a very human kind. But we need not penetrate the text to any great depth to realize that they are profound allegories of the journey of the soul back to God, as indeed are so many traditional narratives. To treat such texts as *only* literary works would betoken our ignorance.

Gai Eaton has remarked of the modern world in general that "our ignorance of the few things that matter is as prodigious as our knowledge of trivialities." The force of this appalling observation is nowhere more apparent than in modern academia. The traditional principle of *adaequatio* affirms that the mode of knowing must be adequate to that which is known. Modern scholarly treatments of traditional texts all too often violate this principle, sometimes in quite flagrant, impudent and impious fashion. We are confronted with the unhappy spectacle of the contemporary scholar, impervious to the spiritual dimensions of the work at hand, strait-jacketing it into the sterile categories of modern thought. No such scholarly enterprise, no matter how prodigious the research nor how ingenious the treatment, can do justice to those dimensions of the text which deal with domains of Reality beyond the reach of an irreligious mentality. A vast labor is often expended in the analysis of just those aspects of the text which are quite marginal to its central purpose. Such scholars need reminding that a thing not worth doing, is not worth doing well! For a conspicuous example of this sort of thing look no further than the recent academic treatment of the Homeric texts where the religious and metaphysical aspects of these works either altogether escape the attention of the scholar or are relegated to the periphery. None of these reproaches can be leveled at the author of *Unveiling the Garden of Love*; Lalita Sinha observes the rigorous protocols of modern scholarship without being captive to the assumptions and attitudes which these days tyrannize much of the Western academy. She is certainly not victim of what René Guénon calls that "passion for research taken as an end in itself... [which is] 'mental restlessness' without end and without issue." No, in her own words, the author has her sights firmly set on "that which lies beyond words" and "That which should not be forsaken."

That the imagery of erotic love is one of the staples of mystical literature is a fact too well known to need any laboring here. But to understand how and why it is so is to understand the nature of traditional symbolism—again, a task often beyond the capacities of the modern researcher. The author of the present volume explicates the true nature of the multivalent symbols which pervade these mystical allegories. Traditional symbols, let it be said, should never be confused with the arbitrary and "flat" sign-systems which so clutter the modern world. To put it as simply as possible, a symbol is a material entity which by its nature participates analogically in a higher order of reality, and is thus a bridge between the different planes of the Real. This is also to say that no traditional symbolism can be understood without a degree of metaphysical discernment. (For readers who may be uncertain about the terms "mystical" and "metaphysical," Schuon has put the matter in a nutshell: "'metaphysical': concerning universal realities considered objectively; 'mystical': concerning the same realities considered subjectively, that is, in relation to the contemplative soul.") In the present case one might refer particularly to the metaphysical acuity needed to grasp the interrelations of Truth, Beauty and Goodness, a nexus that has been torn asunder in the modern world—one need only think, for instance, of the provincial and horizontal manner in which a corrosive modern "philosophy" deals with the etiolated and self-contained 'fields' of epistemology, aesthetics and ethics.

This book offers the reader an exegesis of traditional texts which makes some use of contemporary modes of literary analysis but goes well beyond them to grasp these works in their own terms. This is much easier said than done. Furthermore, the comparison of the two texts is more than the sum of the two parts: the author's fine-grained commentary not only explicates the texts but each is made to illuminate the other. The symbolic music of "the garden of love" resonates with all manner of spiritual leitmotiv—the relationship of human and divine love, the path of *bhakti*, self-surrender, separation and union, holy inebriation, and many other contrapuntal themes dealing with the mysterious alchemy of the soul. In the course of her inquiries the author necessarily ranges far and wide in considering the religious and cultural milieu in which these texts appeared, as well as giving scrupulous attention to textual particularities. She displays both erudition and sensitivity in dealing with cultural context, language, literary convention and genre, whilst at the same time realizing that an understanding of such factors is auxiliary to the central task of expounding not only the literary features but, insofar as is possible, the spiritual *meaning* of these texts—a meaning which is actually inexhaustible if one truly understands the nature of traditional myth, symbol and allegory.

As Mircea Eliade remarked in *The Quest*, many scholars dealing with religious and spiritual subjects "defend themselves against the messages with which their documents are filled. This caution is understandable. One does not live with impunity in intimacy with 'foreign' religious forms.... But many historians of religion end by no longer taking seriously the spiritual worlds they study; they fall back on their personal religious faith, or they take refuge in a materialism or behaviorism impervious to every spiritual shock." Not so in the present case. It is to the author's credit that she approaches *The Story of Layla Majnun* and the *Gitagovinda*, and the traditional understandings of these mystical narratives, precisely in order to understand these "spiritual worlds" and the "messages" of these texts. In brief, she wants not only to learn *about* these texts but to learn *from* them.

It is a melancholy fact that the modern university is now largely ruled by a secular ethos and, under the aegis of so-called "scientific" ideals, given over to the accumulation of a profane "knowledge" which deserves no such name. Nonetheless a handful of scholars continue to labor in the vineyard well into the night, realizing that all "research," all intellectual effort (and for that matter all "art") should be directed to its proper ends—to support the spiritual wayfarer, to nurture wisdom and for the greater glory of God. *Unveiling the Garden of Love* draws freely and fruitfully on the work of distinguished traditionalist authors such as René Guénon, Frithjof Schuon, Ananda Coomaraswamy, Seyyed Hossein Nasr, Martin Lings, and Titus Burckhardt, familiar to students of the *sophia perennis.* What a scandal that their names should so rarely appear in works of modern scholarship! Readers will also find in these pages reference to the work of Eastern pundits and Western writers who have resisted the debilitating effects of a profane ideal of "scholarship"—one may mention such names as Kathleen Raine, Annemarie Schimmel, William Chittick, and S.N. Dasgupta. But the real distinction of the book lies in the author's handling of the materials she has drawn from various quarters, and in the way that these mystical works have been "taken to heart."

None of the remarks above should mislead the reader into supposing that this is an arcane work, fit only for the specialist. Certainly *Unveiling the Garden of Love* will command the close attention and appreciation of scholars. It bids fair to become the standard work on its particular subject. But, by its very nature, mysticism is concerned with the human condition, with our deepest intuitions and yearnings, with that Reality which lies both in the innermost recesses of "the cave of the heart" and infinitely beyond the highest heavens. These are matters which concern every spiritual seeker. The present work offers a very pleasing blend of real scholarship and metaphysical insight. It is also an invitation to a richer spiritual life in which we might yet once again find the First Beloved.

Harry Oldmeadow
Bendigo University

PREFACE

This book is a labor of love. As a comparative study of two masterpieces of literary expression, based on what was initially a PhD research, attention is directed at unveiling similarities and differences of mystical significance between Nizami's *The Story of Layla Majnun* and *The Gitagovinda of Jayadeva: Love Song of the Dark Lord.* The study is conducted on theoretical constructs of Hermeneutics, guided by traditional norms and conventions of Persian and Sanskrit literary expression, and informed by the Traditionalist perspective of religion. These considerations represent the platform for the understanding and interpretation of elements or phenomena in the texts as symbolic expressions of the Sufi and Bhakti mystico-religious traditions.

At the level of literary expression, the study is a focus on the saga of love between two human characters in the Persian work, Layla and Majnun and between a human and divine figura in the Indian work, Radha and Krishna. Beyond this level, an esoteric perspective of Love is considered. This perspective contends that the depiction of human love is symbolic, allegoric, anagogic, and ontological. Accordingly the parallels between the texts are considered in terms of the love between the human soul and God, or the mystical connection.

The attempt to unveil the mystical symbolism of "The Garden of Love" in the individual texts, is based on three major themes, representing cyclical or returning stages of the spiritual Quest. The Quest refers to a process of transformation of the lover, from the human, worldly and materialistic modes of existence, to the divine, celestial and spiritual modes, involving much trial and tribulation. In this context, the first stage or theme is of love in union which also inheres impending separation. Next is the stage of love in separation which involves pain and suffering, as well as pleasure and joy. The final stage, that of love in reunion, represents the end of the journey or the ultimate spiritual station, from which there is no return.

The study finds not only a wealth of common elements, but also shared truths and experiences of the two great mystico-religious traditions represented by the texts in question. Despite the fact that they originate from two apparently diverse cultural and geographical milieus, and employ apparently different forms of expression, there is essentially a relatively high level of equivalence and correspondence at the level of literary phenomena, as well as in the spiritual dimensions of poetry. Thus, the study of phenomenal elements that are different leads to noumenal correspondences and parallels. Ultimately, the works attest to the dictum, Many Paths, One Goal, an idea expressed in identical images by Rumi as "The roads are different, the goal is one" and by Krishna as "All paths lead to me."

I gratefully acknowledge the support of several people. Foremost is Professor Md. Salleh Yaapar who was my Supervisor and Holder of the European Chair of Malay Studies at the International Institute for Asian Studies, Leiden. He is indeed a true teacher who first beckoned me into the "comparative world," and his invaluable guidance, support and suggestions have molded the course of my intellectual and academic development. It is a great honor to express my highest esteem for Sri Swami Damodaranandaji Maharaj and Shaykh Abu Bakr Siraj ad-Din, custodians of their individual spiritual traditions. The momentous transformational encounters, and my profound reverence for each of them have an indelible influence upon this research.

I would like to acknowledge the help of those who have given generously of their time and shared their opinion. Particularly, I wish to mention Abrahim H. Khan, Patrick Laude, Barry McDonald, Ali Lakhani, Vladimir Braginsky, Shakila Manan, Kalpana Ponniah, and P. K. Das.

The patience and sacrifice of my husband, Kumar and the unfailing love of my children, Nisha and Roshen, have given me much comfort. My cherished brother Bijon, my much valued "devil's advocate" Richard, and my fellow travelers, Zailan and Jamil have given me the wherewithal to cope with the tremendous challenges, both academic and personal, I have faced during the course of this research. Last and most important, the infinite grace and loving presence of That which has made every effort possible and every moment worthwhile. *Tat Tvam Asi.*

Prologue

There is no love
but for the First Friend
whose naked glory you hide
under hundreds of veils

Annemarie Schimmel, *Nightingales Under the Snow*, 1997

CHAPTER ONE
UNVEILING THE GARDEN OF LOVE

... whose naked glory you hide
under hundreds of veils.

—Annemarie Schimmel

The Issue at Hand

Man's mystical experience, which is a direct experience of the Divine Presence in the here and now, has been said to be a state which surpasses human understanding or description. Yet, throughout the ages, this experience has been expressed through diverse forms of sacred and traditional art. Thus art functions as a vehicle for expressing the mystical experience. Frithjof Schuon (2003) says that all traditional art belongs in some way or other to the ritual domain, and that art is

> ... a projection of truth and beauty in the world of forms; it is *ipso facto* a projection of archetypes.... It means concentration, a way back to God.... The archetypes of sacred art are celestial inspirations; all other artworks draw their inspiration from the spiritual personality of the artist.

Of all the artistic forms of expression, poetry, specifically that of a mystical nature, plays a central role. In the same way that music is the vehicle, or medium of expression for the musician, and paint the medium for the artist, so is language the medium for the writer. Through this medium, mystical and metaphysical poets and writers have produced abundant and eloquent works extolling their spiritual experiences.

In most religious traditions the mystical experience is established as ineffable and inconceivable, precisely because it is a transcendental, other-worldly, and extra-ordinary experience. That being the case, the question usually posed is: how do words of an ordinary, human language capture and convey an extra-ordinary, transcendental experience? The answer, as attested to by all major religious and literary traditions is, by recourse to the language of symbolism.[1] Humanity uses symbols as a concrete or perceptible means of expressing the experience of abstract, imperceptible, spiritual, and divine realities. Schuon's expression of this is as follows (Coomaraswamy 1981, 252):

> In order to bring the realm of the spiritual and the divine within the range of perception, humanity ... loses the immediate union with the divine and the immediate vision of the spiritual. Then it tries to embody in a tangible or otherwise perceptible form, to materialize what is intangible, and imperceptible. It makes symbols ... and sees in them and through them the spiritual and divine substance that has no likeness and could not otherwise be seen.

At the most heightened state of consciousness, the mystical experience has been perceived as an encounter between two intangible entities, namely, the human soul and Divine Reality. In order to express the abstract encounter therefore, the concrete has to be expediently employed. In this context, the paradigms of love between man and woman, in all its myriad aspects, have most often been employed by mystics as a means of expressing this experience. In portraying this earthly love, however, the concern is usually not with the actual persons figured, but with them as archetypes, and as symbols of divine realities.

It is also of significance that symbolic expression generally focuses on the *process towards union*, rather than on union per se, with the Divine. In diverse mystical traditions this ontological experience has been given emphasis because mystical union is arrived at only through the stages of a long and arduous path.[2] This path, or journey, is expressed by the portrayal of human love-in-separation, in which the lovers are "torn" from each other. The separation is characterized by a searching, or quest, and a journey back to each other, fraught with pain, agony, and intense longing. This state of affairs symbolizes the consciousness of the human soul of its separation from God, and a yearning to return to its Source. This yearning has been hauntingly

[1] In a general sense, symbolism may take the form of images, allegories, parables, metaphors, or figurative expressions. It can also be in the form of characters, types, archetypes, prototypes, or mythical figures.

[2] See Marcoulesco (1993).

portrayed in "The Lament of the Reed," one of the most beautiful Sufi poems ever written. It conveys the plaintive cry of the reed (symbolizing the human soul) being torn from its original place (symbolizing Divine Reality). The great Persian mystic of the thirteenth century, Jalalu'l-Din Rumi), wrote (Ardalan 1998, 106):

> Harken to this Reed forlorn,
> Breathing, ever since 'twas torn
> From its rushy bed, a strain
> Of impassioned love and pain ...
> 'Tis the flame of love that fired me,
> 'Tis the wine of love inspired me.
> Wouldst thou learn how lovers bleed
> Harken, harken to the Reed

In the context of this process towards re-union, two great and dominant traditions, namely the Islamic-Sufi tradition of Persia, and the Hindu-Bhakti tradition of India, have produced literary works of singular beauty and merit in the form of prose, as well as poetry. In particular, two classic poems, Nizami's *Layla Majnun* (Gelpke 1997), and Jayadeva's *Gitagovinda* (Miller 1984), have gained widespread acclaim and canonicity within their individual literary traditions, as well as sanctity in their originating mystico-religious traditions.

Accordingly, there have been literary studies and enquiries carried out on both *Layla Majnun* (henceforth *Layla*) and *Gitagovinda* (henceforth *Govinda*). However, the profundity of these outstanding works cannot be sufficiently appreciated unless the literary elements therein are fully considered and explained in relation to the mystical content. In particular, the importance among mystics of symbols as the means for expressing the ultimate meaning of poems, renders it worthwhile to investigate the literary elements for their underlying mystical meanings. Apart from the literary and mystical meaning, the affinities and commonalities, and the differences and contrasts, between these texts have not yet been considered from a comparative approach. Although scholars such as Toshihiko Izutsu, S.H. Nasr, and Ananda Coomaraswamy have extensively examined philosophical doctrines from a comparative point of view, no one has examined the poetry of these traditions from a comparative perspective.

The issue to be addressed in the present study is the symbolic meaning of expressions in *Layla* and *Govinda*, as representative works of two different literary and mystical traditions. Considering that symbolism is the main criterion of assessing a poem's ultimate meaning among the mystics, it seems worthwhile to investigate the underlying philosophical assumptions of this poetic symbolism. In other words, the study focuses on the inward meaning of outward expressions. Based on a casual observation of the texts in question, it appears that there are similarities, affinities, and commonalities, as well as contrasts, disparities, and differences. This observation presents a challenging prospect for reconciling the manifest, literary elements, with the hidden, mystical dimensions of these elements.

At the literary level, the texts are acknowledged as masterpieces and as classic love stories. *Layla* is one of the best-known legends of the Middle East, of which it is said: "The two lovers of this classic tale are remembered to this day in the poems and songs from the Caucasus to the interior of Africa, and from the Atlantic to the Indian Ocean" ("Nizami" 2001). Similarly, Jayadeva's work is repeatedly referred to as the immortal lyrics of *Gitagovinda*" (Mukherjee 1989).

There have been many retellings of the tragic love story of *Layla*. In several versions and adaptations in the West, in India, and even in popular Persian literature, it has frequently been regarded as a narrative of two ill-fated lovers separated by feuding families, much in the manner of Shakespeare's classic love story, *Romeo & Juliet*.[3] Similarly, *Govinda* has often, even among Indian scholars themselves, been relegated to an account of "the illicit and rapturous love of Radha for Krishna," and perceived merely as an aesthetic rendition of an erotic Indian tale. As individual love stories, the *extent* of literary parallels between the texts remains undiscovered. Consequently, the potential for mutual understanding and enrichment between the two literary traditions has been missed. In this context, it is possible that a comparative and systematic study of literary elements may reveal the extent of parallels between the two texts.

Beyond the extent of apparent literary parallels between *Layla* and *Govinda*, the real *nature* of the parallels between the two texts in question is also unknown. In other words, it has not been ascertained

[3] Adaptations also exist as films, especially in India, the most famous being "Heer Ranjha," and "Heera Panna," depicted as Indian characters, and the Punjabi "Sohni Mehwal," depicted as Middle Eastern, or Moghul, characters.

whether or not the manifest similarities and differences exist only at a superficial, physical, or outward plane, or if there is a deeper, mystical, or inward affinity between them. Therefore, there is a possibility that the literary elements in the texts of two different traditions veil a further dimension. This possibility arises from the idea that there are enduring and universal principles of likeness and correspondence among the world's mystical traditions that come to light when they are closely examined. In this connection, Huston Smith has posed a challenging question about the ubiquity of likenesses of this nature, in a powerful aquatic metaphor. He asks: "What precisely,... is this subterranean water table which, pressurized by truth ... gushes forth wherever and whenever the earth is scratched?" (2001, 140). This question, considered in relation to different religious traditions, applies equally to the Persian-Islamic-Sufi, and the Indian-Hindu-Bhakti, traditions respectively. Thus, an inquiry into comparable concepts in the texts of *Layla* and *Govinda* may well be able to address the question.

Approach to the Issues

In comparing literary elements in the texts of *Layla* and *Govinda* the realities expressed in the two texts will be subjected to intra-textual interpretation and explanation, as well as inter-textual comparison. This will include both similar/parallel expressions as well as contrastive/contrary expressions, pursued at both the literary and the mystical levels of meaning.

The major, underlying principle of approach to *Layla* and *Govinda* is the progress from the lower to the higher level of understanding of human expression. This means that through the interpretation of literary elements, the mystical and esoteric elements will be unveiled. This principle, aptly stated by Reza Shah-Kazemi in relation to the writings of Martin Lings, is especially relevant for stating our purposes. He writes that (Shah-Kazemi 1999, 61, emphasis mine):

> ... interpretation of the image furnishes us with a key for comprehending the works.... His manner of treating this subject always carries the reader from the realm of *forms* to that of the *Essence*, from the *particular* to the *Universal*, and from the *symbol* to the *Archetype*.

A reading of the texts based on this principle allows multiple levels of interpretation. Foregrounding literary variations among the texts, this work initially brings out the nature of textual and outward similarities, as well as differences. Subsequently, the esoteric or underlying spiritual principles of the Islamic-Sufi tradition discerned from *Layla*, is compared with that of the Hindu-Bhakti tradition evinced from *Govinda*. In this way the question of whether or not there is a significant equivalence between the texts at the literary and spiritual levels may be reliably ascertained.

Within the above context, the hermeneutic approach, focusing specifically on the ideas developed by Hans-Georg Gadamer and Paul Ricoeur, forms the basis of enquiry. This approach is informed by the Traditionalist perspective which is in fact intrinsic to hermeneutics, even though the Traditionalists deal mainly with traditional and spiritual principles, rather than with poetry. The key concepts and features of hermeneutics, as well as the Traditionalist perspective, are summarized in the ensuing paragraphs.

The term hermeneutics originated in the classical Greek tradition. Its etymology can be traced to Hermes, the messenger of the Greek god Zeus (Jupiter in Latin). Zeus is identified, among other things, as the transmitter of Olympian messages into a language understandable to the lowly mortals (Quito 1990, 8). He is also known as the god of sleep, of alchemy and transformation, and of boundaries, who guides the newly dead to the underworld. "Hermeneutics" as related to interpretation derives from the Greek term *hẹrmeneuein* meaning "to interpret." In this context it has three senses: to interpret poetry orally; to explain; and to translate. This term is closely associated with *hermeneutike mantike*, the technique of oracle interpretation, whereas poets are referred to as ***hermenes ton theon***, "interpreters of the gods" (Preminger 1993, 516). Hermeneutics has come to mean "the process of bringing a thing or situation from unintelligibility to understanding" (Palmer 1969, 3). In the same context, it is associated with "revealing the hidden" (Preminger 1993, 517). On this basis, hermeneutics, and more specifically, spiritual hermeneutics, has been particularly applied to the interpretation of works of divine origin, including the Vedas and the Koran. In the Hindu tradition, the counterpart of hermeneutics is *brahmavidya*, meaning "the supreme science."[4] On the other hand, the Arabic term *ta'wil*, meaning "to cause to return" or to lead something back to its beginning or origin, is a legitimate form of hermeneutics in Islamic literary criticism.[5]

Hermeneutics has reemerged as an important discipline in the human sciences, particularly in philosophy and literature. The philosophers directly responsible in the nineteenth and twentieth centuries are of the German and French schools. Notable of the former group are, F.D.E. Schleiermacher, Martin Heidegger, and Hans-Georg Gadamer, whereas taking center stage of the latter group are Paul Ricoeur and Jacques Derrida.

Although differing from each other in terms of features developed in the notion of hermeneutics, both Hans-Georg Gadamer (1989), and Paul Ricoeur (1985), underscore its philosophical and ontological nature. In opposing its consideration as a methodological, and therefore scientific, process, Gadamer says that truth eludes the methodical individual and hence, method retards, if not subverts, the truth. In other words, we reach the truth not methodically but dialectically (Quito 1990, 51). In the same vein, although Ricoeur does not rule out hermeneutics as a method, he discards the objective, rigid, structured method of the natural sciences. He (1985, 94) says:

> The question of truth is no longer the question of method; it is the question of the manifestation of being, for a being whose existence consists in understanding being.

[4] *Brahmavidya* is considered an introspective tool, with which the inspired *rishis* (literally "seers") who lived ascetic and celibate lives (*brahmacharya*) in the forest hermitages (*ashram*) of ancient India analyzed the awareness of human experience to see if there was anything in it that was absolute. "Supreme" because where other sciences studied the external world, *brahmavidya* sought knowledge of an underlying reality which would inform all other studies and activities. The discoveries of *brahmavidya* are *shruti*, i.e., records of the direct encounter with the divine transmitted through *shabda*, literally, "sound" or "that which is heard." See the Introduction by Eknath Easwaran in his translation of the *Bhagavad Gita* (1986, 4-5).

[5] *Ta'wil* refers specifically to spiritual exegesis of the revealed truths contained in religious sources. In the Islamic literary tradition, it is an esoteric form of interpretation to achieve the inner understanding of the text, arrived at by means of symbolic interpretation. However, penetrating the significance of a symbol is done by intuitively sensing the original spiritual experience attained by the author of the text, and not through rational elucidation. See Md. Salleh Yaapar (1988, 44-45).

From the hermeneutic perspective, Ricoeur's understanding of symbol highlights the revelatory function of a symbol. An apparent meaning points analogically to a second meaning which is not given otherwise. In this context, his idea of the "architecture of meaning" is explained in the following manner (Blaikie 1995, 154):

> The symbol as it stands means more than one thing; there are different levels of meaning contained in it. The most obvious, or literal meaning hides the figurative meaning but at the same time it also discloses it, since the figurative meaning cannot be grasped except through the literal meaning.

However it should be remembered that even though all symbols are signs, every sign is not a symbol. A symbol enjoys a "double intentionality." Therefore while a sign manifests other than itself, it does not invite thought. Signs perform indicative function while symbols also have an added dimension: they perform a revelatory function.

In the hermeneutical definition, a text is viewed as a projection of the human world, in that it imitates the world in a relation of *mimesis* and *poesis.* This means that the text is not merely a copy or duplication of the world, but an author's creative and intentional act, conveying a particular discourse. Further, the text entails a specific context which is determined by its "historical tradition," or "culture," or "worldview," and situated in a particular milieu, i.e. its location in time and space. This milieu constitutes the historicity of the text. As the author's act is his construction of the human reality situated in a particular context, his text should therefore be understood through its historicity, rather than as an autonomous entity.

In this context, it is important to the process of understanding and interpreting a text to be aware that the author and his text, and the reader (or interpreter), originate from different cultures or traditions, or, in Gadamer's terms, different "horizons." This difference invariably influences and colors the interpreter's understanding. Consequently, there has to occur a "fusion of horizons," in order for interpretation to take place. This is a process whereby the horizons of the text are merged with the horizons of the reader. According to Ricoeur, several elements are inherent in this process. One is *Aneignung* or appropriation, meaning "genuinely to make one's own what is initially alien" (1981, 18). Appropriation requires the correct attitude in approaching a text. In relation to the text, this attitude is one of sympathy. The aim is to "hear" or "see" what lies beyond the words of a text. In doing so, the interpreter's openness to the relevant tradition will allow the text to reveal itself to the interpreter. One has to look beyond what is said in the everyday meaning of the language, to what is being taken for granted, while it is being said (Blaikie 1995, 64). In allowing the text to reveal itself, the anteriority of the text, or what stands "in front" of it, comes into play. The notion of anteriority is explained by Ricoeur (1986, 68) as follows:

> Ultimately, what the reader appropriates is a *proposed world*, which is not behind the text, as a hidden intention would be, but *in front of it* as that which the work unfolds, discovers, reveals. Henceforth, to understand is *to understand oneself in front of the text.* It is not a question of imposing upon the text our finite capacity of understanding, but of exposing ourselves to the text and receiving from it an enlarged self.

Acceptance, and thereby a fuller appreciation, is enabled when the nature of the interaction between the self and the text "ceases to appear as a kind of possession, (and) implies instead a moment of dis-possession of the narcissistic ego" (1986, 68). In this context an important contrastive differentiation is held between "self" and "ego," whereby it is the text, "with its universal power of unveiling, which gives a *self* to the *ego*" (1986, 68).

If in relation to the text, appropriation requires the correct attitude, in relation to the interpreter, appropriation requires a suspension of the self. This involves the encounter between the self and the text, which is becoming aware of his own deep-seated assumptions, prejudices, or horizon of meaning, with regard to the nature of the experience or the object being studied. Without the encounter between the self and the text, preconceived notions would otherwise remain unknown or ignored. Awareness, and subsequently a relinquishment, of prejudices, brings about a suspension of presupposition and judgment, as well as a critical self-consciousness and, ultimately, a transformation or metamorphosis. In this case metamorphosis is understood as a relinquishment of the self as it were, by the interpreter, to the objective guidance and support of the text. Subsequently, a genuine understanding is achieved, not only of what is written together with its inherent traits, but also of what he is himself, as a part of the meaning of the text.

It is equally important to be aware that the subject matter of the text is answering a particular question. Therefore, rather than attempt an "objective" interpretation, it is the responsibility of the interpreter first to reconstruct the question that the text is answering, and subsequently, to engage in a conversation or dialogue about it. For both Gadamer and Ricoeur, dialogue involves dialectics, whereby all contradictions and conflicting forces that come into play have to be worked out in the process of investigating the truth.

A consequence of the encounter between the interpreter and the text is that the interpreter's horizons are altered and thereby, broadened. Ricoeur describes this as "an ultimate expansion of consciousness" (1986, 68). By this he does not mean that the interpreter is trying to discover what the text or the author "really means," but rather that he is basically "becoming" an "experiencer" of the tradition that opens or reveals itself to him. In this context, hermeneutics means "bridging the gap between one's familiar world and the meaning that resides in an alien world" (Blaikie 1995, 64). Thus, as has been emphasized by most scholars of hermeneutics, "Understanding is not reconstruction, but mediation" (Linge, in Blaikie 1995, 64). The direct effect of mediation may be seen as the establishment of a connection between the self and the other at a level such that both the interpreter and the text are mutually transformed.

In consideration of all of the above attitudes, views, notions, contexts, and concepts, understanding is an ontological condition of mankind. Besides, in view of the fact that language is the conveyor of meaning, it allows us not only to understand a particular experience, but also the world in which it occurs. In this connection, Gadamer argues that even from the world of our own language we can grasp the world of another language. This view is explained as follows (Gadamer 1989 65):

> ... as language has a universal function of providing human beings with a world of shared understanding, and (as) hermeneutics is linguistic in nature, hermeneutics itself also has universal significance.

Accordingly, it is possible for the interpreter to identify elements of universal significance in literary works, when he adopts the foregoing approach to interpretation. It also allows for subjectivity in recovering meaning. Subjectivity is important, for there cannot be only one true, original, meaning in a human expression, even for the author himself. Consequently, meaning is always open-ended. In Gadamer's words, "Art demands interpretation because of its inexhaustible ambiguity. It cannot be satisfactorily translated in terms of conceptual knowledge" (Gadamer 1989 65).

The problematic of different horizons, particularly in the modern (as opposed to the traditional) worldview, is that there has occurred a gradual and almost complete estrangement between the secular and the spiritual realities, which in effect is held by Ricoeur to be an estrangement from meaning itself. In order to recover this meaning, as well as to bridge the distances, points of view, horizons, or tensions between the other and the self, the fusion of horizons is advocated, in which appropriation occurs. Furthermore, appropriation takes place not arbitrarily or subjectively, but bound by the authority of tradition. Thus appropriation facilitates the unveiling of meaning in the text, and thereby establishes an ongoing dialogue between the writer and the reader. It is the establishment of such a dialogue that is considered as ultimately fulfilling the purpose and function of the text. In Ricoeur's words, "... reading is the concrete act in which the destiny of the text is fulfilled. It is at the very heart of reading that explanation and interpretation are indefinitely opposed and reconciled" (1986, 92).

The basic principles of the Traditionalist perspective, which informs the study and understanding of mystical symbols, may be understood as follows: The Traditionalists adhere to principles of *scientia sacra*, or the sacred science, which originates from primordial traditions. They contend that behind apparent or exoteric differences of religious forms there exists an inward or esoteric core of common spiritual Truth, unanimously attested to by the sages and the mystics of the revealed religions. This truth has been called the *sophia perennis* or "perennial wisdom," and those who subscribe to this view are often referred to as perennialists or perennial philosophers.

The objective of the earliest Traditionalists in the twentieth century, René Guénon and Frithjof Schuon, was to reveal the spiritual dimensions and essential truths inherent in symbols, and the universal applications of this perspective. Its outstanding advocates like Ananda Coomaraswamy, Titus Burckhardt, Martin Lings, and Seyyed Hossein Nasr, have upheld and continued these efforts by scholarship that is more academic in character. Nasr's version of the perennial philosophy has largely been responsible for its acceptance in Western academia and for its application to the comparative study of religions (Hahn 2001, xvii).

The application of the ideas of the Traditionalists that are particularly relevant to the needs of the present work is specifically to augment our understanding of the forms of expression, rather than to address issues of doctrine and metaphysics of the differing mystical traditions. These may be summarized as follows: Firstly, higher levels of reality are expressed in symbolic language. Secondly, that different traditions represent these realities by different symbols. Thirdly, and consequently, the meanings of traditional symbols are determined by the individual traditions.

The main distinction between the interpretation of conventional literary symbols, and traditional, spiritual symbols is that the former are subjective, arbitrary, individual, or creative expressions of the poet, whereas the latter is objective and has a precision in reference according to its particular tradition. In fact, in the Traditionalists' view, symbolism is seen as an "exact science," and symbols represent the "technical" terms that authors employ in their works, which are recognized by members of that tradition. It is this recognition that facilitates the interpretation of symbols that are specific to a culture and religion.[6] This particularity of meaning reinforces and confirms the importance mentioned earlier, of appropriation in hermeneutics. The basis of appropriation is that interpretation of spiritual meaning takes place not arbitrarily or subjectively, but bound by the authority of tradition.

By unveiling the inward, quintessential meaning of expressions in *Layla* and *Govinda*, the true worth of these texts as traditional works of art can be unveiled. Ultimately, the blooms of these gardens of love could be regarded as expressions of the Inexpressible.

[6] See Coomaraswamy (1989, 131). For an excellent elucidation of the particularity in meaning of sacred symbols, see Ghazi bin Muhammad (2001, 85-108).

Limits and Boundaries

The comparative study of *Layla* and *Govinda* is based on English translations of the texts in question. Their particulars are tabulated below:

Texts	Layla	Govinda
ORIGINAL WORKS	*Leyli o Majnun* (one out of five *mathnawi* in a collection entitled *Panj Ganj (Five Treasures)*	*Gitagovinda* (in the tradition of performed recitation (*ragakavya*))
LANGUAGE	Persian	Sanskrit
AUTHOR	Nizami (pen-name for Abu Muhammad Ilyas ibn Usuf ibn Zaki Mu'ayyad), mystic poet of Ganjar, Ayzerbaijan, Persia (Iran)	Goswami Jayadeva, wandering seer-poet of Kindubilva, Bengal, India
PERIOD OF PRODUCTION	Latter half of 12th century	Latter half of 12th century
TRANSLATED WORKS	*The Story of Layla and Majnun*	*Love Song of the Dark Lord: The Gitagovinda of Jayadeva*
TRANSLATORS	Rudolf Gelpke, translator and editor. Final chapter translated by Zia Inayat Khan and Omid Safi.	Barbara Stoler Miller, editor and translator
LANGUAGE	English	English
PUBLICATION	New Lebanon, New York: Omega Publications, 1997	New Delhi: Motilal Banarsidass, 1977

Figure 1: Publication Background of Texts Being Studied

As has been mentioned previously, the literary interest in the texts is of paramount interest, although the spiritual and philosophical interests are considered as an integral part of the works in question. That is to say, the focus will primarily be on literary mechanisms and devices that are ingeniously and intentionally utilized by the authors to convey realities, experiences, notions, and viewpoints. Stated differently, the present work is an attempt to pluck the "blossoms" from the gardens of love in *Layla* and *Govinda* to behold their resplendence, and to admire their fragrance.

The examination of the similarities and differences between *Layla* and *Govinda* is circumscribed significantly by two foundational and interrelated issues, that of language and genre, and requires a disclaimer. With regard to the issue of language, both texts are English translations, of which critical acclaim has been high. However, it is necessary to point out that the reliance, by necessity, entirely on the English translations, has diminished a full appreciation of the complexities of the works. In fact, some scholars maintain that the texts cannot be studied in their translated versions for the intended purposes. This is because, in medieval court poetry of both the Persian and Sanskrit literary traditions,[7] such special intricacies as the ambiguity of language, deliberate ambivalence in expression, emphasis on connotative and suggestive meanings of vocabulary, free use of imagery, frequent literary, scriptural, and other references, and allusions intrinsic to aesthetic and devotional expressions, are all highly effective forms and devices abundantly employed in the original languages. The general consensus of opinion is that translation is inadequate and unsuited for transforming these features into the English language. Furthermore, a high degree of interpretation is not only unavoidable, but incumbent upon the translator in the process of transforming one language into another. In the words of Hans-Georg Gadamer, "every translation is at the same time an interpretation" (1989, 346). As is widely acknowledged, and as will be explained subsequently, the process of interpretation is a highly complex, rigorous process that requires active participation on many levels of informed awareness, specific attitudes, and modes of approach.

As to the issue of genre, there are also limitations. In the case of *Layla*, whereas the original is "a tragic poem in the tradition of courtly love" (Levy 1969, 83), Gelpke's translation has been rendered in narrative prose, with some exceptions where poetic form is retained in

[7] Note that the "cross-fertilization," and thereby the resemblance, between these two literary traditions is not unexpected considering their shared linguistic roots in the Indo-Iranian and Indo-European languages. This factor has been discussed by many scholars. It is dealt with at length in several works of Muhammad Bukhari Lubis (see 1990).

terms of rhyme and rhythm.[8] In Persian literature, as is the case for the original *Layla*, poems are always rhymed, within the principal verse form of the *mathnawi*. The *mathnawi* is particularly employed for heroic, romantic, or narrative verse, whereas the *ghazal* (the Western genres being the ode or the lyric) which appears in parts of *Layla*, is a comparatively short poem, usually amorous or mystical and varying from four to sixteen couplets, all on one rhyme.

As for the English version of *Govinda*, although it is preserved in the original style of a poem of twelve cantos containing twenty-four songs, it, similarly, has inevitably lost out on the rhyming patterns. Besides, as stated by the translator herself, "The *Gitagovinda*,... has a wealth of meaning embedded in structurally intricate forms and concepts drawn from various levels of Indian literary tradition" (Miller 1984, 7). She also confirms that "as the relations among words are fluid, any translation of *Gitagovinda* is necessarily tentative" (Miller 1984, 43). Besides, in terms of mode of expression, the original poem is a particular type of drama, the *ragakavya* which is customarily performed (acted, sung, danced, etc.), and therefore to be approached and interpreted in ways that are quite different from those of English poetry (Miller 1984, 43). In the words of Lee Seigel, who has adopted a literal approach in his translation of *Govinda* (1978, 234): "The ideals, aims, subtleties, constructions, standards ... are so utterly different from those of English poetry."

It is also held that the greatest charm of Persian and Sanskrit poetry lies in its musical effects. Just as the integration of sensual lyrics and plaintive cadences of the *ghazal*, situated within the original *mathnawi*, complements and enhances the musical effect of the original *Layla*, so the original *Govinda*, written in the form of devotional songs (*bhajan*), and set in various musical modes (*raga*) and beats (*taal*), evokes a certain emotion and response in its practitioner/audience, during a performance.[9] Consequently, the incorporation and transmission of these elements in the English translation is a practical difficulty. Furthermore, this limitation is a particular shortcoming because it is

[8] Cf. XXIV:75, LIII:174.

[9] For example, the presentation of *bhajans* in "Kavi Jayadeva's Gita-govinda."

related to the acoustic or auditory effects of the original texts, an element that is critical to the study of literary devices.

For the practicalities cited above, it may be that full justice cannot be done to the original texts. The endeavor is nevertheless undertaken on the following premises. Firstly, on the understanding that the translations represent "secondary" sources. Secondly, the study is confined to the translated texts as observable evidence of literary elements. Finally, on the premise of the sub-discipline of Comparative Literature, that without translated texts, in this case constituting authoritative translations, the world's greatest works would be unattainable and inaccessible between one culture and another.

This work is by no means a comprehensive account of all the paradigms of love in the texts in question, nor is it necessary to be so. Consequently, the analysis of expressions is not exhaustive. Rather, single, and in some cases several, representative examples of expressions of a particular notion, concept, element, or aspect of love will be interpreted and explicated. In this context, it should be made clear that in both the cases of *Layla* and *Govinda*, what is being studied here is the later, *probably* posthumous Sufi reading of Nizami's poem, and the *obviously* Sahajiya reading of Jayadeva's poem. This adoption and adaptation of the works by mystics of the individual traditions constitutes another parallel between Nizami and Jayadeva. For the reason stated above, the core of discussion revolves around key episodes of the two poems which are essential for the mystical (Sufi and Bhakti) interpretation, and not on the text in entirety.

Towards a Contribution

The present work anticipates its primary contribution to be towards a better understanding of these two works in terms of affinities in literary elements and subject matter, as well as an enhanced awareness of their perennial and universal significance.. The ramifications of this discovery may make a small contribution in identifying commonalities that lie beyond the surface of apparently distinct, and sometimes contrasting, religious and cultural traditions. In view of this, certain parallels in the mystical traditions of Islamic Sufism of Persia and Hindu Bhaktism of India may emerge.

As a corollary to the above, this work hopes to supplement the limited corpus of comparative studies available in English on these two mystical texts. As access to most extant studies are limited by language, i.e., Arabic or Hindi, and thereby by readership, i.e., to the Middle Eastern or Arabic-literate readers and to the sub-continent of India, this fills a niche in inquiries conducted in English on the topic.

Finally, it is the hope that a greater awareness of, and sustained interest in, the common wealth and universality of the spiritual and perennial dimension in man's existence may be promoted by this book. In the context of ever-widening gulfs in the relationship between cultures of the world, and the contemporary emphasis of secularism and material gains, such awareness is viewed as essential to mutual appreciation, harmony, and acceptance.

The material in this book is divided thematically. The first two chapters are to provide basic information on the subject matter of the comparative study, and the milieu and some fundamental aspects of interpretation of the texts, such as literary conventions and mystico-religious norms, of both the Persian-Sufi and Indian-Bhakti traditions underpinning the texts of *Layla* and *Govinda* respectively. This is followed by four chapters of analysis and comparison to determine the nature and extent of the similarities and affinities, as well as the differences and contrasts, between the texts. Each of these chapters presents aspects of a particular mystical theme, namely, of initial union, of separation, and of reunion. The final chapter concludes the work by summarizing principal findings and implications.

CHAPTER TWO

COLORS OF LOVE: SOME IDEALS OF TRADITIONAL PERSIAN AND INDIAN LITERATURE

> All the arts strive to express the same idea,... [but] it is of interest and importance to enquire by what different methods they have respectively attained to them.
>
> —C. E. Wilson (1974)

Prior to commencing a comparative study of the texts it is necessary to delineate the specific regard in which these works are held in their originating literary traditions. *Layla* and *Govinda* constitute works of art, expressing the Persian-Islamic-Sufi, and Indian-Hindu-Bhakti, traditions respectively.[1] Consequently, the production of these works is based on literary norms and conventions of their individual traditions. Furthermore, like all traditional works of art, they are perceived as possessing specific symbolic and spiritual functions and ideals, such as to illuminate or intensify the mystery of metaphysical, non-empirical dimensions of reality. As shall be seen in the study of some common symbols, from the mundane, outer dimension, each text allows a supra-mundane, inner dimension and symbolic relevance and level of interpretation.

Although all texts must be interpreted before their meanings can be understood or divulged, literary texts require the most interpretation or "reading." Scholars like Mishra (1998, 81) emphasize that:

[1] For convenience, and unless otherwise specified, all future reference to the Persian-Islamic-Sufi tradition will henceforth be by the term "Sufi," and to the Indian-Hindu-Bhakti tradition, by the term "Bhakti," to denote the respective geographical, literary, and spiritual traditions as the milieu of the works.

> ... of all texts it is to the literary that the term interpretation is most often applied. This is because the literary—and especially the literary work of art—is consciously designed as a network of dense semantic configurations that requires the most systematic acts of interpretation. It is in the literary that nothing is redundant; every word, every period, even its layout, carry [*sic*] meaning. One emphasizes the act of interpretation because the coming into being of a literary text is the result of a dialectical process along an axis that involves both the text and the reader.

Here, two points are significant, namely the conscious design of literary texts, and the dialectic process between text and reader. Both are fundamental considerations in the hermeneutical approach to determining meaning. In this approach, a text "starts" with the author consciously and unconsciously "encoding" meaning and "ends" with the reader "decoding" that meaning. In this process, the "traditional" reader has a significant role, as kindred spirit or participant (*sahrdaya*), having a shared universe of discourse. On the same principles, a "modern" reader may also participate in that discourse, divorced though he is from the original time-space constructs. The point being made is that interpretation may be informed by underlying codes of discourse shared by author and reader.

In light of the above perception, the interpretation and discussion in this chapter proceeds along three major divisions. The first attempts to contextualize the works in line with the hermeneutical approach. Thus it identifies the particular historical periods of their production in order to facilitate an understanding of "the individual author's originary actions and their purposes" (Md. Salleh 1995, 11). The subsequent section discusses literary expression of the mystical experience, focusing on some generalities and commonalities between the relevant traditions, as well as specific modes of expression of the mystical experience in the Sufi and Bhakti traditions. The final section highlights a particular, and common, view in which the mystical experience is universally perceived, namely the concept of *unio mystica*. This is the process towards union and absorption of the human soul into God. The stages of *unio mystica* constitute the grid upon which the comparison will attempt to chart the similarities and differences in dominant symbols of love as portrayed in the texts. Stated in another way, the study illustrates the stages of *unio mystica* in the Sufi and Bhakti traditions, conveyed by way of literary expression.

Taken together, the three sections mentioned above constitute the conceptual framework upon which rests the entire comparative study of the two works in question. Thus it attempts to trace the path symbolically traveled by the lovers in question, i.e.,·Layla-Majnun in *Layla* and Radha-Krishna in *Govinda*, both from the literary, outward, level (its substance), and the mystical, inward, level (its essence).

Milieu, Historicity, and Ahistoricity

The milieu of a text includes its historicity. This is the historical context of the production of a text in terms of its social, political, and economic environments. These environments are factors that provide a dependable basis for the interpretation and understanding of any literary work being studied. Consequently, this section will consider the milieus of *Layla* and *Govinda*, respectively.

The consideration of the milieu of Layla encompasses both the author, Nizami, and his work, *Layla*, within the context of Sufi literature. In Levy's accounts (1969), Nizami's poetry falls within the classical era of Persian literature also referred to as the Golden Age. This age spans the pre- and post-Islamic medieval era, a period which witnessed the rise and fall of several great empires in Persia, or Iran, as it is referred to by its people. Persian political rule changed hands from the pre-Islamic Sasanian kings, to the stronghold of Arabic influence from the seventh century onwards, and ultimately, to the development and maturity of the national language and literature by the end of the fifteenth century. Scholars like Levy attribute the evolution of Sufism in Iran intimately to the literary sources of Iranian Sufism. Among other genres, the Persians employed the *mathnawi*, or rhyming couples, for heroic, and didactic narratives, of which the greatest exponents exponents were Sana'i Nizami, Rumi, Sa'di, and Jami (Arberry 1977,14). Besides the *mathnawi*, panegyrics—the mode of laudatory, eulogic, and hyperbolic expression dedicating works to rulers—was exploited by poets seeking royal patronage for their sustenance.

In the wake of Sufism, religious and didactic poetry became an integral part of literary works, and the mystic experience found symbolic expression in the works of writers, among them Nizami. In fact, an illustrious poet of mysticism like Jami is said to have been a great admirer and imitator of Nizami (Arberry 1977, 123). .

Nizami lived and died in Ganja, a town in Khorasan (part of modern-day Azerbaijan), *c.* 1140-1209. Although the actual dates of his life are uncertain, it is established that he flourished in the latter half of the twelfth century. In this period, Persia was dominated by Turk rulers, particularly the Saljuqs, the Ghaznavids, and the Atabegs. These rulers paid generously for poetry, especially if it served their propaganda and purpose.

Hailed by scholars of Persian literature as the greatest exponent of romantic epic poetry in Persian literature (Levy 1969, 81), Nizami is also referred to as a genius of universal significance, "the first in Persian literature worthy to take place beside Firdausi" (Arberry 1977, 122). Living in the Saljuq-Ghaznavid periods, Nizami enjoyed the patronage of several Persian monarchs, such as the Shirvan-Shah and Atabeg rulers (Arberry 1977, 23). Nizami was commissioned by a Transcaucasian chieftain, Shervanshah to write the story of Layla-Majnun (Gelpke 1997, xiii). However, little is documented about Nizami's personal life, apart from the facts that he was orphaned at a tender age, that he lived austerely, turning for consolation to religion, and living a life of piety. Nizami's gift for poetry reflected this characteristic of his life, as well as his admiration for mystical compositions of earlier writers. True to the tradition of Islamic literature, authors like Nizami were partial to *nazira*, or responses to earlier writers. In this regard, *Laila and Majnun* is no exception. According to Braginsky (1998, 609 fn. 17):

> For purposes of *nazira*, the poet, in utilizing as many elements as possible from the works of his predecessors, tries to outdo him in terms of artistic worth and deeper elaboration of theme, or ornament the work with new nuances and colors or unusual interpretations to the storyline, or create unexpected modifications to a particular scene in the work, and so on. The number of *nazira* is countless. For example there are tens, if not hundreds, in *Laila and Majnun.*

Nizami is admired in Persian-speaking lands for the originality of his writing, and especially for his clarity of style, due mainly to his incorporation of the colloquial styles as a mode of creative expression. In addition, and unlike his contemporaries, his use of ancient legends lays emphasis on the human aspects of his characters rather than the superhuman or heroic aspects (Levy 1969, 81). Undoubtedly these characteristics made his work "realistic" and intelligible to all levels of society, and thus his audience could readily identify with them.

Nizami is believed to have drawn inspiration from other Persian mystic poets, particularly Firdausi and Sana'i, composing for the most part odes (*qasidah*), lyrics (*ghazal*), and rhyming couplets (*mathnawi*). His reputation, however, rests mainly upon the genre of the *mathnawi*, particularly through his *magnum opus*, the *Panj Ganj* (Five Treasures).[2] This outstanding work comprises five long poems, all written in the *mathnawi* verse form, a genre which Nizami is acknowledged to have developed and perfected. *Panj Ganj* includes a didactic poem, a romantic epic, a philosophical portrait of Alexander the Great, a series of anecdotal stories of King Bahram, and *Leyli o-Majnun*, as the original Persian version of *Layla* was referred to. With regard to the literary worth of *Panj Ganj*, there is a consensus of positive opinion among scholars, including those in the West. For example, despite the Orientalist tenor of the remark, Levy acknowledges that the *Panj Ganj* (1969, 92):

> must be regarded as achieving a high standard by any literary criterion, for there lies in them a great store of poetic imagination displaying an abundance of glamorous pictures. Their fault is that all is too rich, too dazzling in imagery, so that the mind turns for relief to something sober and less glittering.

In similar vein, the Egyptian scholar M. Gh. Hilal concludes that it was Nizami who transformed the legend of Layla and Majnun into a work of art of timeless value (Gelpke 1997, xii).

It is important to bear in mind that there have been numerous texts and versions of the story of Layla and Majnun. In the sixteenth century, Hatifi, Jami's nephew and a noted poet, composed *Laila u Majnun*, which was translated by Sir William Jones in 1788 (Arberry 1958, 447). Nizami's version in the Persian *mathnawi* form was begun in 1188, based upon the ancient Arabian true story of Qays and Layla (Arberry 1958, 124). Qays, of the North-Arabic tribe of Amir, lived and suffered for his Layla about 500 years before Nizami wrote his poem (Gelpke 1997, xi). However, as has been argued by notable scholars, manuscripts of Nizami's *Layla* vary significantly. In 1836, a "skilful version" of Nizami's poem, published by James Atkinson,

[2] This work is better known by its Arabic title, *Khamseh* or *Khamsa* (quintet).

features the final episode, in which "the ... lovers are dead and their friend Zaid realizes in a dream the mystical import of their immortal love" (Arberry 1958, 124). In 1960, Rudolf Gelpke, who translated Nizami's *Layla* into English, published an abridged version. This version is in prose, and ends with the death of Majnun at Layla's grave. This means that Gelpke's translation left out the "final episode" mentioned above. A more recent version of Gelpke's translation has been republished in 1997 by Inayat Khan, who translated this final episode from Nizami's original Persian version into English and reinstated it in Gelpke's translation. This is the version used for this study, chosen because firstly, despite the fact that Gelpke's version is abridged, his translation has been hailed as authoritative; secondly, because Khan's addition is considered as completing Gelpke's version; thirdly, because Khan's authority within the Sufi tradition is significant; and, finally, because it is the most recent and comprehensive version in English.

In considering the foregoing particulars of both author and text, it is important to mention that the extent of the mystical, or Sufi, content of Nizami's *Layla*, and its true nature, has often been questioned by various quarters. One view is that Nizami's rendition is merely a conglomeration of parts of different versions and accounts of the well-known story in Islamic folklore. Another view highlights the historical origin and content of the story. Similarly, the opinion that the story originates in the pre-Islamic Arab-speaking world equally holds sway. Another view of it is that it is a tragic poem of courtly love. A different perspective holds that Majnun constitutes an archetypal literary figure epitomizing the madness of love-in-separation in a worldly context. A further view is that the story of Layla-Majnun has merely been adopted by the Sufis as a fitting vehicle for expressing the mystical experience, and has thus subsequently been given a spiritual interpretation by them. Basically, what is directly relevant to the present study is that some writers understand Nizami's poem as a Sufi work and others do not (Braginsky 2004). Among the former are Schimmel, Schuon, Hodgson, Gelpke, Braginsky, and De Bruijn from the West, as well as Hamzah Fansuri, Baharuddin Ahmad, and Daud Baharom in the Malay world. Among the latter group, Meisami is probably the most resolute opponent of the reading of the work as a Sufi poem, but even she admits mystical elements in Nizami's *Haft Paykar* (Braginsky 2004).

It may well be that all of the above are legitimate views, and accurate to varying degrees. In any case, from observable elements of the work and those regarding the author, or verifiable "evidence," the present work contends that Nizami's *Layla* is a deliberate and purposeful Sufi expression. Generally, this is apparent from the setting of the text. Besides, from the geographical context upon which Nizami's creation of *Layla* rests, it may be ascertained that its cultural background is Persian-Islamic. Furthermore, it is a work authored in the twelfth century, a temporal construct within which the intimate connection between the artistic and the spiritual *weltanschauung* was still robust. To elaborate, all art of the time, as an embodiment of a traditional culture, had a profoundly religious significance. Therefore an artistic, literary, or aesthetic expression such as *Layla* was not at any time removed from its spiritual constructs or sacred dimension.

Therefore, even if Nizami is not universally acknowledged solely as a mystic-poet, the religious element in his work is irrefutable. Besides, Nizami is on record as incorporating outstanding hymns in honor of the Prophet which have become models for later poets, and "his descriptions of Muhammad, the ideal servant of God, show all the poetical elegance in which his epical poetry in general excels" (Schimmel 1982, 196). These tendencies in Nizami can be substantiated by similar observable textual characteristics of *Layla*: the genre of the *mathnawi* as medium of expression; the ubiquitous religious associations; the apparent musical quality of the text; and the exceptional lyrical beauty of expression. This last characteristic may be viewed from the Platonic dictum that "Beauty is the splendor of the True" (Schuon 1995, 23). Furthermore, as the analysis hopes to demonstrate in due course, *Layla* displays a great deal of textual elements that correspond to the "technical terms of the Sufis" (Arberry 1977, xvii). For example, the doctrines of love, union, separation, annihilation, ecstasy, and intoxication, reflect and express ideals associated with the Sufi mystical experience.

It is significant that Schuon, renowned originator of the Traditionalist school of thought and a revered Sufi shaykh, perceives Layla as synonymous with the Divine. In *Road to the Heart*, a rare compilation of mystical poems written in English, he eulogizes "Layla" in a poem of the same title (1995, 11):

She may be dark, a deep and silent night,
Yet she is beautiful, a wondrous sight.
By greedy men she never will be seen;
Her peerless body hides behind a screen.

Her breasts are like the sun, now East, now West;
They are the pilgrim's refuge and his rest;
She gives him joy and peace with tender lips
And with the rapture of her dancing hips.

Closer to the present work in place and time, a scholar of Sufism from the Malay world, Baharuddin Ahmad, equates *Layla* to other great Sufi works in theorizing about its association with Islamic literature in general. According to Baharuddin, Layla and Majnun are perceived as "types." He writes (1992, xxiii-xxiv) with keen insight that:

> Prose is employed in Islamic literature in a quite different way from modern Western literature.... Characterization in the *hikayat* typifies "someone" who is also "anyone." It does not refer to particular embodied or material characters but to "types," or sorts which represent "man"; or, more precisely, a good character represents "paramount qualities in man," and an evil character represents the evil in man; this is a universal reflection of the Realities of life and of existence. In Nizami's *hikayat*, Majnun in *Lila dan Majnun*, can be anyone who falls in love, who encounters the depths of love, who experiences love and becomes aware that love is the embodiment of a special attribute beyond compare, wondrous, and of immense worth. That love comes from Allah and is likened to grace which at one level is shared with his special creature, which is man.

Moreover, Baharuddin not only recognizes the work, but also its author, as being in the league of other well-known Sufi poets like Rumi. In expressing this in striking metaphors of beauty and majesty, two of the foremost Divine attributes, he writes (1992, xix):

> When the spiritual meaning is clear, its form becomes as clear as the sun shining at noon devoid of shadow.... Works of Ibn 'Arabi, Khayyam, and Hafez can be compared to the sun at noon from which meaning directly shines forth into form. It is like the Divine Majesty (*al-Jalal*) that discloses the Reality of Truth, whereas works of Rumi, Ibn Farid, 'Attar, and Nizami are like the waning sun, or

like the moon; providing shade, cool, and Divine Grace, the aspect of *al-Jamal*, Divine Beauty.

From Baharuddin's opinion it is possible to infer that in essence, neither the Sufi content, nor the author's credibility as mystic-poet is disputed. In fact it may be said that he takes for granted that *Layla* is a Sufi text, and Nizami, a mystic-poet.

A textual-structural consideration may be put forward to conclude the argument that the mystical element in *Layla* is not incidental but reflective of the author's originary intentions. It is significant that in the final chapter of *Layla*, the dream sequence is recounted by Zayd,[3] a saintly persona in the Sufi tradition. In this episode, the lovers are portrayed as reunited and experiencing perfection in Paradise. This constitutes a fitting closure to their story both at the literary and at the spiritual levels. At the literary level, the recognizable "happy ending" preempts the possibility of the love story ending as a tragedy of Aristotelian proportions. Furthermore the reunion conforms to the ideal of poetic justice. At the spiritual level, the lovers' reunion is consistent with Islamic metaphysical concepts of salvation, deliverance, reward in the hereafter, and so on.

On the basis of all the above considerations, the text may speak for itself as a work of deliberate Sufi expression. In this context it describes the story of the love between the Divine, symbolically represented as Layla, and the spiritual aspirant, symbolically represented as Majnun. Further, it is a model of poetic expression *par excellence* of the Sufi quest for final annihilation and subsistence in God. And finally, that at both the literary and spiritual levels it is an allegory expressing the process of union of the human soul with God. The foregoing views, of Nizami's *Layla* have been voiced constantly and consistently, as has been pointed out. However, they still remain views; they have yet to be substantiated by reference to textual evidence, and understanding of their symbolic significance. This is what the study of expressions hopes to establish in the course of scrutiny in subsequent chapters.

Turning to Jayadeva's work, again the milieu of both author and text are considered in tandem. It appears that the poet Jayadeva

[3] The episode in the final chapter also exists in other versions of *Layla*.

flourished in the same time frame as Nizami, namely, the second half of the twelfth century. Jayadeva's origins are in the ancient village of Kendubilva, the modern-day Kenduli in West Bengal. Like Nizami, Jayadeva too enjoyed royal patronage, specifically at the court of Lakshmana-Sena, the last Hindu king of Bengal, who bestowed upon him the title of *Kaviraj*, King of Poets (Chatterji 1981, 3). In the reign of the Senas, Vaishnavism began to gain popularity.[4] In this regard, "the first Bengali Vaishnava poet to sing the sweet immortal songs of Radha-Krishna was Jayadeva" (Chatterji 1981, 118).

In the absence of written records, legends abound in association with Jayadeva. They tell of a harmonious domestic life, and his love and pride for his wife, Padmavati, is apparent in his work. In *Govinda*, apart from several direct references to her, he describes himself as *Padmavati-carana carana-cakravarti*, meaning "the veritable suzerain to cause the feet of Padmavati to move in dance" (Chatterji 1981, 9).[5] Apart from being acclaimed as an inspired poetical genius, Jayadeva was honored as a Vaishnava *sant*, or saint, who had received the special grace of Krishna himself.

The significance of these aspects of Jayadeva's life may be specifically contextualized by pointing out that in the traditional Indian worldview, all art functions in an integrated manner as a vehicle of worship, and also possesses sacrality and sacred functions. Consequently, Jayadeva's work, his life, his love, and his religious devotion may be seen to be complementary and inextricably interconnected aspects of his artistic worldview. In the same context, and especially in the Vaishnava tradition, *Govinda* obtained the status of a religious work and Jayadeva was hailed as *Adi-Kavi*, "Foremost or Perfected Poet" of his time. Again, such exaltation is a discernible trait of the traditional Indian *weltanschauung*, as has been borne out through the ages by the phenomenon of the saint-poet, exemplified by literary giants such as Valmiki, Vyasa, Kalidasa and the "modern" poet, Tagore, all of whom

[4] A Vaishnava is a worshipper of Vishnu, of whom Krishna is a manifestation or *avatara*. Incidentally, the name Jayadeva, meaning "victorious Lord," is also an epithet of Krishna.

[5] Legend also has it that Padmavati was intended by her parents to be dedicated to the temple of Jagannatha as a *devadasi* or temple dancer, and was consequently an adept in classical dance and music. However Vishnu himself directed the father to marry her to Jayadeva instead. See Chatterji (1981, 8-9).

are venerated and perceived as integral to the Indian mystico-religious traditions. In brief, in the traditional Hindu perception, the artistic role of the poet is almost synonymous with the religious role.

Although Jayadeva's fame rests mainly upon *Govinda*, he is nevertheless almost universally acknowledged as preeminent among the greatest of the Sanskrit poets. To a large measure, this preeminence is ascribed to the fact that he fruitfully straddled two important periods in Indian literature. The first is that of classical, "high" Sanskrit poetry, which was in its final stages by the end of the twelfth century, and the second, the advent of the new *bhasa* or "Vernacular Age," referring to the indigenous or regional languages like Bengali, through which devotional poetry found expression. In Chatterji's words, "Jayadeva ... stands at the *yuga-sandhi*, a confluence of two epochs.... [He] can truly be called 'the Last of the Ancients, and the First of the Moderns' in Indian Poetry" (1981, 2). It is said that Jayadeva's utilization and promotion of the vernacular, with "its Sanskrit so totally unmannered and full of vernacular cadences and rhythms" (1981, 2) in *Govinda*, secured not only the popularity of the text, but also its sustainability and appeal. In fact, it profoundly influenced the scholars and the masses, and invariably, the literature of India.[6] It may be noted here that the use of colloquial forms of expression in Nizami's poetry, as mentioned before, had precisely the same effect in establishing his popularity and esteem among all levels of society in Persian culture.

Presently, verses of the *Govinda* in different versions have been recorded and rendered as devotional songs of the highest order throughout the length and breadth of the Indian sub-continent, from Gujarat in the West to Bengal in the East, and Nepal in the North to Madras in the South. Again a parallel may be drawn in this respect to *Layla*, in connection with its popularity to the present day. In Persian- and Urdu-speaking cultures, and especially in the Indian subcontinent, the persona of Layla features prominently in musical renditions, stories, film versions, and religious songs, of which the *qawwali* is a notable genre.

By the foregoing contextualization of *Govinda* within the traditional Indian worldview of art, its religious and spiritual implications

[6] Not only has *Govinda* influenced Indian religious literature, but also song, dance, drama, music, and painting. Cf. Vatsyayan (2001).

may be discerned. However, similar to the case of *Layla*, *Govinda* has equally given rise to differences in perception. According to Braginsky (2004):

> its author—as Dasgupta and Stoler Miller showed only too convincingly—did not belong to Sahajiya. However, thanks to Caitanya's efforts, his poem was included in the Sahajiya cult and reinterpreted accordingly.

Dasgupta refutes the idea that *Govinda* is an expression of Jayadeva's longing to unite with the Supreme. He writes (1962, 125):

> If we analyze the *Gita-govinda* of Jayadeva we shall find not a single statement which shows the poet's desires to have union with Krishna as Radha had, he only sings praises ... and hankers after a chance just to have a peep into the divine *lila*,... [as] the highest spiritual gain which these poets could think of.

Furthermore, the religious status of the text has often been rejected by "orthodox," "religiously correct" readers, and there is controversy over the religious viewpoint of Jayadeva (Mishra 1998, 113). Apart from that, it has been condemned for its eroticism by the seventeenth century aesthetician, Jannatha, in his *Rasagangadhara* (Miller 1984, ix).

It is possible however, on one hand, to accommodate *Govinda* within the purview of Hindu religious literature. As Dasgupta goes on to specify, in what seems to contradict his earlier position, that Vaishnava poets like Jayadeva placed themselves in the position of the *gopis*, the female companions of Radha, who ever longed for the opportunity to witness from a distance, rather than participate in, "the eternal love-making of Radha and Krishna in the supra-natural land of Vrindavana" (Dasgupta 1962, 125). On the other hand, the orthodox, negative viewpoint pointed out by Mishra may be surmounted by an allegorical reading of the portrayal of eroticism, as well as by the tantric viewpoint of human sexuality as a channel for sublimation and transformation.

Notwithstanding the censorious perceptions therefore, the prevailing view, including those of authorities like Milton Singer and David Kinsley, strongly affirms the central position of *Govinda* within the Hindu mystical tradition and recognizes Jayadeva as a mystic-poet.

Much mention has been made of the terms "mystic," "Sufi," and "Bhakta," to refer to the practitioner of mystico-religious traditions. The first is a generic term, the second refers to the Persian-Islamic mystic, and the third to the Indian-Hindu mystic. In this regard it is necessary, as a preliminary measure, to know the defining characteristics and fundamental aspects of the mystic as a general term, as well as of particular aspects of the Sufi and the Bhakta, in order to realize the profound spiritual implications and applications of the doctrines, the terms, and the practices of the mystics of the respective traditions that emerge from literary or creative expressions. This is indispensable to the interpretation of the literary phenomena, and to a full understanding of the mystical dimension of the texts being studied.

The English term "mystic" derives from the word Greek *mu*, literally, "to close," as applied to the secret rites and lessons of the Greek mysteries. Equally in the Greek context, these rites were things about which "the mouth was closed."[7] Mysticism has also been said to contain (Schimmel 1975, 3):

> something mysterious, not to be reached by ordinary means or by intellectual effort ... [and] understood from the root common to the words mystic and mystery, Greek *myein*, "to close the eyes."

In the Islamic context, a similar *hadith* (Prophetic Tradition goes, "Who knows God, his tongue is tied." Jalal al-Din Rumi, the Sufi poet *par excellence*, has also conveyed gems of equal brilliance in this regard: "Close your lips, close your eyes, and close your ears, Laugh at me, if you do not see the secret of the Truth." Basically, what the aphorisms imply by "close" the "eyes" is that the mystic sees not with the human faculty of sight but with the eye of the Heart. A dictionary definition of the adjective "mystic" corroborates its denotation as "secret, concealed, or hidden meaning or nature, enigmatic, mysterious, all of which are applied to inner esoteric doctrines of a religion" (NSOED). In early Christian times, the term was applied to an exponent of

[7] Pythagoras prescribed that his disciples observe a five year course of silence before they were admitted to his mystic path.

mystical theology, or a person who maintained the validity and the supreme importance of mystical theology. Subsequently, it came to be applied to a person who seeks, by contemplation and self-surrender, to obtain union with or absorption into God, or who believes in the possibility of the spiritual apprehension of knowledge inaccessible to the intellect (NSOED).

Briefly, mysticism can be defined as love of the Absolute, because what makes the seeker capable of bearing, even of welcoming all the tests God puts upon him in order to purify his soul, is none other than Divine Love (Schimmel 1975, 4). The mystic's perception of his relation with God is on two interconnecting and integrated planes. In this context, religion is the exoteric dimension or outer shell, within which lies mysticism, the esoteric dimension or inner kernel of his existence. In physical terms, religion relates to the body, and mysticism to the heart. In metaphysical terms, religion is the phenomenon/substance and mysticism is the noumenon/essence. Man's position between the outward and the inward has been expressed as follows (Schuon 1976, 182):

> Man's mission is precisely to join the vision of "the Outward" to that of "the Inward"; to be at once witness to God as Principle and to God as Manifestation of Theophany....

From this quote it may be discerned that in the mystic's perspective, man is essentially a link between the Creator and creation.

The salient features of mysticism and metaphysics that are of direct relevance to the study comprise various intersecting notions such as union, separation, return, path, spiritual guide, spiritual poverty, center, and identity. To facilitate understanding of how each tradition symbolically expresses these aspects, they will first be described in this chapter, and subsequently applied to the texts in the following chapters of analysis. For the purpose of highlighting the affinities as well as the differences between the traditions, the discussion on the features mentioned starts with the Bhakti tradition for reasons of chronology, which will soon become apparent.

Hinduism has no particular founder or temporal origin. It is characterized by an immense range of sources, doctrines, and practices, encompassing sources like the Vedas and the *Bhagavad Gita*, which are believed to be ahistorical, and historical sources like the

Upanishads, the *Mahabharata*, and the *Aryanakas*. Both types of sources are accepted as knowledge of the Truth, although the former is qualified as direct, revealed knowledge (*sruti*), and the latter as transmitted knowledge (*smrti*).[8]

The explanation has been given that the root of the adjective *hindu* is the noun *hidi*. The *hidi* is a man who moves on the path of spirituality, and who "chooses to abandon all worldly pleasures and passions for the sake of spiritual upliftment" (Sharma 2003). The preferred term among Hindus with which to refer to Hinduism is *sanatana dharma*. The word *sanatana* means primordial, all-pervasive, everlasting, ever-present, without beginning or end. Although *dharma* is often translated as "religion" in English, the Sanskrit term has a much wider and more complex sense, meaning the natural law, order, and harmony that is divinely ordained.

Quite in contrast to Hinduism, the religion of Islam has a founder, Prophet Muhammad, whose historical origins are in Arabia of the seventh century. The Qur'an is the final authority and credo for all who claim Islam as their religion. The principle of Revelation of the Word of God to the Prophet is essentially the same as that of the Vedas in Hinduism, as pointed out by Burckhardt (1973, 45):

> The Veda, like the Qur'an, subsists from all eternity in the Divine Intellect and its "descent" is brought about by virtue of the primordiality of sound. The rishis, like the prophets, received it by inspiration, visual and auditory, and transmitted it just as they had seen and heard it without any mental discrimination on their part.

Islam, meaning submission to the will of Allah, is also known as *ad-Din*, a divinely prescribed way of life. Just as the Hindu tradition admits the Vedas as revealed and intuited scriptural sources, in Islam the Qur'an is the revealed source, which is also accompanied by the *hadith*, or sayings from the Prophetic Tradition. Apart from his say-

[8] In Hindu belief *sruti* is handed down by way of "seers" who "saw" the Truth while in a state of deep mystical consciousness (*turiyam*). To "see" in this context is not different from what has been mentioned about seeing with the eye of the Heart. In this case the human being was merely a channel through which direct knowledge of the Divine was revealed. On the other hand, *smrti*, knowledge which is "heard" (*sabda*) through "sound" (*nad*) acknowledges the intrusion of the human consciousness, although acquired in a similar heightened state.

ings, the personality of the Prophet himself provides a tremendous spiritual influence and model to his community, whereby he is venerated as the Perfect Man, *Insan al-Kamil* (Schimmel 1975, 27).

The Hindu concept of God is constituted of Brahman, which is the Transcendent or unmanifest (*nirguna*) aspect, and which encompasses the Immanent or manifest (*saguna*) aspect. This second aspect gives rise to worship of personal loving god(s). On the other hand, Islam is a monotheistic religion, characterized by its singularity of the concept of God (Allah), and the founder (the Prophet Muhammad). As the divinely revealed testification (*Shahadah*) goes: "There is no god but God; Muhammad is the Messenger of God" (*La ilaha illa'Llah; Muhammadun Rasulu Llah*) (Lings 1981, 75). Notwithstanding its unequivocally monotheistic basis, however, the *Shahadah* too includes the notion of dual aspects of Ultimate Reality. This has been understood by the Sufis as follows: the first line refers to the transcendent aspect of God, and the second to the immanent or theophanic aspect personified in the Prophet, and complementing and completing this notion.

The basic difference is that the immanent aspect finds expression in the notion of the supernal beings (deities or "gods") in the Hindu faith, whereas in Islam the fundamental question of "the duality of meanings inherent in the Divine injunctions concerning human things" (Schuon 1984, 86) is prefigured in the name of the Prophet. Muhammad indicates the limited and relative aspect of the manifestation of the Spirit, and denotes the support of this manifestation, or the Word as such. *Rasulu Llah* indicates the Universal Reality of this same manifestation, likewise found in the distinction between the human and Divine nature of the *Avatara* (Schuon 1984, 86).

In chronological terms, if Hinduism represents the earliest Primordial Tradition, Islam is the youngest of the great Revelations. The relationship between the two forms of religion is succinctly expressed as follows by Schuon (1975, 83):

> Islam is the last Revelation of the present cycle of terrestrial humanity. Consequently between these two religious forms there is a cyclic or cosmic relationship, that, as such, is not fortuitous.

This indicates a cyclic relation between the Primordial Tradition and its renewal and reaffirmation in Islam. Comparable concepts of this relation are expressed in poetry, as will be illustrated in the course of our study of the texts in subsequent chapters.

Specifically, for the Vaishnava Bhakta, the "loving God" mentioned above is none other than Krishna. For the Vaishnava, the immanent aspect of Vishnu is the manifestation of Krishna as *Avatara.* Thus a Vaishnava is a worshipper, or Bhakta, of Vishnu/Krishna. The concept of *Avatara* is commonly understood in English to be a bodily manifestation. However, the Sanskrit word *Avatara* includes a further, esoteric, significance, namely that of a descent of God, or incarnation. In the esoteric sense, the *Avatara* is an embodiment not of flesh, but of the essential, divine attributes of Brahman. Therefore although the *Avataras* exist in the earthly realm, they are eternally existent and free from the laws of matter, time, and space, or material realities. This is expressed in the Vedas as: "The *Avatara* descends from the kingdom of God for creating and maintaining the material manifestation" (*Chaitanya-caritamrita* 2:20).[9] In similar vein, Krishna says in the *Bhagavad Gita*: "To deliver the pious, to destroy evil, to reestablish *dharma*, I descend Myself from age to age" (4:8). In this regard, Divine Descent is in accordance with the law of decline that governs every cycle of terrestrial humanity, when it loses its vitality and has moved away from its origins/primordiality (Schuon 1984, 82).

In popular religion, Krishna is one of many deities or demi-gods, who appeals to particular human types or personalities.[10] However, the monotheistic tendency of Vaishanava bhaktas' singular devotion to Krishna is mentioned in the Gita as: "Those who worship Me with devotion, meditating on My transcendental form, to them I carry what they lack and preserve what they have" (9:22). This can be stated as follows: Krishna is Vishnu is Brahman. Furthermore, the Vedas state:[11]

[9] In "What is an Avatar" from The Avatar Site, http://www.avatara.org/essay.html (21 July 1999).

[10] For example, devotees of Murugan as the god of valor, bravery, virility, or of Saraswati as goddess of knowledge, intellectual prowess, purity, assume those attributes and become those personalities. Thus, Krishna is the god of love. At a higher level, these gods are Deities, or Divine Archetypes.

[11] Quoted from "Dancing with Siva," Online Master Course of Himalayan Academy by Satguru Siva Subramuniyaswami, Lesson 45, http://www.gurudeva.org/lesson.shtml (29 May 2002).

> Truly, God is One; there can be no second. He alone governs these worlds with His powers. He stands facing beings. He, the herdsman, after bringing forth all worlds, reabsorbs them at the end of time.

At the ultimate level, devotion is directed solely to Krishna as *Avatara* of Vishnu, the *saguna* aspect of *nirguna* Brahman. In addition, Krishna is the One, Supreme Lord of the Vaishnava Bhakta who does not worship any other demi-god.

As for the phenomenon of polytheism, contrary to popular misconception in Hinduism, it does not mean multiple gods that pervade creation,[12] but rather, it refers to the innumerable attributes of the Supreme Brahman. Thus an Infinite (symbolized by the figure 330 million) Supreme Being is epitomized by multiple names, forms, and functions. A different understanding is that these "gods" refer to the *devas*, acknowledged as the intermediary celestial beings who manage the affairs of the world. The concept of celestial being has a parallel with the numerous angels (*malaikat*) of the Islamic tradition.

In the above framework, Vishnu is that aspect of Brahman or Ultimate Reality that is associated with the preservation or sustenance of Creation.[13] For the Vaishnava Bhakta, this relation is expressed in his devotion to Krishna as that between lover and Supreme Beloved.[14]

[12] In popular belief, most Hindus attest to the existence of three gods; others profess belief in 330 million gods.

[13] The sustaining aspect is the second of the ternary aspects of the transcendent Brahman, the first being Creation, and the third, Dissolution. These may be explained as follows: Brahma is the aspect associated with *kriya* (literally, creation, action). From this root word *kriya* comes the term *Prakrti*. *Prakrti*, also referred to as Shakti, is perceived as the feminine or creative principle and vital energy, which is also the immanent aspect of Brahman, and which complements *Purusha* or the male principle, Brahma. Thus *Purusha-Prakriti* refers to the Creator-Creation relationship. In this context, the male character of Krishna (God) may be perceived as *Purusha* and that of the female character, Radha (human), as *Prakriti*. In *Govinda*, the character of Radha epitomizes the love attitude of the devotee towards God.

The third aspect of Brahman is Shiva, associated with the dissolution, or rather, the reabsorption of Creation into Brahman. Thus the cycle of creation (birth), sustenance (life), and destruction (death) attains completion when the immanent aspects or qualities of Brahman are reintegrated with the transcendent aspect.

[14] The man-God relationship is variously referred to as *atman-Paramatman* (soul-super Soul), *atman*-Brahman, *jiva-Ishvara*, Shiva-Shakti, deity-devotee, the relative-Absolute, etc. In the specific Vaishnava/Bhakti perspective, the supra-natural, eternal

This relationship is the structure upon which Vaishnava Bhakti doctrine synthesizes the principle of the ineffable Brahman with the direct, corporeal experience of God. In this respect the following explanation is of special relevance (Dasgupta 1969, 123):

> The Ultimate Being ... may be conceived in three of its states, either as the unqualified Brahman, or as the Paramatman, or as Bhagavan, the active and qualified God. Krsna as Bhagavan possesses three powers, the *Svarupa-sakti*, i.e. the power which He possesses by virtue of His ultimate nature, *Jiva-sakti* or the power through which all the beings are produced..., and the *Maya-sakti*, through which evolves the material world.... Radha and Krsna are one and the same in the ultimate principle.... Why then the apparent separation of Radha from Krsna? It is for the self-realization of Krsna. God has within His nature two aspects, the enjoyer and the enjoyed, and without the reality of the enjoyed He cannot realize His own nature....

Thus, following from the nature of the Ultimate Reality as such, it is the inseparable relation between the Creator and His creature that is represented in the eternal love-dalliance (*lila*) of Krishna with Radha in the supernal garden of love, Vrndavana (the cosmos). Echoes of this principle of inalienable Divine-human interconnectedness and unity are expressed in the metaphor of the "hidden treasure" in the Islamic *hadith qudsi* that has been referred to previously.

Whereas originally the canonical and classical Sanskrit texts like the *Bhagavad Gita* and the *Mahabharata* laid emphasis on the intellectual tradition in devotionalism, by the time of Jayadeva's era devotion emphasized emotion instead (Mishra 1998, 99). In this regard, the spiritual world is made meaningful not through philosophy but through emotion, particularly the emotion of love. And, thus, for Vaishnava contemporaries of Jayadeva the connection between emo-

archetype of this relationship is expressed in the temporal, earthly manifestations. The historical personages of Radha, the cowherdess, and Krishna, the cowherd, in the geographical location of Vrndavana in pastoral terms, represent the connection between the *gopi* (literally cowherdess, symbolizing man) and Govinda (literally the cowherd Krishna, representing God). In the terms *gopi* and Govinda, the prefix *go/gow* denotes the cow, which symbolizes the abundance of God's creation. Incidentally, this is one of the reasons that the cow is a symbol of the Divine for the Hindu.

tion and eroticism is a close one. Consequently, as both constitute expressions of the Bhakta's love for God—as may be observed from the text of *Govinda*—the depiction of "profane" love, *kama*, may be read both as a medium of transformation and as a symbolic expression of "sacred" love, *prema*.[15] In fact, both types of love are considered different ends of a spectrum, whereby *prema* derives not from suppression, but sublimation, of *kama*. Thus the two are not antinomical but homologous. It remains to be seen, however, whether Jayadeva's *Govinda* conforms to, as well as reflects, the foregoing general characteristics of Bhakti literature of his time.

In the Indian tradition, the Sahajjiya Bhaktas yielded a large body of literature. Their devotional poems especially, including those of Jayadeva, had a considerable influence upon the literature of the Vaishnava poets of Bengal. Bhakti expression was characterized by a wide variety of social and ideological traits, and the forms of Bhakti or devotion in Hinduism may be broadly characterized by different but overlapping characteristics and practices of individual Bhakti sects. However, the categories of Bhaktism have been simplified to be convenient for our purposes.

In light of the above explanation, "Vaishnava poets of Bengal" refers particularly to religious poets of Bengal like Jayadeva, who were Bhaktas of Krishna as the *Avatara* of Vishnu. Furthermore, followers of a mystical path (Sk. *panth,* similar to Ar. *tariqa*) of Bengal Vaishnavism, the *Sahaja* sect, have identified Jayadeva as one of its exponents along with other illustrious figures such as Gosvami and Caitanya (Dasgupta, 1969, 115). Thus, Jayadeva's religious denomination is Vaishnava, his spiritual affiliation is Bhaktism, and the particular sect is *Sahaja.*

Sahaja literally means "easy," "simple," "spontaneous." These qualities refer to man's spiritual goal, which is the return to his real, original state. In another sense, according to *sahaja yoga* and tantric doctrine,[16] the *yogin* or practitioner seeks, through physical discipline,

[15] Akin to the difference between the profane *Eros* and the sacred *Caritas/Agape* Love in the Judeo-Christian traditions.

[16] In seeking authoritative support, the *sahajjiyas* attributed their secret, "unconventional" *yogic/tantric* practices to great Vaishnava poets and thinkers. In turn, the literary representation of the poets is couched in enigmatic language and paradoxical style, comprehensible only to adepts and the initiated. Central to their doctrine is the

to perfect himself by attaining the state of *sahaja*. Towards this aim the body has to be harmonized by achieving, within the bodily *cakras* or centers of vital energy, a balance of the left side (*ida/ali*) with the right side (*pingala/kali*), in the *susumna*, or middle (vertebral column). In this context, *sahaja* means "the middle way," and thus the *sahajjiya* is the spiritual aspirant who has attained or entered this middle, or perfected state. Thus the Vaishnava Sahajjiya practices refer to the Bhakta's path of synthesis between the dichotomies and polarities of *kama* (carnal desire) and *prema* (pure love). In Hindu mysticism this is also seen as the synthesis between sexual and transcendental bliss, or between the Shiva-Shakti Principle, or between the renunciate and the man of the world, etc., depending on the individual sect or mystical affiliation. In this context, Bhaktism encapsulates the principle that all truth underlying the macrocosm of the universe as a whole is contained in the microcosm of the human body. All of these hierarchies of being or stages have may be related to the literary and poetic expression in the text of *Govinda*.

Literary Expression of the Mystical Experience

It is a fact that different cultures are structured such that difference in outward form is actively and dynamically maintained by each community, be it at the social, or religious, or at any level. The extract of C. E. Wilson's view (1974) quoted as an epigraph to this chapter relates to this principle. He says:

> All the arts strive to express the same thing, the idea, the spirit, the soul, the invisible, the infinite ... but..., it is of interest and importance to enquire by what different methods they have respectively attained to them. The difference arises mainly from religion, but this may lead to a considerable difference in the mode of expression.

Naturally then, being from different literary traditions, the expressions in the two texts are governed and regulated by their individual conventions and poetics. Similarly, in the context of the different religious traditions, the sacrality of the texts is true for a particular community

control of the sex-pleasure so as to transform it into transcendental bliss, which is at the same time conducive to the health, both of body and mind. See Dasgupta (1969, 112-115).

only, and not so outside it. Notwithstanding the exclusive nature of outward form, however, there are also some broad characteristics that are inclusive in nature, i.e., shared by diverse cultures, and expressed directly or indirectly in their literary works.

A major element that is shared in mystical and poetic expression is the portrayal of human love to represent Divine Love. As the focal point of our study, this refers ultimately to Love of the highest level (*ishq* in Persian and *prema* in Sanskrit), namely the love between Creator and creature, or man. In both the Persian and Indian traditions, this Love is regarded as the governing principle of the universe.[17] It constitutes for the mystic the end, rather than a means to an end. This is the principle expressed symbolically through the portrayal of human love, depicted customarily in a garden setting.

Of all the dimensions and aspects of human love, such as parent-child or sibling love, it is the man-woman love relationship that is most often explored and exploited as a poetic device to conjure the Divine-human connection. Moreover, it is not the ordinary man-woman love relationship that is depicted, but the kind that knows no laws. This kind of depiction is a particularly common defining characteristic of mystical poetry. To elaborate: apart from the portrayal of the relationship of love being mutually intense, reciprocal, and overwhelming in nature, it often involves the breach or infringement of usual social norms and standards of decorum of a community. Furthermore, such a breach becomes the established prerequisite and the norm of poetic expression. This characteristic also explains the occurrence of erotic portrayal and language in mystical expression. In portraying love for God, however, a difference is maintained between the types of love. In Hindu terms *kama* and *prema* form opposite ends of a spectrum. The former involves sexual desire as an end in itself, whereas the latter involves sexual desire as a platform, or means towards a selfless and intense state appropriate for spiritual transformation of the devotee.

A further defining characteristic of the kind of love portrayed is that the object of desire, namely, union with the beloved, is both the problem and the solution, the poison and the antidote, the point of departure and of return. For all these reasons, the portrayal of worldly

[17] This principle of Love sets mysticism apart from religion, which is generally based on the principle of reward and punishment.

love is intentionally employed as the most appropriate medium for representing the complex array of human emotions and experiences pertaining to Divine Love. This has been put across convincingly by Colin Turner, a translator of the original Persian text, with reference to Nizami's portrayal in *Layla*. In his words: [18]

> [The] striking originality lies in his masterful psychological portrayal of the complexity of human emotions when faced with the "love that knows no laws." The lightness of heart that falling in love can bring; the thrill of mutual affection; the sorrows of separation; the pains of doubt and jealousy; the bitterness of love betrayed; the grief that comes with loss—Nizami maps the whole of the mysterious world of love, leaving no region uncharted.

In this respect, the themes common to both *Layla* and *Govinda*, that of union and separation, may be considered in elaborating this point. At the literary or phenomenal level, the lovers' agony of separation from each other is the poison, and the ecstasy of their reunion its only antidote. But beyond the phenomenality of this interpretation, however, a possible spiritual interpretation of this theme is the necessity and significance of the portrayal of the state of estrangement of the human soul from the Divine, with both texts upholding the Divine as the point of departure and return.

A further device employed in the depiction of love in both the Persian and Indian mystical traditions is the utilization of sensual, particularly auditory, effects. Music, and all manner of musical effects such as rhythm and repetition, is purposefully employed to evoke and stimulate particular emotions, attitudes, and sentiments on the part of the audience. This is directly because in the traditional worldview, the spiritual quality inherent in music offers the possibility of fulfilling the human spiritual thirst . In the dynamics of author-audience participation, therefore, this device of evocation maximizes the poem's effect, and functions as an ontological platform. That is, it obtains a particular state of being, namely one which, on the part of the reader, is unreservedly and positively empathetic towards the writer's expression . In fact, in the context of the traditional milieu, this response is evoked by

[18] In the foreword to his translation, "Layla and Majnun: The Classic Love Story of Persian Literature" (2002).

all art upon an audience. As has been mentioned in the beginning of this chapter, audience and writer share a universe of discourse, in the sense that the spectator does not think of itself merely as an audience but as a "community of believers."[19] In this context, the connection between art and religion becomes evident, with art functioning as a medium of expression of a particular religious tradition in attaining a special knowledge of the spiritual mysteries, or gnosis (NSOED).

In considering the relation between poetry and religion, however, a major difference between purely literary symbols and religious symbols has to be maintained. The former are fluid in meaning because they are individual, subjective, and may be interpreted in relation to context and metatext, or suggest new meaning and usage within the framework of verifiable realities; whereas the latter are collective, objective, specific, and immutable, and serve to illuminate or intensify the mystery of non-verifiable dimensions of Divine Realities. Again, phenomena ostensibly display differences which hold true only for a particular culture or community. Consequently, by taking into account the fact that "each religion is universal by virtue of its essence, and particular by reason of its form" (Shah-Kazemi 1999, 55), it is possible to reconcile the outward truths with the inward principles inherent in the texts.

A further shared form of expression in mysticism is the concept of gardens as a setting. From earliest till present times, the garden has been idealized in different ways by different societies. The commonality in most traditions is usually the setting of an idyllic, earthly garden, conjuring celestial images (Ar. *firdausi*, Sk.*swargah*). The commonly-held significance of the garden, is that of Divine protection and deliverance. An interesting and significant fact is that the Persian word for garden, *jannah*, means both garden and paradise. According to Nurbakhsh, leader of the Sufi Nimatullahi *tariqa*, Paradise symbolizes the station of theophanies, whether of effects, Acts, Attributes, or the Essence.

Furthermore, the connection of the meaning of "protection" with "garden" can be found in the Hebrew meaning of the word for garden, *gan* (and *bagan* in Bengali), which carries connotations of "to

[19] In Sanskrit referred to as *sahrdaya*, "a man whose heart is at one with the author's." See Greenblatt (1990, 15), quoted in Mishra (1998, 19).

shade," in the way a tree offers shade from the sun and shelter from the rain (Stein 1993, 38). Consequently, the setting for the episodes of union and reunion of the lovers in *Layla* is that of a beautiful garden, whereas the entire depiction of *Govinda* is set against "Brindaban forest," an extant location with established connotations of paradise in the Hindu tradition (referred to in the Bhagavad Gita as *Goloka Vrindavana*).

Thus the setting of the garden plays a parallel role in the texts. The following excerpts of garden imagery from *Layla* are self-evident:

> She was the most beautiful garden and Majnun was a torch of longing. She planted the rose-bush; he watered it with his tears....
>
> In every plane tree the ringdoves cooed their love-stories, and on the topmost branch the nightingale was sitting, sighing like Majnun; while below, the rose lifted her head out of her calyx towards the bird, like Layla.... On one such happy day, when the roses were in full bloom, Layla came with some friends into the garden, to enjoy themselves among the beautiful flowers like the maidens in the garden of paradise.

There are elements in these examples that convey its specific milieu: the "rose," the "nightingale" and the "maidens in the garden of paradise" (or *houris*) are distinctly Arabic-Islamic. Yet it reminds us that Layla and Majnun can be anyone who falls in love, who encounters the depths of love, who experiences love and becomes aware that love is the embodiment of a special attribute beyond compare, wondrous, and of immense worth (Baharuddin 1992, xxiii-xxiv).

Although in *Govinda* the actual location is the forest, the garden is central to the rich imagery of wild nature. This is amply demonstrated by the following verses (I:33; I:36) of "The First Song":

> Budding mango trees tremble from the embrace of rising vines.
> Brindaban forest is washed by meandering Jumna river waters.
>
> Crying sounds of cuckoos, mating on mango shoots
> Shaken as bees seek honey scents of opening buds....

Trees figure prominently in this setting, especially—typical of the Indian convention—mango trees,[20] regularly occurring in juxtaposition with lovers and their union.

Furthermore, echoes of Majnun as the "torch of longing" in the garden in *Layla* are echoed in images of "flames" in the following verse in *Govinda* (II:20):

> Wind from a lakeside garden
> Coaxing buds on new asoka branches
> Into clusters of scarlet flowers
> Is only fanning the flames to burn me.

The beauty and bounty of nature provides the perfect setting for love in *Govinda.* In both the above examples, the lush natural surroundings convey the sense of pleasure the lovers have in each other. Again, although the setting is distinctly Indian in details such as the "Jumna river" and "asoka branches," at the same time they remind us that the union of the lovers is not bound to a particular time or place.

In this context gardens function symbolically in referring to particular existential realities, the earthly gardens signifying a worldly reality, which in turn signify a Divine Reality. In other words, the "real," earthly gardens have a relative reality, and the sacred gardens, an absolute Reality. The connection of the gardens, as the setting of the love stories, with the religious dimension, is thus apparent: it represents a refuge from the world.

There is also another significance to this concept of the garden. It is both protecting (a masculine attribute) and protected (a feminine attribute). Furthermore, in many Eastern cultures, the garden is a sexual symbol and a metaphor for woman's sexual arousal and desire. For example, in the Hebraic tradition, particularly in the *Song of Songs*, this is explicitly stated (Stein 1993, 43).

Based on the foregoing connections between the garden and love and its consummation, it is indeed appropriate that the love between man and woman is depicted within a garden setting. This is the particular context in which the phrase "Garden of Love" in the title of this work is understood, and the context in which it attempts an

[20] In the Hindu tradition, the mango tree is a symbol of fertility and regeneration. For this reason, mango leaves and branches are an indispensable part of Hindu marriages.

"unveiling" of the similarities and differences between the Persian and Indian "Gardens."

To recapitulate the general points about commonalities in modes of expression and its relation to the examination and comparison of the texts in hand, the issue to be addressed is the essential nature of the differences and similarities. This may shed light on questions such as: Do *Layla* and *Govinda* have an adequately spiritual interpretation in the first place? And: Is the spiritual interpretation appropriate and sufficient for attesting to commonalities between the Persian and Indian traditions? And beyond that: Does this give room to verify the Traditionalist perspective of the transcendent unity of religions? In the course of comparison and analysis, and of discovering the nature and the extent of the similarities and differences in the two texts, it is hoped these questions may be addressed.

The Stages of *Unio Mystica*

Unio Mystica, or the ultimate point of identification with the Divine, is arrived at through a process of transformation. The elucidation of this process in this section is partly an adaptation of the ideas and metaphysical categories formulated by Meister Eckhart and explained by Whitall N. Perry (1981) involving the stages and processes relevant to the development of the human soul on the mystic path. The particulars of each spiritual stage or phase will be outlined in the ensuing discussion, together with the equivalences in viewpoint of the stages within the Persian and Indian traditions. The relevant stages may be regarded as a cyclical projection of man's spiritual potentialities, as schematized below:

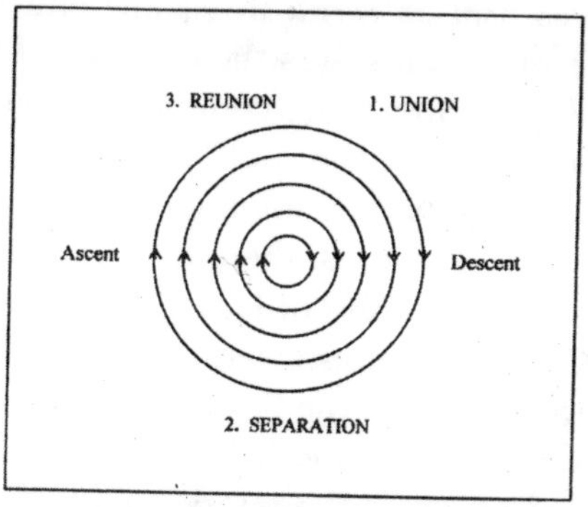

Figure 2: Stages of Mystical Development and Spiritual States

In Figure 2, three broad processes of mystical development are mentioned, namely, "union," "separation," and "reunion." As indicated in the diagram, the process or journey is cyclical, in that "union" entails "descent," whereas "reunion" entails "ascent." In terms of existential states, "1" refers to the spiritual-causal plane of existence, or *spiritus*; "2" to the gross-material plane, or *corpus*; and "3" to the subtle-spiritual plane, or *animus*. In whichever perspective they are viewed, the cycles are not on a level plane, but rather on higher or lower planes of existence. This is the archetypal spiritual journey in which man undergoes consecutive, recurring experiences of separation and union, or "death" and "life." But each time he "dies" and is "reborn," he moves closer to the ultimate state.

Although the first and third stages, that of "union" and "reunion," are placed at the same level in the diagram, they differ qualitatively. "Union" refers to the state of initial union, a state of innocence and ignorance. It is the primordial state of the soul, and reflects the original, paradisiacal divinity in man. In Islamic terms, this existential state is associated with spirit or *ruh*, and in Hinduism with *atman*. Thus, although this state concerns the bliss of ignorance (or innocence of the worldly state) it is also the bliss of knowledge (referring to the proximity with Spirit). In mystico-poetic expression, indications of impending separation or covert references to a fall from this state are ubiquitous.

"Separation" is contrary to union in that it deals with the "fall" of man from his divine state, and the severance of the self from its Center. In this context it is penitential in nature and necessitates processes of reconstruction and purification at the material level of the self, referred to as *jism* or *sarira* in Islamic and Hindu terminology respectively. The process involves the crushing of the self or ego, and entails great trial and tribulation, commonly referred to in Christian terms as "the dark night of the soul." However, for the mystic, this process is voluntary, embarked upon by the sole motivation of Love (*ishq* or *prema*). In other words, the underlying motive of Love is not as means to an end (the reward of Heaven) but the end in itself (Love for Love's sake). Thus, the mystic path of the Sufi (*turuq/suluk*) or of the Bhakta (*marga/panth*) to the Beloved is depicted by the travails of the soul. In conveying the existential state of separation, a key characteristic of mystical poetry is the interweaving of expressions of both pleasure and pain.

"Reunion," as mentioned, is differentiated qualitatively from "union," and denotes the state of union regained by the human soul after the experience of earthly realities, or "separation." This state is similar to the bliss of "union" in that it refers to the spiritual state. However, it is different in that it is concerned not with the bliss of innocence, but that of intellectual penetration. Basically, penetration is not of the mind *(al-'aql/ manas)* but of the heart (*al-qalb/ buddhi*). The process of conscious realization involves the awakening to the wholeness of the pre-existing and pre-eternal self or soul and grasping of, this innate power of the Ultimate. This power increasingly overwhelms the finite self with the Infinite. The spiritual aspirant's consciousness of his essential identity with the Ultimate involves the experiential awakening to a pre-existing condition of oneness or unity.

When this realization matures sufficiently, the spiritual aspirant or Bhakta may rightly utter the startling assertion, *Aham Brahmasmi*, "I am Brahman," or, as a Sufi spontaneous utterance of realization (*shathiyyat*) has been expressed, *ana-al-Haqq*, "I am the Truth." Thus reunion refers to a spiritual return in which the soul realizes its true Self, and the veil of *maya* is rent, leading to a direct vision of, and identification with, Ultimate Reality. This refers to the stage of gnosis, or Enlightenment, which enables the soul to regain perfection, and to be in union with God. It is referred to as *ma'rifa* in Islam and *jnana/ samadhi* in Hinduism. In mystical terms it involves a leaving behind of all attachments, and at the highest stage, extinction in God and subsistence in God (*al-fana'/al-baqa'*) in Sufi terms, or absorption in Brahman and dissolution in Brahman (*jivanmukti-moksha*),[21] in Bhakti terms. Poetic expression of the state of union regained is invariably marked by the paradox of "return" (to the origins) and "no return" (from the origins).

Each of the foregoing stages mentioned are not neat and discrete, but overlapping and recursive in nature, involving the experience of the aspirant in a direct and personal spiritual encounter. The understanding of the series of narrative events in the texts in the following chapters is based upon these stages and principles. In this manner,

[21] *Mundaka Upanishad* 3:2.9: "Absolute knowledge of Brahman is to become Brahman."

hopefully the blossoms of initial union, thorns of subsequent separation, and garden of final reunion may be properly recognized, compared, and appreciated.

CHAPTER THREE

BLOOMS OF LOVE'S GARDEN: INITIAL UNION AND SEPARATION IN UNION

Together they had inhaled the
scent of a flower, its name
unknown, its magic great.

(*Layla*, II:5)

Exciting your Yadu kinsmen....
Like sunlight inciting lotuses to bloom.
Triumph, God of Triumph, Hari!

(*Govinda*, I:19)

As mentioned in the preceding chapter, conventions and ideals of traditional literary works convey a message by indirect means. A common means is through the medium of stories. This is also true of the texts of *Layla* and *Govinda*. *Layla* recounts the story of two human lovers who experience love at first sight. As this state of affairs is unheard-of and not tolerated by the community, the encounter of the lovers is drastically cut short. Forced apart by family objections, by Majnun's consequent madness, and by Layla's arranged marriage to Ibn Salam, the lovers are torn and tortured by the separation from each other. Undergoing anguish, and pining for each other for the rest of their earthly lives, both lovers ultimately die. They are, however, reunited eternally in Paradise, where they enjoy infinite bliss in each other's presence. The tale of *Govinda*, on the other hand, begins with the young Krishna, Divine Lover of human cowherdesses or *gopis*, and his passionate encounter with one particular *gopi*, Radha, on the banks of the Jumna river. Radha is jealous of Krishna's dalliances with countless other *gopis* and she leaves him in a rage. This separation takes its toll, and both realize they cannot survive without each other. Finally all is forgiven, and they are reunited in an idyllic encounter celebrated with promises of unconditional and enduring devotion to one another. Thus, both texts convey a distinct story line or narrative. Even though the original works are poems, in translation, *Layla* is rendered in lyrical prose and *Govinda* in narrative poetry.

Apart from the narrative aspect, both texts are expressed in enigmatic language which can yield diverse levels of meaning and interpretation. It is possible to interpret this sort of expression through the approach of hermeneutics, facilitated by knowledge of, and reference to, the individual originating mystico-religious traditions of the texts. In this way, one can study and compare the outer, formal aspects of the texts, to derive their inherent, essential meaning. Using this approach, this study embarks on the analysis, interpretation, and comparison of the many-hued garbs of the Layla-Majnun and Radha-Krishna love stories that bloom in the gardens of *Layla* and *Govinda*.

In this, and following three chapters the outward meanings of literary "phenomena" that is, particular features, will be studied and compared. The two literary phenomena selected are, setting and characterization.. Subsequently, the study will proceed to the inward dimensions of these phenomena. These involve their spiritual and mystical implications, or the "noumena" inherent in them. This chapter deals with the first of the three phases of mystical development put forward in the schematization, namely, the initial or primordial state of union. The discussion on this state deals with two different aspects, the first being the initial union and bliss of the lovers, and the second, the element of separation in their union.

The State of Initial Union

The nature, condition, or qualities of the depiction of the union of the lovers, will be examined from the standpoint of two literary elements mentioned. Specifically, the setting and the characterization are understood in relation to the lovers and the nature of their love in union. To this end, the discussion includes the techniques and devices employed by the individual authors in conveying their message, and interpreted in the context of the individual cultural milieus of *Layla* and *Govinda*.

Setting is a basic aspect of any literary work. Although basic, it has an important role and function in enhancing a work, and affords ample basis for interpretation and comparison, as will be shown in this section. The setting of a work involves the entire environment of a story, including physical and natural location, historical period, and socio-cultural milieu portrayed in the work. Environment also includes extra-physical, or abstract elements such as atmosphere, mood, tone, etc. Moreover, environment includes the internal "landscape" of human emotions, which may be reflected by, or invoked through, an appropriate external scene or depiction. A general setting creates the entire frame of the work, and specific settings are usually attached to various episodes of a plot (Myers 1989, 277).

The setting of *Layla* alternates between two main locations in an Arabized Persia of the twelfth century. One is the opulent setting of palace and garden, and the other, the arid, harsh, desert landscape. The former is for the most part urban in character, inhabited by "noble families of various tribes" (II:4) such as the families of the protagonists, whereas the latter constitutes a wilderness inhabited by wild beasts. However, in this chapter, only the former is discussed, as it represents the setting of the lovers' initial meeting and union.

In *Govinda*, the entire setting of the union is rustic. Thus, there is an observable difference from *Layla* : the setting of place in *Layla* is urban and rural, whereas that of *Govinda* is rural. The love story of Radha and Krishna takes place in an idyllic Indian forest in the season of spring. *Govinda* is a song of one particular aspect of Krishna, the cowherd lover. Consequently, the story of cowherd lovers is set against a corresponding natural scene, that of a forest.

The particular location where the lovers meet in *Layla* is a school. This locality may be construed as the world of Layla-Majnun, which affords them all the delights and pleasures of love; it is there that they "inhaled the scent of a flower, its name unknown, its magic great" (II:5). In this world of initial union, the lovers dispense with the elements of "education" such as spelling and counting, and instead are immersed in "learning" about each other. Their conduct is reflected by charming puns like, "Their minds were freed from spelling by love's spell" and, "The others learned to count—while they could tell that nothing ever counts but tenderness" (II:6).

In taking a step back from the point of the lovers' meeting at school to the early life of Qays, we see that it begins in an opulent setting. His father is the ruler of a prosperous kingdom, and he is born in a palace. Subsequently, the son is entrusted to "a learned man to whom distinguished Arabs took their children" (II:4).[1] These textual facts may be read at a deeper level of understanding. Qays' birthplace and noble family background may be construed as symbolizing the

[1] In this Persian work, there appears to be an anomaly in the reference to "Arabs" rather than Persians. This may be an allusion to the origins of the folk tale in the Arabic context.

plenitude of man's divine origin. As for Layla, apart from the information that she too is from a noble family, there are no details about her origins. This evokes a sense of mystery in connection with Layla, which contrasts with Qays. It allows the interpretation that there is no information about her origins because there is no origin. In other words, Layla symbolizes the uncreated, Divine Being of which there is no beginning, and no end.

Furthermore, the "learned man," denoting the school teacher to whom Qays is entrusted, is not merely a teacher in the secular understanding of instruction. Rather he represents the Shaykh or spiritual guide of the seeker. The Shaykh's all-important role is to guide the pupil and deliver him into the spiritual life. This may be substantiated by the information that from the teacher Qays should learn "everything of use in this world" (II:4). There are two important aspects of spiritual import in this information. One, "everything" refers to the one thing that is "of use" in the mystic's world, namely the spiritual life. And two, "in this world" refers to man's earthly existence. In this existence the world is perceived as a learning experience. Consequently, it is represented as a school. Thus, there are two interpretations of the school setting. The first is that the initial union of the lover with the Beloved occurs in a primordial setting, meaning in a world which is still in its primary, pure state. The second is that the spiritual guide shows the seeker or the initiate, in the subsequent material world, the spiritual path as the way to regain this original state. Thus the "Fall" of Qays represents the spiritual aspirant's worldly existence.

Turning to the case of precise location in *Govinda*, the lovers' initial physical union takes place in "Brindaban forest ... washed by meandering Jumna river waters" (I:33). Here, their "secret passions" triumph, and here, Krishna, fatigued from sexual union with Radha, rests (I:17):

> ... on the soft slope of Sri's breast....
> Fondling wanton forest garlands.

This depiction, similar to *Layla*, paints a world in which none but the lovers exist. Although this is not directly stated, as it is in *Layla*, it may be inferred from the notable absence of any other character at this point in time. The only other characters in the work, the *gopis*, emerge after the separation occurs between Radha and Krishna.

Similarly, although it is not directly stated in *Govinda*, as in *Layla*, that they are in a paradise, the idyllic depiction of Brindaban forest conveys that, like Layla and Majnun, Radha and Krishna are in a natural, paradisiacal environment, namely, Brindaban.[2] The opening lines of the poem evoke a sense of darkness through interwoven, natural images in each successive line, as may be observed from the highlighted words in the following extract of the opening verse (I:1):

Clouds thicken the sky.
Tamala[3] *trees darken* the forest.
The *night frightens* him....
Passing *trees* in *thickets* on the way,
Until *secret* passions of Radha and Madhava
Triumph on the Jumna riverbank.

In this manner, the darkness of the setting unfolds in a contracting succession of concentric circles, to convey the lovers' union as a secret, hidden occurrence. This notion may be schematized as follows:

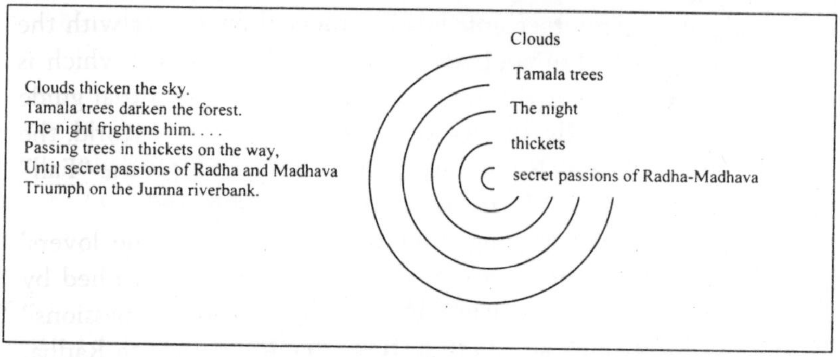

Figure 3.1: Schematization of Physical Space in the Union of *Govinda*

[2] In the *Bhagavad Gita*, Brindaban is referred to as *Goloka Vrndavana* the realm of cows, Brindaban) and *Krsnaloka* (the realm of Krsna).

[3] The *tamala* is a large, shady, flowering tree with a dark bark. Its flowers are used for incantation rites, *puja*, and are believed to grant enjoyment and salvation. Its shade is proverbial, believed to give as much comfort as a mother's womb. See Miller (1984, 216). This association with the womb is also evocative of the return to primordial origins.

This presentation of setting may be related to a spiritual perspective of the lovers' union, referring to the mystery of the primordial state of union with the Divine. The inward movement towards the secret union of the lovers resembles the archetypal *mandala* in Hindu mysticism. The word *mandala* in Sanskrit is a compound of *manda*, which means "essence," and the suffix *-la*, meaning "container" or "possessor." Thus, "a container of essence" or "sphere of the essence." From this etymology, the *mandala* shares with the depiction in *Govinda*, a common characteristic of a circle, having a center or axis and directional headings.

As a cosmological symbol, the *mandala* is a place where microcosm and macrocosm unite, a place where the inner world, or the Self, and the outer world, or the Universe, come together in the body. Thus the body represents the entire universe. In this context, the *mandala* signifies union or harmony of Self and Universe, the inner world and outer world. Thus, the *mandala* is a visual, diagrammatic representation of the universe or macrocosm, which is conventionally used as the focal point for meditation. The goal of this concentration or focus is to be ceaselessly centered on the innermost, which is the highest, level of one's being. At the microcosmic level, centers of energy, referred to as *cakras*, inhere in the human body

Meditation involves the repetition of a *mantra* or invocation of Divine Names. Basically the word *mantra* comprises the root *man-*, or mind, and *-tra*, which combines the notions of "tranquility" and its outcome, "freedom." In many religious traditions the Holy Name is kept secret—an underlying principle being, that which is sacred is secret. In the Hindu tradition, the secrecy of the Holy Name is found in the guidelines concerning a Vedic invocation, the *Gayatri Mantra*, or mother of all *mantras*. This *mantra* is believed to have been revealed only in part, for to reveal all would unleash unbounded power, and be too overwhelming for the uninitiated. It is in this context that in the *guru sampradaya*, or tradition of the spiritual guide, the *guru* utters a specific *mantra* in the ears of the initiate, appropriate to the individual's status or station, signifying revelation of the Holy Name to one who has qualified as an adept.

There is a complementary aspect of the *mantra*, namely, of contemplation which involves a *yantra*,[4] or mechanism. The *yantra* is a sacred tool of contemplation on the Transcendent, Absolute Brahman. Thus it is an icon which, like "all other visible symbols, establishes a bridge from the sensible to the spiritual" (Schuon 1984, 72). The basis of meditation as explained in the *Bhagavad Gita*, in which Arjuna asks Krishna, "How should I meditate on You? In what various forms are You to be contemplated, O Blessed Lord?" (10:17), is in Krishna's answer, "I am the Self O Gudakesa,[5] seated in the heart of all creatures. I am the Beginning, the Middle, and the End of all beings" (10:21). On this basis, the *mantra-yantra* is the vehicle which carries the devotee on the path to *jivan mukti*, liberation-while-living.

Seen in the above context, the circles conveying the lovers' union evoke the *mandala* at the macrocosmic level, which in turn, correspond with microcosmic levels of the human consciousness of the lover. Thus the "Triumph" or secret consummation of the love of Radha-Krishna may be interpreted as a union of the highest order, one that achieves the ultimate destination, *paramam gatim.* Within the schema of the setting represented in the above diagram, mention of the Jumna river as the site of the union is especially significant. The site represents the element water, which is a major symbol in most religious traditions. In Hinduism it is an archetype of purity, and purification. In *bhumi loka*, the earthly realm, water is used for religious purification. The source of the Ganga-Jumna rivers is said to be in *swarga loka*, the heavenly realm,[6] and thus the water of the earthly Jumna not only symbolizes, but is in itself, purity and sanctification. Water also has a rejuvenating and transforming power. In this context, the river banks of Jumna evoke a transcendental atmosphere, and the union of Radha-Krishna is perceived as a rejuvenating, spiritual "triumph."

In *Layla*, the setting of the union of the lovers is characterized by exclusivity. In projecting this characteristic, a virtual garden is evoked through images of garden and nature, and sustained by analo-

[4] The *yantra* is a geometric design that functions as an aid to meditation.

[5] Meaning, "one who has conquered the darkness." See Swami Prabhupada (1971, 519).

[6] Or, *Goloka Vrndavana* and *Krsnaloka*, as mentioned earlier.

gies and comparisons between the characters and their surroundings. It is said of Layla that "even the milk she drank turned into the color of roses on her lips and cheeks" (II:5). Another floral metaphor goes, "Together they had inhaled the scent of a flower" (II:5). Similarly, it is said of Majnun that he was a "carefully protected flower in the happy garden of childhood" (I:3). Thus, the existence of the lovers is contained within an exclusive garden in which, as long as no one has noticed, "they went on ... enjoying the sweet scent" (II:5). This conveys that their relationship excludes everyone and everything else, as they "turned their backs on the world" (I:7). The school constitutes their world which becomes transformed by their love into a garden of paradise, where the lovers, "enjoying their paradise" (III:7), drink "the wine of oblivion" (II:7).

Based on the above depiction, the mandalic interpretation of the union in *Govinda* may be applied to *Layla* in an identical context. Although it differs phenomenally in setting, a similar pattern of concentric circles of the lovers' union as a secret, hidden occurrence, emerges. This pattern may be illustrated by the following diagram.

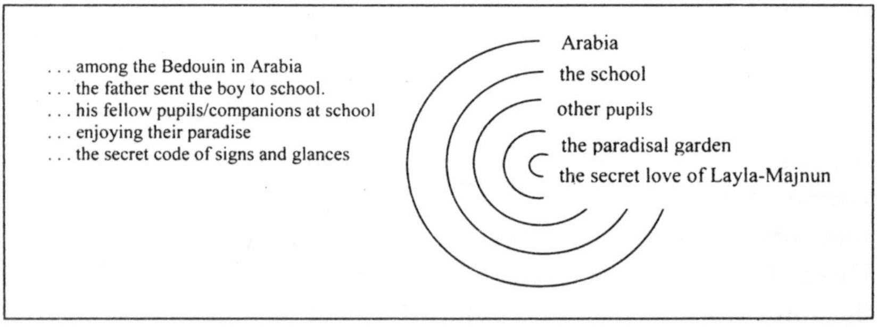

Figure 3.2: Schematization of Physical Space in the Union of *Layla*

Although the elements of physical space do not appear in a single paragraph and in sequence as they do in *Govinda*, they provide an ample basis for constructing a similar pattern. While in *Govinda* the schema of the union evokes the three doctrines of Hindu mysticism, namely, the *mandala*, the *cakra*, and *yantra-mantra* in *Layla* it may be related to three corresponding Sufi doctrines. They are, the *latifa* or seven stages or centers, the arabesque design, and *fikr-zikr*, the principle of contemplation and meditation.

The Sufi initiate strives for attainment of a rigorous balance between the human body or microcosm and the universe, or macrocosm. This process basically occurs through seven *latifa*, hierarchical stages or spheres or centers (Ardalan & Bakhtiar 1973, 132n). Each of these seven stages signifies a special relationship between the seven centers of the body and the seven Prophets. The balance is "needed to visualize inwardly what one sensibly feels and to feel inwardly what one visually sees" (Ardalan & Bakhtiar 1973, 132n). Thus the possible significance of the fact that Qays first sets eyes on Layla at school "when he was seven years old" (I:3), is that he is at a particular level of consciousness and thus qualified to begin the journey to God. This is signalled by the number seven, which in many spiritual traditions is an auspicious number. In a manner similar to the Bhakta, the journey of the Sufi involves contemplation or *fikr.* The contemplation may be upon a graphic representation of the cosmos by means of a geometric, arabesque pattern. This pattern is a reflection of the cosmos, thus forming a "mental itinerary" for the contemplative mind (Ardalan & Bakhtiar 1973, 30). It envisions the Garden of Paradise, and the cosmic processes within all things. The arabesque thus relates metaphysically to the Quranic verse, "He is the First (*al-Awwal*) and the Last (*al-Akhir*), the Manifest (*al-Zahir*) and the Hidden (*al-Batin*); and He knows infinitely all things" (Quran LVII:3), the essence of which is strikingly reminiscent of the verse of the *Bhagavad Gita* quoted above. Further, this contemplation is facilitated by the practice of *zikr*, or remembrance of God, through religious formulas and repetition of the Divine Names. Similar to the Hindu tradition, in Islam the 99 Most Beautiful Names of Allah are revealed, whereas his essential Name is hidden from those without proper initiation (Ardalan & Bakhtiar 1973, 30).

The relevance of the above practices and processes to the lovers in union in *Layla* may be seen from the following description of the lovers' state of complete concentration and absorption upon each other in the garden (II:5):

> ... (they) drank by day and dreamed by night, and the more they drank the deeper they became immersed in each other. Their eyes became blind and their ears deaf to the school and the world.

in a manner suggestive of the deep contemplation and practice of remembrance of the Sufi. From the foregoing comparison therefore, it may be said that the texts illustrate corresponding and equivalent representations of the setting of union, reflecting Bhakti and Sufi notions of union with God.

The setting may be understood in relation to a particular feature, namely the quality of plenitude. In *Layla*, as has been pointed out, Qays is from a family background of wealth and nobility. This is apparent from the diction in portraying both bounty and magnanimity in relation to his father, who is (I:1):

> ... a *great lord*, a Sayyid, who *ruled* over the Banu Amir. No other country *flourished* like his and Zephyr carried the *sweet scent* of his *glory* to the farthest horizons. *Success* and *merit* made him a *Sultan* of the Arabs and his *wealth* equalled that of Korah.
>
> He had a *kind* heart for the poor and for them his *purse* was always open. To strangers he was a *generous* host and in all his *enterprises* he *succeeded* as if *good luck* were part of him, as the stone is part of the fruit....
>
> ... *respected* like a *caliph*,... he who otherwise *possessed everything* he desired.... (emphasis mine).

The above passages are heavily laden with images of plenitude, as can be seen from the emphasized words in the description. Accordingly, elements in the depiction of the setting reflect and correspond to these qualities through descriptions of a similar tenor, of what occurs in the immediate human environment following the birth of Qays (I:2):

> ... the happy father opened wide the door of his treasury. Everyone was to share his happiness and the great event was celebrated with shouts of joy and words of blessing.

Every other word in the above passage evokes an atmosphere of plenitude. The celebration and commemoration that prevails in the above description is sustained in the depiction of Qays flourishing in his growing years: "Playful and joyful, he grew year by year, a carefully protected flower in the happy garden of childhood" (I:3). Consequently, when the meeting of the lovers takes place, the floral imagery and abundance is continued: "How happy this first flowering of love for Qays and Layla!" (III:6). Furthermore, forces of nature reinforce the effect of the lovers in a state of union, in a visibly integral way (III:7):

> Just as Joseph came out of his pit, so the sun, a golden orange, ascends every morning from the hem of the horizon like a precious toy in the sky;... So Layla also shone forth in her morning. Every day she grew more beautiful.

In keeping with this portrayal of the lovers, there is a sense of fullness in their love—"A bearer had come and filled their cups to the brim" (II:5)—evoking a quality of superabundance.

Plenitude in terms of material riches in *Layla* is apparently lacking in *Govinda.* This may be explained by the fact that, as mentioned earlier, the entire setting of *Govinda* is rustic. Nevertheless, what is lacking in terms of material riches is replaced by the portrayal of natural richness, i.e. a verdant forest setting in *Govinda.* As seen in the quotations provided earlier in regard to location, there is also a sense of superabundance in the physical union of Radha and Krishna, projected in recurring images of nature. The imagery is fashioned from elements like trees, thickets, rivers, garlands, etc., and sustained by liberal references to natural elements such as "the wild Himalayan goose on lakes" (I:18), "sunlight inciting lotuses to bloom" (I:19), the "fierce eagle Garuda" (I:20), "the fresh rain clouds," "night birds" (I:23), and so on. Taken together, these nature images in the depiction allow the reader to virtually see, touch, hear, smell, and taste the abundance. Further, these sensory images convey a super-sensory state of being.

From the foregoing arguments and examples, a commonality in the setting in *Layla* and *Govinda* is that the state of union is characterized by plenitude. In this connection it is interesting to mention briefly here, a point of difference between the setting of the first stage of union and the next stage, separation, in both works. In *Layla*, the separation of the lovers occurs primarily in a contrasting desert setting that is bare and harsh, appropriate to the condition of separation. However, in *Govinda*, there is no change in setting, and separation occurs in the same, lush setting. An attempt will be made to address this point of difference in the following paragraphs.

The question of setting may be related to the issue of historical and ahistorical realities. It is noted that the setting in *Layla* has a historical reality, meaning it belongs to a particular time and place, i.e. an Arabized-Islamized Persia that is consistent with the time of production of Nizami's text, namely the twelfth century. On this basis, at the literal level the phenomenon of the human characters concerns a male madly and recklessly in love with a female. However, this phenomenon has a symbolic and mystical significance. For the Sufi, Layla symbolizes the Divine Beloved, and Majnun, the human soul longing for the Divine, or the longing of man for restoration to his Divine origin. In this way, the love story in *Layla* is of two separate orders, the worldly and the spiritual.

In contrast, the love story of Radha and Krishna in *Govinda* is set in primordial times, representing an ahistoric and mythic reality. This means that although Bhaktism and esoterism are phenomena of the Iron Age or *Kali Yuga*, the love story in *Govinda* represents and participates in a reality of the Golden Age, *Dwapara Yuga*, involving primordial humans and an *avatara.* Thus the story follows the logic of the doctrine of Krishna and Divine intervention; the "Brindaban" referred to is one and the same as the celestial *Goloka Vrindavana*, and for the human, it is, to borrow a Christian expression, on earth as it is in Heaven. Thus man embodies primordial perfection and divinity, projected and manifested in the earthly domain. In the words of John Herlihy, Adamic,[7] or primordial man (2003):

> affirms the Divine Principle in the human form by virtue of his being made "in the image" (*imago Dei*)[8] of a Divine Being..., his human nature expressed totality and completeness.... He could see things directly ... and he symbolically walked with God.

In the same vein, "Primordial man saw God everywhere,... and he was not enclosed in the alternative 'flesh or spirit'" (Schuon 2003). This is the particular context in which the setting of *Govinda* is understood.

[7] In Sanskrit, *Adi* (*purusha*) meaning First or Foremost (man), and the Hindi/Urdu *aadmi*, meaning man or person, have an equivalent semantic significance as Adam.

[8] In a similar context, in Hindu myths the Sanskrit term *devi* is thus applied to Radha in relation to her "divine" status, and the perception of her as a "deity."

And thus, like *Layla*, it may also be understood in two ways: a direct and literal manner, as well as an anagogic and symbolic manner.

Characterization is one of the most important means by which a literary writer projects certain ideas into a work. The love relations of Layla-Majnun and Radha-Krishna, studied from various aspects of characterization, may shed light on its essential significance. This involves (Myers 1989, 44):

> the presentation of fictitious people whose composite physical descriptions, attitudes, motives, and actions are lifelike enough for the reader to accept as representing real people.... The proper selection and the particularization of detail make for characters that are specific, but which contain universal significance.

With reference to the above definition of characterization, the literal meaning, as well as the literary implications relating to the male and female protagonists of *Layla* and *Govinda* in the state of initial union can be better understood. In their characterization, the names, the physical attributes, the qualities, and the actions of both pairs of lovers from the individual texts, and how they convey the idea of initial union, are of particular interest.

The characters in question are identified both by appellations and by epithets. The former is defined as a designation, a name, and a title, whereas the latter as a word or phrase expressing a quality or attribute regarded as characteristic of the person mentioned (NSOED). The ensuing discussion is confined to the particular forms of reference that reflect and convey the state of initial union of the lovers, starting with the female protagonists.

Layla is introduced as follows (II:5):

> The name of this miracle of creation was Layla. Does not "Layl" mean "night" in Arabic? And dark as the night was the color of her hair.

In this introduction, Layla conjures up a mystery. Instrumental to this are, the reference to her as a miracle in the first sentence, its literal meaning in the second, and associations with "dark," "night," and "hair". In subsequent descriptions, her looks are associated with images of light and darkness, such as, "her face was a torch, with ravens weaving their wings around it" (II:4), and reference to her hair as "under the dark shadow of her hair" (II:4), and "dark as the night was the color of her hair" (II:5). All of these expressions emphasize and deepen the sense of mystery. In other words, the physical description of Layla constructs a sense of the mysterious, that is, something that cannot be easily perceived or apprehended.

It is interesting that although there occur many indirect or elliptical references to, and descriptions of, Layla in the text, she has only one name. This fact has important implications at the religious or exoteric level, as well as at the spiritual or esoteric level. Firstly, the association with the religious context is to be found in the *Shahadah*, the foremost profession of faith in the Islamic religious tradition. The attestation *La ilaha illa'Llah*, "there is no god but God" reflects the characteristic monotheism of Islam. This monotheistic element is reflected in the particularity and the singularity of reference to Layla as a symbol of the Divine Beloved. Besides, Layla's name has a phonetic resemblance to the first segment of the attestation, *la-ilah*. Secondly, in the spiritual context, "night" is an epithet justly bestowed on Layla, because night symbolizes Unity and Oneness or union in the Sufi tradition. Unity involves the annihilation of the mystic's "being" before, and into, the only real Being. Thus the mystical formulation of the *Shahadah* is "There is nothing existent save God" (Schimmel 1982, 22). This point about annihilation and non-existence will be taken up further in reference to the discussion on Majnun in subsequent paragraphs.

Another aspect of Layla is in reference to the moon in the examples, "They kept the new moon hidden from the fool" (III:9), and "Layla, his moon" (V:14). This form of reference to her may be interpreted as representative of epitomizing the nature of the union of the lovers: each reflects, and is reflected in, the other. It also indicates that their relationship is a union of mutuality and complementarity.

As to the name of the female protagonist in *Govinda*, although she is referred to in several ways, the focus is on one name, Radha. Speculations of scholars trace the Sanskrit word *radha* to Vedic and Puranic origins. It is associated with *radhas*, a common noun referring to a woman as "beloved" and "desired." Others suggest that it means "satisfaction," and "perfection," and most scholarly interpretations indicate something or someone that "fulfills a need" (Miller 1984, 56). All of these interpretations suggest that the name Radha has a dimension of fulfilling or of complementing something else. In this regard, Radha in the state of union may be contextualized as fulfilling Krishna's needs, and of complementing his perfection. This has been taken further, to say that Radha is none other than Krishna's feminine aspect.[9]

As for the male protagonist in *Layla*, it should be pointed out that the name of "Majnun," meaning "mad," and his entailing characteristic of madness, emerges only after "Qays" is overwhelmed by the separation from Layla. Therefore, the discussion on the state of original union between the lovers only considers the name of Qays. In other words, he is referred to by the name Qays when the state of initial union prevails, and by the name Majnun after separation occurs. The association of this name with separation can be substantiated by the mention in *Layla* that (I:8):

> ... his heart was no longer at one with his reason. If reason asked him to avoid his love, his heart fell ill with longing for her. Away from her, Qays found no peace....

The above quotation can be interpreted as, without Layla there is no Qays, but only Majnun. This is underpinned by explicit statements such as, "his heart suddenly lost its balance" (II:9), and "The reins had slipped from the rider's hand" (IV:10). These expressions obviously contrast with the nature of initial union, which will be further discussed in the following paragraphs.

When Qays is born, it is said that he "looked like the moon ... and his parents gave him the name of Qays" (I:3). Here it may be added that "Qays" literally means "moon" in Arabic. A particular attribute of the moon is its glow, which is reflected from the light of the sun. In short, moonlight is a reflection of sunlight. It is also important to remember that although the moon is always there, it is visible only as a nocturnal phenomenon, or in the darkness of night. These elements of the moon may be applied to Qays and the state of his unity with Layla. Just as the moon exists only at night, so too, Qays exists only in Layla. In this connection it may be said that Qays is literally and metaphorically a reflection, or mirror, of Layla. This is indicated in the expressions "Qays' soul was a mirror for Layla's beauty" (III:8). Stated

[9] According to practitioners of the Sahajiyya-Vaishnava devotees of Bengal.

differently, without Layla, Qays becomes a non-entity (and assumes the character of Majnun), just as without the darkness, the moon cannot be perceived.

The mystical interpretation of Majnun's nonentity on one level, is that as the lover whose heart was no longer at one with his reason, he personifies the "loss of discerning intellect through the overwhelming power of Love" (Schimmel 1982, 75). On another level, it refers to annihilation and non-existence of the self mentioned previously in relation to the mystical formulation of the *Shahadah.* The heart has to be cleaned and emptied, so that the Divine Spirit can dwell in it (Schimmel 1982, 234, n87). This state is *fana'*, the necessary state of annihilation in the material life required of the mystic in order to gain eternal life.

The characteristics of the connection of the lovers discussed above are strikingly encapsulated in a passage describing Qays' attempts to steal a glimpse of Layla (V:14):

> The curtain was withdrawn and in the entrance of the tent unveiled in the light of day, clearly visible against the dark interior, Layla was sitting; Layla, his moon.
>
> Majnun sighed deeply. Now Layla saw him, and they recognized in the mirror of each other's face their own fear, their own pain and love.

If Layla as the symbol of the Divine Beloved is referred to by only one name, by contrast, Krishna, the divine figure and male protagonist in *Govinda*, is referred to by numerous names, although the foremost one is Krishna. It would be interesting and challenging to reconcile this difference as will be attempted in the ensuing discussion.

The understanding of the title of *Govinda* may shed some light in this direction. The particular community in *Govinda*, although limited to the protagonists and the *gopis*, or cowherdesses, is apparently rustic. The literal meaning of *gita* is "song," whereas *govinda* is "cowherd." Thus it means "song of the cowherd." Besides, Krishna means "black" or "dark." This explains the "Dark Lord" in the translation of the English version of *Govinda* used for this study. Scholars suggest that the word *govinda* originates from *gopendra*, the term to denote the cowherd caste. In turn, *gopendra* is derived from *gopa* and *gopi*, meaning the male and female cowherd respectively.[10] In this context, the words "dark" and "cowherd" would naturally have a close relationship because it is entirely probable that a cowherd, continually exposed to the sun in tending his herd, would become dark-skinned. In this context, Krishna is the Dark Lord who is portrayed as the cowherd lover in the poem.

Apart from the literal meaning, darkness is associated with the unseen or unmanifest, or a mysterious entity. In this regard, the cowherd Krishna, who is the Dark Lord, represents the unmanifest and unknowable Brahman. These particular meanings and associations of the name of Krishna exhibit a close parallel to the meanings and associations of the name of Layla. On a different level of interpretation, the syllable *go* means "universe," *vin* means "joy," and *da* means "to give." Thus *govinda* is "One who gives joy to the universe" (Hariharananda 2003).

At the same time, Krishna is associated also with the moon, and light: "The earth clings (to him).... Like a speck of dust caught on the crescent moon" (I:7). Thus, Krishna is associated with both the night and the moon, or darkness and light. Similarly, Layla, meaning "night," and described as "like the Arabian moon" (II:4), is associated with both the night and the moon, darkness and light. The parallel associations exist not only between the names of Layla and Krishna, but also between Qays and Radha. Qays, symbolizing the human soul, means "moon," just as Radha, representing the devotee, is described as "moon-face" (I:23). Stated differently, both Qays and Radha, the human entity in the human-divine relationship, are associated with the moon. This point of similarity between the two pairs of lovers is spelled out in Krishna's plea to Radha in the line: "Let your moon face lure my nightbird eyes" (I:23).

The terms of reference to the lovers in union in *Govinda* are particularly interesting. In major religious traditions of the world, it is conventional to represent the relationship between the Lord and His congregation in cattle and livestock imagery. Thus the representa-

[10] Both terms originate from the word *gow*, meaning cow. Hence another of Krishna's epithets is Gopal. The term *gopi* represents the topos in the Hindu tradition in specific relation to "the cowherdesses of Brindaban forest who were the female companions of Krishna," a definition of *gopi*, which interestingly enough appears as an entry in the Oxford Dictionary. Cf. NSOED.

tion reflects two complementary entities, the herd and the herder.[11] Similarly in the Hindu tradition, the entity of herder/Divinity is represented by Krishna, the cowherd.[12] The cow is specifically associated with Krishna, epitomized in the epithet "Govinda," and referred to in Vedic texts as *Tam ekam govindam*, meaning "You are Govinda, the pleasure of the senses and the cows." In this context, the cow is understood as symbolic of the senses, and Govinda is the object of all human pleasure. Thus, there is only one cowherd in *Govinda*, i.e. one representation of the Divine entity. In other words, no matter by what name He is called, the reference is to Krishna alone.

Since the Lord is the cowherd, one would assume that the human entity or worshipper would be represented by "herd" (plural reference) or "cow" (singular reference). However, in *Govinda* the devotee is represented by *gopi*, meaning cowherdess. Thus, the devotee is symbolized by Radha and her companions who are cowherdesses, rather than by the cow, or the herd. The term *gopi*, referring to Radha or the devotee, gives room for extrapolation because it indicates that the cowherd and the cowherdess are in a relation of equal standing. This notion of equality can be applied to the union of Radha and Krishna, as lover and Beloved. It means that in the state of union, Radha and Krishna are equal, and not Lord and serf, nor Master and servant. The difference is that whereas the master-servant relationship represents a religious view of the Divine-human connection, the cowherd-cowherdess relationship represents a mystical view. Within its milieu, *Govinda* is an expression of Vaishnava Bhakti, the spiritual movement of "Devotion to Vishnu-Krishna." Therefore it represents a mystical and spiritual viewpoint. Thus, although Bhakti literally means "devotion," the focus is not only on the religious devotion of the servant to the Lord, but primarily the mystical, selfless devotion of pure love, *prema*, between lover and Beloved.[13] This may be substantiated by the

[11] In Christianity, the reference is to the Shepherd (Jesus) and His flock (the followers).

[12] "Cow" indicates the singular form, and "herd" the plural. Further, "cowherd" refers to the male gender, "cowherdess" to the female, and "herder" to the neuter.

[13] This will be further validated from expressions in subsequent parts of the discussion.

terminology of parity applied to the Radha-Krishna relationship in the text, which is consistent with the mystical viewpoint.

In a different interpretation of Krishna's name, *Kri-* in Sanskrit refers to "creation," and *-shna* derives from *Vishnu. Vish-* means "all-pervader," and refers to the uncreated, preserving energy of Brahman. Thus the name Krishna incorporates both creation and the uncreated aspect of the Ultimate Reality. Indeed, in the Hindu religious context, Krishna embodies both the immanent and the transcendent aspects of God. In line with this view, in *Govinda*, Krishna is represented not only as the Lover, or the Beloved, but also as the cosmic power of *Kali Yuga*, the Dark Age (Miller 1977, 23). There are manifold references to this power. An example may be found in the lines of "The First Song," which is a hymn to Krishna as *avatara* at the beginning of the poem (I:19):

> You defeat the venomous serpent Kaliya,
> ... Triumph, God of Triumph, Hari!

Here, Krishna, as Hari or Enlightenment, triumphs over the Dark Age, referred to as "the venomous serpent Kaliya." In this context, the serpent appears as an archetype of evil and destruction as often represented in the major religious traditions of the world. The word Kali- in this instance refers to the context of *kala* as time, as well as darkness. In this verse the particular time/age of Krishna's triumph is *Kali Yuga*, Dark Age, referring to the present age. In this context, the Dark Age is portrayed as the "venomous serpent," an archetype of evil and destruction, in contrast to Hari as the Divine archetype of salvation. Other evidences of Krishna's power and triumph over *Kali* are: "Recalling Hari's feet is elixir against fevers of this dark time" (XII:19) and "he calms my fear of dark time" (II:8).

Within the Hindu religious tradition, two aspects of Krishna are apparent: one, which expresses his awesome aspect, and the other, his beautiful aspect. These aspects are apparent in *Govinda*. References to the awesome aspect are found in the verses of extolment or hymns. These verses vividly portray his "ten incarnate forms" (I:16). In each form, Krishna is referred to by an epithet (I:5-14). One is "form of the Fish," (*Minasarira*), which alludes to man's salvation from the deluge by Krishna. Consistent with the conditions of the deluge in this ancient myth, Krishna assumes the form of a giant fish (Miller 1984,

21). Another epithet of Krishna is "form of Rama" (*Ramasarira*), or Perfection in Man. Rama's purpose is to destroy the demon (in man), represented by Ravana, the force of evil that threatens the world. In this context, the Divine-human connection is that of Brahman-Vishnu-Rama-Perfection prevailing over

man-beast-demon-imperfection. Here again, the motif of man's salvation through Divine intervention is apparent. Thus, each of the epithets mentioned (I:16), in invoking a particular aspect of Krishna's supremacy has an esoteric interpretation that is consistent with the Age in which the *avatara* appears.

The relevance of the incarnations to the state of union between Krishna and Radha may be stated as follows: Krishna represents the projection or descent of God's Presence into the material world, or creation, of which Radha is a part. Thus, his physical encounter with Radha in Brindaban, and the identification of Krishna by his various names and forms has the special function of expressing the durability and sustainability of the divine-human connection.

Based on the above discussion, the phenomenon of the singularity of the name of Layla, representing the Divine in *Layla*, may be reconciled with the many names of the Divine, Krishna in *Govinda*. Whereas the singularity of the name of Layla clearly reflects the strictly monotheistic conception of God in Islam, the many names of Krishna refer to his many forms or aspects in Hinduism. It is this factor that has often been the source of a misconstrued understanding as polytheism in Hinduism. The multiplicity of names and forms signifies unbounded Divine qualities and powers. In other words, Krishna is Supreme, both in terms of being Almighty, and being the One God. This is the element of "monotheism" for the Vaishnava Bhakta.

Apart from the awesome aspect of avataric destroyer, Krishna is also Divine Beloved, characterized by his beautiful and bountiful aspects in the depiction of initial union. He is referred to by the name Madhava, which is a derivative of *madhu*, "honey." Honey is commonly associated with nectar, which in turn represents an agent of immortality, or elixir of life. Thus Madhava is immortality, or the eternal connection of God and man, as illustrated by the following lines (V:7):

> Madhava still waits for you
> In Love's most sacred thicket,

> Where you perfected love together.

Another epithet, Hari, meaning "springtime," has obvious associations of renewal and regeneration. For example, in the lines (IX:2):

> Hari comes when spring winds, bearing honey, blow.
> What greater pleasure exists in the world, friend?

the name illustrates the close association with spring, which in turns evokes a sense of the everlasting or eternal. Hari also means "light," and is associated with illumination in the line "Seeing Hari light the deep thicket" (XI:13). Thus Krishna is enlightenment. In both cases the names Madhava and Hari suggest that the union of Radha-Krishna epitomizes the relation between man and God, a relation which is characterized by the qualities of eternity and enlightenment.

In the depiction of union in *Layla*, beauty is a keynote of the portrayal of the protagonists in the state of union. There is a profusion of evidence in the beginning of the work to indicate that both the lovers are exceedingly attractive. From the start, Layla is described in detailed and recurring metaphors of beauty, such as "a jewel such as seldom seen," "as slender as a cypress tree," with "eyes like those of a gazelle," a face like "a lamp, or rather a torch," and "equipped with lustrous eyes" (II:4). In fact, it is explicitly stated that "everyday she grew more beautiful" (III:7). Similarly, in a depiction of outstanding merit, Qays' smile is likened to "a rose whose petals have opened overnight, like a diamond which transforms the darkness of the world into sheer light" (I:2). Furthermore it is stated that "the boy's beauty grew to perfection," and that "people told of his beauty like a fairy tale" (I:3).

These recurring expressions present images of beauty in *Layla*. The beauty of the characters of Layla and Majnun symbolize the mystery of Divine Beauty, *jamal* in the Sufi tradition. Thus, Layla represents the beautiful aspect of God, and Qays, the reflected manifestation of that beauty in man. It is interesting to note that, at this point of the narrative, the aspect of *jalal*, Divine Majesty, which is the opposite and harmonizing aspect of *jamal*, is not mentioned. This is indeed appropriate to the context of the state of earthly union being portrayed, because the dual aspects of *jamal* and *jalal* are particularly applicable to the earthly realities and the human condition of separation, whereas the state of primordial union relates primarily to the Divine realities.

In this regard, the presentation differs from *Govinda*. Both the awesome and the beautiful aspects of Krishna are present in the depiction of union. The reason for the difference may be ascribed to the fact that the concept of *avatara* exists in the Hindu religious tradition, whereas it does not in the Islamic tradition. As an incarnation of the transcendent Brahman, Krishna assumes form, such that in man's perception of his connection to God the physical and the spiritual states are not dichotomized. In this context the earthly presence of the *avatara* means that the divine and human realities are also not dichotomized. Thus although the earthly existence is determined by the doctrine of *karma*,[14] the Bhakta of the right disposition may experience a sensual knowledge of the *avatara* in his human existence. In a nutshell, there is a vertical movement from God to man, in which Krishna descends to man.

In contrast, the doctrine of the "Fall" of man in the Semitic traditions, which includes Islam, distinguishes the Divine from the earthly state. This is expressed in *Layla* as, "Heavily falls he who has never had a fall before" (II:5). This fall is a prefiguration of the separation of man from the Divine or Paradisiacal state, as a precondition to the seeking and regaining of his primordial union. In the Hindu tradition evil or disharmony in man's earthly existence is a precondition of the *avatara*'s descent, and His instrumental reconstruction and restoration of the original, divine nature of man. This aspect of restoration is expressed in *Govinda* as (I:21):

> Watching with long omniscient lotus-petal eyes
> You free us from bonds of existence,
> Preserving life in the world's three realms

In the Islamic tradition, the dual aspects of *jamal* and *jalal* work together upon the lover in the earthly state, "to make him die to him-

[14] *Karma* is the cosmic law of cause and effect that upholds *dharma*, harmony and balance in creation. In the Christian tradition this is illustrated by the maxim: As you sow, so shall you reap. Thus when harmony is threatened, the *avatara* incarnates from age to age (*Bhagavad Gita* IV:9).

self and gain a new life in God" (Schimmel 1982, 26). The following lines of Majnun's verses allude to this idea (XLVI:156):

> Two riddles to the world we represent,
> One answer each the other's deep lament.
> But if our parting severs us in two,
> One radiant light envelops me and you,
> As from another world though blocked and barred
> What there is one, down here is forced apart.

From this verse, it may be inferred that the seeker, or the Sufi, may experience the existential state of unity in which "the uncreated Divine Spirit descends into the created spirit of the lover" (Schimmel 1982, 31). Here again, there is a vertical movement from the Divine to the human, wherein both the Beauty and Majesty of God descends upon man.

The similarities and differences of the two traditions in the expression of the mystical connection in these instances may be summed up as follows: On the one hand, the similarity between the Sufi and the Bhakta lies in the underlying principle of vertical or Divine descent. On the other, the difference lies in the conception of the human-Divine connection: in Sufism, the union of the Divine and human Spirit is of an essential nature, meaning, united in essence. In contrast, in Bhaktism, the union is of a consubstantial nature, meaning, united in substance and essence.[15] This consubstantial quality of the *avatara* is commonly mistaken for substantiality. The mistake is the source of the denigration of the concept of *avatara*, and its reduction to worship of the human form. As argued previously in relation to the many names and forms of Krishna, consubstantiality does not incorporate idolatry as understood in popular Hinduism. This is confirmed in the *Bhagavad Gita*: "Fools deride Me when I descend in the human form. They do not know My transcendental nature and My supreme dominion over all that be" (9:11).

[15] In Christian theology, the notion of consubstantiality relates to the Trinity of the Father, the Son, and the Holy Ghost, whereas in Hinduism it refers to Krishna embodying the ternary aspects of the Supreme Brahman, as Brahma, Vishnu, and Shiva.

In the initial depiction of union, there is little articulation of the physical appearance of Krishna, except for the direct statement that his "beauty is fresh as rain clouds" (I:23), and that his eyes are "night birds" (I:23). If the avataric epithets in the earlier paragraphs deal with the awesome aspect of Krishna, then these descriptions express his beauty. The element of beauty in general, with regard to his physical appearance, and the association with the night in particular, are points of similarity with *Layla* mentioned in a previous discussion.

Rather than expressing the physical attributes of Krishna, however, the focus is on His nature. On one hand, the expression "If remembering Hari enriches your heart, If his arts of seduction arouse you...." (I:4), suggests his sexual prowess, true to the context of his erotic play with the cowherdesses in Brindaban forest (Miller 1984, 23). This element may be associated with the substantial, or material aspect of his nature, or immanence. On the other hand, both the information that he is "Moved by deep compassion" (I:13), and the description "The sun's jewel light encircles you as you break the bond of existence" (I:18), constitute abstractions. This element may be associated with the essence, or metaphysical aspect of his nature. In this context, references to the lotus in association with Krishna are particularly worthy of note: "Nails on (his) soft lotus hands," and "water (that) falls from lotus toenails to purify creatures" (I:8, 9). These examples share a common factor, namely the reference to the lotus. With regard to Krishna, they refer to the aspect of the transformation of human existence.[16] This particular set of examples may also be seen in the context of union. The lotus reflects the intimate interaction between the lovers in that it deals with the paradigm of transformation or alchemy of Krishna's (God) effect upon Radha (the human soul). In other words, couched in the floral image of the corporeal bloom dwells the Divine image of the multifaceted, incorporeal lotus of the Self.

As for Radha, there is also little description of her physical appearance in the initial depiction of union. An exception is in the lines:

> tender-limbed Radha wandered
> Like a flowering creeper in the forest wilderness,

[16] This will be dealt with at length at the level of inward meaning.

> Seeking Krishna in his many haunts.

The second line, although limited in form, constitutes the "dense description and complex ideas" mentioned previously with regard to content in the Miller quotation. The image of the creeper conveys a vivid suggestion of the nature of the human-divine relationship. Just as the creeper requires an upright support to survive and thrive, so equally, man has no existence without divine support. The example suggests the complementarity of Divine Grace and human will. This has been expressed eloquently as "Where there is a Way there is a Will" (Connaughton 2003-4). In spite of human frailties, man has certain qualities to surmount this deficiency. The creeper's physical incapacity is combined with its strong tendency to survive, just as Radha is "tender-limbed," yet "seeks" or relentlessly pursues Krishna.

The analogy of the tender-limbed Radha who wanders like a flowering creeper may be seen as the keynote of the mystical quest. "Tender-limbed" refers to her heart that is pliant and yielding, while the name "Radha," as previously explained, indicates her opposite and harmonizing position in relation to Krishna. The word "wandered" evokes the forlorn and bewildered nature of the seeker, and Radha's likeness to a "*flowering* creeper" distinguishes her from other creepers. This reference identifies the Bhakta or seeker (as opposed to other humans) as one who possesses the potential to flower and blossom forth in their spiritual aspirations. This is confirmed by the expression that Radha does not give up the quest easily, but seeks "Krishna in his many haunts." The "many haunts" suggest Krishna's omnipresence, and multitudinous forms. In brief, one has to seek in order to find that which is everywhere, all the time.

It is significant that in the depiction of initial union, the only other description of Radha's appearance draws a likeness of her to the moon. In the lines (I:23):

> Your eyes are night birds drinking from Sri's moon face.
> Triumph, God of Triumph, Hari!

she is identified by the epithet "Sri," identified with Savitri, meaning "vivifier." In this context, the reference to Sri's "moon face" conveys that she is lustrous and luminous, and thus a metaphor of light. Incidentally this quality of luminosity is reminiscent of Layla's "lustrous eyes" (II:5). In these lines, Radha is the object of Krishna's admiration, and associated with the moon and light, is a perfect foil for Krishna, associated with the night and darkness. Furthermore, the element of darkness in Krishna is complemented in the next line by the epithet Hari, light or illumination, by which the "God of Triumph" prevails. In this instance, the metaphors of light and darkness highlight and complement each other with regard to both the lovers. The identification of the lovers by the epithets Sri and Hari convey the divine nature of the union. Sri is also a variant form of reference to *Sakti* which represents *Prakrti*, the divine feminine energies, whereas Hari is a variant form of reference to *Purusha*, the divine masculine energies which "triumph" or prevail. In this instance, *Purusha-Prakrti* are prefigurations of Hari and Sri, God and man.

An aspect of the characterization which is significant in the initial stage of union is the age of the protagonists. In *Layla*, there are covert and overt indications of the ages of Qays and Layla. Qays' age, at seven years, is given in the reference to "the violet-colored down of his first beard," which "began to shimmer on his tulip cheeks." Further, it is mentioned that his beauty drew the attention of all when he was ten years old, in the expression "when he had reached his first decennium" (I:3). Moreover, at the beginning of the narrative, several forms of reference to Qays give clues about his age. For example, he is referred to repeatedly as "the boy" (I:3, II:4), and as "young Qays" (II:5). As for Layla, the indication that she is of tender age is given by the reference to her as "the young gazelle" (III:9). Besides, indications of time employed in reference to her, such as "Layla shone forth in her morning" (III:7) and "the new moon" (III:9), function as metaphors of youth. In these instances, the words "morning" in the first example, and "new" in the second, are the indicators.

The fact that Layla and Majnun are still at school, implies that neither of them is a grown-up, and the expressions "They were children and did not realize…." (II:5), and "the children did not notice…." (III:6), confirm this explicitly. Moreover, the characteristic of the young to be completely self-absorbed in whatever they are involved in, is suggested in these expressions. This is reinforced by the quality of innocence that is typical of children's behavior, represented in the lines, "He was drowned ... before he knew that there was such a thing" and "He had already given his heart ... before he understood what he was giving away" (II:5).

The images of youth concerning the characters are set against images of nature concerning time. In other words, the references to time are reflections of the age and nature of their relationship. In expressions such as "the moon after fourteen days" (I:3), "this first flowering of love" (III:6), and "the young day donned his morning coat" (V:13), the images of nature are consistent with youth, which in turn reflects the stage of primordiality. Finally, there is an allusion to the Edenic state in the reference to "their naked love" (III:8). This accentuates the image of primordiality in the portrayal of love in union. These figurative and metaphorical forms of expression allow the interpretation that the lovers are young, and the youth of the lovers reflects a primordial state of union. Thus it may be established that the school symbolizes the original union of the protagonists through its association with innocence, lack of experience, and knowledge, immaturity of the "self" which attains its maturity only after the stage of separation, that is, the mystical journey (Braginsky 2004).

It may be noted that, not long after the separation, Layla is married off to someone else. This means that she is of marriageable age, and, compared to the explicit information that Qays goes to school and first sees Layla when "he was seven years old" (I:3), it is possible that Layla is older than him. An interesting speculation and interpretation may be made in this regard at a deeper level of significance, on inward meaning. If Layla is older than Majnun, then it is consistent with the idea of her as a symbol of the Divine that is eternal, compared to Majnun as a symbol of man who is temporal. Stated differently, man's lifespan is minute, compared to the eternity of God.

Similarly in *Govinda*, the female, human character, Radha is older than the male, Divine character, Krishna. In Hindu myths, Radha and the *gopis* are represented as *parakiya*, meaning "a woman who belongs to another." This means that in spite of being wives of other men, the *gopis* are inexorably attracted to Krishna. In *Govinda*, we find that whenever they hear the "Sweet notes from his alluring flute echo nectar from his lips" (II:2) they abandon home and hearth in a frenzy of intoxication. Furthermore, confirmation that Radha is a mature female may be drawn from the reference to "the soft slope of her breast" (I:25). From this expression, it can be inferred that she is physically or bodily well-endowed, and a woman capable of the passionate sexual encounters with Krishna, as depicted. In comparative terms, Radha, just like Layla, is older, and another man's wife, whereas Krishna is a young adolescent, just like Qays.

This is a topos that the Hindu audience is familiar with. In the tradition, Radha is another man's wife, and Krishna is a child. This may also be verified from the textual depiction of their initial union. Krishna's fear of the dark, in the expression "the night frightens him" (I:1), indicates that he is a child. "Nanda," who is Krishna's foster-father orders Radha to "take him home" (I:1) meaning that Krishna is entrusted to a grown-up, i.e. Radha.

With regard to Krishna, it is accepted in the Hindu religious tradition that Krishna's existence in the material world was approximately 3500 years ago, and that the period of his life among the *gopis* occurs when he is ten years old. The youth of Krishna reflects his association with man in his primordial state. Primordial man is attributed with qualities of beatitude, spontaneity, freedom, and all the characteristics that are attributed to Krishna the child. Similarly, the pleasurable focus and concentration of the child protagonist is identical to that of a child enjoying play with his reflection in the mirror. In this play there is neither man nor woman. In Hindu terminology it is the meeting of *atma* with *Paramatma*, and the primordial connection of *adi purusha*, literally "first, or foremost, man," with Krishna is similar to the Islamic concept of the connection between Adamic/Edenic man and Allah.

In addressing various literal and literary aspects of expressions regarding the depiction of union between the lovers in both texts, it has become apparent that the nature of their love is characterized by certain qualities like perfection, pleasure, goodness, innocence, and joy. Furthermore, the relationship is one of reciprocity and mutuality, as has been illustrated in relation to the point about the equality of status between the lover and the Beloved. In discussing the nature of the love relation, it is of relevance to take into account another aspect of the relation, namely the quality of exclusivity.

The exclusivity of the union is illustrated by the element of secrecy. This element has three motifs. The first is privacy, referring to the fact that the union of the lovers is hidden from others. The second involves concealment, which refers to the lovers' attempts to keep their love from discovery. The third is incontinence, meaning that the secret cannot be contained, and this entails revelation.

In *Layla* the element of secrecy is augured by the fact that even as a child, Qays' development "remained a secret, hidden from every eye." Subsequently, in the period of union with Layla, the secret is known only to themselves, even in the midst of others, as strikingly illustrated by the expression: "Did the others understand what they saw? Could they decipher the secret code of signs and glances?" (III:7). However, later on, their love reaches a point when it seems almost inevitable that (III:8):

> Their eyes and lips could now no longer shield
> The tender secret which each glance revealed.

In other words, the very glances which once concealed their love, now reveal it. As a belated measure of caution, the lovers try to (III:8):

> ... mend the torn veil, to protect their naked love from the world, to hide their longing for each other, to tame their glances and to seal their lips.

but without success. When the point is reached that Qays is no longer able to contain his love, he loses his reason, and the Majnun in him emerges. This is the point where they become separated from each other. It reduces Qays to Majnun, and Layla, to tears. As narrated, without Majnun, Layla would "drop the curtain and shed lonely tears" (III:10).

In this regard, it may be asked how the lovers' secret fares by comparison, in *Govinda*. In the opening verse it is apparent that the initial union takes place in seclusion (I:1):

> Until secret passions of Radha and Madhava
> Triumph on the Jumna riverbank.

In fact, indications of the secret nature of their trysts are copious in the text:

> I reach the lonely forest hut where he secretly lies at night. (II:11)

> I murmur like a cuckoo; he masters love's secret rite. (II:15)

> She secretly draws you with deer musk to resemble the god of love. (IV:6)

> He ventures in secret to savor your passion, dressed for love's delight. (V:8)

Apart from similarity with regard to seclusion, there is also similarity in attempts to preserve the secret under the cover of darkness

> Go to the darkened thicket, friend! Hide in a cloak of night! (V:11)

> Two lovers meeting in darkness.... (V:18)

In these examples from *Govinda* there are obvious parallels with *Layla* with regard to the symbolic connection of darkness and secrecy with union. Despite attempts to conceal their love by meeting in darkness, however, the secret is revealed. Instrumental to this exposure are "familiar voices" (V:18):

> When familiar voices reveal
> That they ventured into the dark.

While in the above lines the revealers of the secret are possibly human, the following lines show that nature too, is instrumental to the "betrayal" (VII:1):

> As night came
> The moon displayed cratered stains,
> Seeming to flaunt its guilt
> In betraying secret paths
> Of adulterous women.

When once, night was an ally, and the cover of darkness, protection, at this point it is the adversary, and moonlight the traitor. Light not only betrays the secret, but also "flaunts" it, displaying "cratered stains." In this instance, the "guilt" is two-fold: the moon's betrayal of "secret paths," and the women's betrayal of their spouses. Consequently, when the secret is revealed, the lovers are separated (VII:2):

> Lonely Radha
> Cried her pain aloud
> In pitiful sobbing.

Radha is left lonely and sobbing, just as Layla weeps alone on being parted from Qays. The difference is that whereas Layla weeps in silence and seclusion, Radha "cried her pain aloud" for all to see.

In these instances, there emerges a parallel pattern in *Layla* and *Govinda* with regard to the notion of exclusivity. The concealment of the union begins with initial success, continues with cracks in the wall, results in exposure of the secret, and ends with the consequential separation of the lovers.[17] This pattern of secrecy and concealment may be given several interpretations in spiritual terms. At one level, the nature of the human-divine union is an unfathomable mystery, and thus regarded as a secret. An ancient saying, "that which is sacred, is secret" points to the close relation of "secret" with mystery and ineffability. And the obvious phonetic similarity in the words "sacred" and "secret" cannot be missed in supporting this view. Similarly, there is a close etymological relation between the word "secret" and "mystery." The Latin word *mysterium* is a derivative of the Greek *musterion*, meaning "secret thing or ceremony." *Musterion* is the origin of *mustikos*, meaning "secret," and *mustes*, "initiated person." Thus the English word "mystic" is a derivative of these words and concepts. The definition of "mystic" in the general and literal sense is (NSOED):

> a hidden or secret thing; a thing beyond human knowledge or comprehension; a riddle, an enigma, a puzzle; a person or thing not understood.

This definition entails that the secret is one to which only the initiated are admitted. However in the religious and spiritual sense, the word "mystic" is defined as (NSOED):

> A religious belief based on divine revelation, *esp.* a doctrine of faith involving difficulties which human reason is incapable of solving.

[17] The mention of "ends with separation" here has a relative meaning, depending on its context. On the one hand, it may be seen as an "end" in the context of "the end of the beginning (union)." On the other hand, it may be seen as a "beginning," in the context of "the beginning of the end (separation)." Depending on the point of view, it may refer either to the end of the beginning, or the beginning of the end. However, as circularity of movement is a defining characteristic of the mystical process, union and separation are preconditions of each other. Thus separation is both a beginning and an end.

Based on this understanding, the depiction of the union of the lovers in both the texts may be said to originate from the metaphysical dimension, relating to man's primordial state of total innocence and the soul's divine state of perfection. It is through the earthly and material experience, however, and of living amongst "the others" (III:7) and the "familiar voices" (V:18) in the world, that man becomes aware of himself, conscious of his origin, and inspired to return to this original state.[18] Thus, as a step in the direction of accessing this worldly experience it is necessary for the secret to be revealed, as occurs in both texts.

Furthermore, as the adage goes, "truth will out," and so the secret is impossible to be contained despite all caution and prudence. Particularly, as the "truth" relates to "the Truth," or God, no force can conceal it. This idea is represented by the phenomenon of incontinence, and betrayal of the secret of the union of the lovers. As indirect clarification *Layla* expresses this notion in metaphors of betrayal, concealment, and revelation, such as (III:8):

> Like the musk-deer, love, betrayed by its scent, cannot hide; like the sun, it penetrates clouds.

and (XVI:50):

> ... his eyes betrayed his feelings, and he repeated smilingly "Layla ..., nothing but Layla."

In *Govinda*, there is a direct indication that the moon is instrumental in the disclosure of the secret of "adulterous women," as quoted before (VII:1).

Furthermore, Radha does not conceal her passion, but "shows" it (VII:22):

> Her rapt face shows the passion her lips feel kissing him
> With deer musk he draws the form of a stag on the moon.

[18] In relation to the Hindu doctrine of detachment, the human experience is expressed as "being *in* the world, but not *of* it." The *Bhagavad Gita* says: "One who performs his duty without attachment, surrendering the results unto the Supreme God, is not affected by sinful action, as the lotus leaf is untouched by water" (5:11).

The remarkable similarity of imagery in the above examples may be noted here. In *Layla*, reference is made to the "musk-deer" whereas in *Govinda* it is to "deer musk." In both traditions, musk or scent, has mystical symbolism. In the Sufi tradition, the musk-deer leaves a fragrant trace, which may indicate the way to the source of the fragrance, which is the Divine Beloved (Schimmel 1982, 81), whereas the deer and stag in Hinduism symbolize both sexual and spiritual union. Furthermore, with regard to incontinence, Majnun's "eyes betrayed his feelings," whereas Radha's "rapt face shows the passion." Again, both texts evoke betrayal through display of irrepressible emotions. In *Layla*, this irrepressibility is associated with the sun "that penetrates clouds" and in *Govinda*, with "the moon." Here, both are light metaphors. Thus, the expression is parallel in the texts in conveying that the truth is brought to light. Stated differently, the Truth is Illumination.

A final characteristic associated with the nature of the initial union of Layla and Majnun that will be dealt with, is that of intoxication. This notion is initially suggested by a description of Layla's mouth, from which flows "such overwhelming sweetness" (II:5). Further on, it is explicitly introduced, in a metaphor of cup-bearer and drunkenness. The pair of lovers are captivated by each other, and become "drunk" in each other as they "drank by day and dreamed by night." In fact, the more they "drank the deeper they became immersed in each other" (II:6). Again, the notion of primordiality is presented through the information that "He who is drunk for the first time, becomes deeply drunk indeed" (II:5). In other words, the drunkenness experienced is none other than the first. Further, it is said that the lovers were "drinking the wine of oblivion" (III:7), which finally and inevitably causes them to become "deeply intoxicated by their dreams" (III:8).

If in the initial stage of union in *Layla*, intoxication is specified as being caused by "drinking," in *Govinda* this is suggested: it is mentioned that Krishna is "drinking" from Radha's "moon-face." The word "drinking" evokes the element of drunkenness or intoxication as a consequence of the bliss of union. Further, it indicates that Radha, in association with the moon, is an image or reflection of the "drinker."

The above quotations from both texts indicate the lovers' experience of a state of drunkenness. In the beginning, the exclusivity of the love is facilitated by secrecy. When others look at them, "Could they decipher the secret code of signs and glances?" (III:7). This means that all but themselves are excluded from the secret. However, just as a person is without full control of his faculties as an effect of alcohol, so too are the lovers unable to control the effects of their intoxication with each other. When secrecy is not, or cannot, be maintained, exclusivity is no longer possible, and the lovers lose the paradise of their early love.

Thus the effect of intoxication on the lovers is two-fold. They are afflicted by blindness and incontinence. The former refers to the lovers' state of awareness of their surroundings. In *Layla*, there is reference to the fact that "their eyes became blind and their ears deaf to the school and the world" (II:6), and to the "blind happiness" (III:7) of Qays. Indirectly, there is a diminishing of clarity and awareness, "Was not a shadow already falling ... even if the children did not notice it?" (III:6), and mention that "the wine of oblivion" (III:7) has overtaken them. The latter effect, incontinence, refers to the lack of their ability to contain, or conceal their love: "Like the musk-deer, love, betrayed by its scent, cannot hide; like the sun, it penetrates clouds" (III:8). In this regard, it has been suggested that it is not the parents' interference that causes their separation, but the effects of the intoxication of love upon Qays. In the words of Khan (1997, xx):

> In his book of profound meditations on *'ishq*, the *Sawanih*, Ahmad Ghazali (d. 1126) suggests that it was not family politics but Majnun's inability to remain conscious in the presence of Layla that kept the tragic lovers apart.

In *Govinda*, as Radha struggles to understand why Krishna stays away from her, she asks (VII:11):

> Is he roaming blindly near the dark forest?
> Or does my lover's anguished mind so tangle the path
> That he cannot come into this thicket of vines
> And sweet swamp reeds where we promised to meet?

In this verse, both the conditions of blindness and incontinence are expressed. Radha assumes that Krishna is keeping away from her, and "roaming blindly." Furthermore, his mind is so "anguished" that it "tangles" the path such that he cannot find her. It is interesting that the human character (Radha) assumes that it is the divine figure

(Krishna) who cannot find her, rather than the other way around. This point will be taken up in a different section.

With regard to the issue of cultural conventions, one may observe the presentation of a common element in both works, namely, the transgression of norms. Both authors project the love story in a unique, extraordinary, and memorable way, albeit within the mold of the individual literary traditions. The "extraordinariness" in this instance refers firstly to what the particular form of transgression is, and secondly to how that transgression is presented. As the following discussion shows, the transgression is presented in different ways.

Two elements which constitute transgression of social norms in *Layla* are, an illicit love affair and intoxication. The norms of Persian-Islamic society dictated highly restricted social interactions between men and women, and arranged marriages as the common practice. In this scenario, a love affair prior to marriage is aberrant. Consequently, "love played a much larger role in fantasy than in real life" (Brians 2001). In spite of this, Layla and Majnun engage in a real-life love affair. In fact, by falling in love, Qays and Layla are falling into a scandalous madness (Brians 2001). Thus the literary depiction presents a transgression of cultural norms as a means to convey the extraordinariness of the love affair. Similarly, the drinking of wine is strictly forbidden in the Islamic religious tradition. For this reason, there cannot be portrayal of "drinking" or "drunkenness" in a positive light. But because the condition of being "in-love" is so similar to the condition of being "intoxicated," the metaphor of intoxication is used to represent the similarity between the two states or conditions. For this reason too, the symbolism of intoxication is popular in mystical expression. Just as intoxication means, for the ordinary person, the loss of awareness of one's immediate environment, for the mystic "the goal of love is loss of awareness of all but God" (Schimmel 1982, 9). Thus mystical intoxication is not from the wine of the grape but rather from the pre-eternal wine of love (Schimmel 1982, 78). True enough, in literary expression the drunkenness of the lovers in *Layla* is not due to wine of the grape but to the wine "of oblivion" (III:7), of "the sweet scent" (II:5), of "their dreams" (III:8), and so on. In a later part of the story, after separation has occurred, this is spelled out as (V:14):

> Layla held in her hand the glass of wine scented with musk. Majnun had not touched the wine, yet he was drunk with its sweet smell....

In *Govinda*, on the other hand, the extraordinariness of the love is expressed by the particular transgression of adultery. This is frowned upon in any culture, more so within a traditional setting. But for Radha, the *parakiya* woman, the rules of morality no longer have a place in her clandestine rendezvous with Krishna on the banks of the Jumna on a moonlit night in spring. As for Krishna, he is the upholder of "the holy Veda" (I:5), and yet indulges in amorous dalliances with other men's wives. In this regard, it is possible that the point made by the poet is that their union is indeed something beyond the realm of the ordinary and the commonplace. This is also the view of Dimock (1966, 56-57):

> The relationship of Krishna to the *gopis* is beyond ordinary standards of morality..., only *parakiya* results in the *prema*, the intense desire for the satisfaction of the beloved, which is the characteristic, to be emulated by the Bhakta.... The pain of separation, possible only in *parakiya*, and the resultant constant dwelling of the minds of the *gopis* on Krishna, is their salvation.

There are two elements in this view, that from the mystical understanding, mitigate the transgression. The first is that the *prema* of the Bhakta is not an ordinary love of desire and self-gratification, but on the contrary, one that seeks only the satisfaction of the beloved. The second is that, the portrayal and evocation of such a love necessitates the element of separation, possible only in loving someone who belongs to another. It is the pain of separation that, for the Vaishnava, draws interest away from worldly concerns and leads to the meditation on Krishna and leads to attainment of him (Dimock 1966, 56-57). In this attitude and interpretation, there is a close parallel to the Sufi tradition regarding the goal of love being the loss of awareness of all but God.

The phenomenon of social transgression in both *Layla* and *Govinda* may thus be explained in light of the mystical viewpoint. Each sort of transgression, i.e. a love affair and drunkenness in the former, and adultery in the latter, has its own implications within its individual cultural context. However, the contravention of norms evokes the same response, namely a sense of the extraordinary and the supernormal. In literary terms, the intensity of passion that can be expressed by a portrayal of forbidden love has a far greater impact than that evoked by a permitted or lawful one. This is a common practice in artistic expression that has also been utilized to the same end in mystical expression.

Separation in Union

In ending this chapter on the many facets of love and the lovers in union, the discussion will address a vital component of the portrayal of initial union, namely the element of separation in union. This element has been left to the end, and the discussion on it is necessarily short, owing to the fact that it constitutes a minor and imperceptible proportion of the depiction of love in union. Nevertheless, it has an important significance, as the following discussion attempts to show.

In the case of *Layla*, the first hint of separation is given when the lovers "became drunk" (II:5). When this happens, it is followed by a foreshadowing regarding the extent of the lovers' condition: "heavily falls he who has never had a fall before" (II:5). Juxtaposed with expression of the height of the lovers' bliss, "How happy this first flowering of love for Qays and Layla!", comes another foreshadowing: "Can such happiness last?" "Was not a shadow already falling over their radiance ... what did they know about the ways and laws of this world?" (III:6). This quotation gives a clear indication of both impending disaster and the lovers' youth and innocence.

A subsequent hint is given in Qays' reaction when he notices that he is no longer alone with Layla. When his companions, mesmerized by her beauty, begin to stare at her, "a bitter taste mingled with the sweet scent of his love" (III:7). That is, when the total exclusivity of the lovers' union ceases, the spell of initial perfection is broken. When this happens, "A small crack appeared in his blind happiness, he had a foreboding of what was to come; but it was too late" (III:7). Despite the forebodings, however, the young lovers rashly "turned their backs on the world" (III:7). Another wrong move! In the same paragraph, the reader is informed that by doing so, the lovers made it easy "for their enemies to set their traps" (III:7). Following this turn of events, the lovers awaken to "the pointing fingers, to hear the reproaches, the derision, the whisperings ... " (III:8), and realizing their blindness, attempt to "mend the torn veil" (III:8). Despite their attempts, however, they fail to conceal their love, as it proves impossible to stem the tide of their overwhelming love, as has been discussed before. As a result, the secret is revealed and Qays' heart "suddenly lost its balance" (III:9). That is when Qays becomes Majnun.

From the above expressions, it is apparent that the account of the initial stage of union between the lovers in *Layla* is riddled with foreshadowing and anticipation of impending separation. As has been shown in the diagram on "real time" devoted to the portrayal on initial union, approximately three out of the six pages following their first meeting deal with union per se, whereas the element of separation exists intrinsically throughout the narrative prior to actual, physical separation.

In the case of *Govinda*, similar mention has been made of the coverage of actual union. Between verse 1, in which union between the lovers is mentioned, and verse 26, in which Radha wanders in the wilderness seeking Krishna, there are only two other verses specifying union (verses 17 and 25). In short, 3 out of the first 25 verses deal with union per se. It is pertinent to pose the question at this point: what is the purpose of liberally intermingling the verses of the lovers' union with the verses of extolment, prior to the portrayal of separation? A possible assumption is that it serves to present the possibility and the reality of separation in a subtle and imperceptible manner. This assumption may be substantiated by the following argument.

As has been explained earlier, there are two objects of extolment, Jayadeva and Krishna. In the first instance, there is a subtle modification of tenses in words and phrases. In verse 2, Jayadeva projects himself as unrivalled "king of bards" (I:2). Whereas the union of the lovers in verse 1 is in the present tense, mentioned as "secret passions ... *Triumph*...," it is referred to in the past tense in verse 2, as "When Krishna *loved* Sri." Furthermore, when the poet claims in the present tense in verse 3 that "only Jayadeva *divines* the pure design of words" this is followed in verse 4 by the phrase, "if *remembering* Hari enriches your heart." In this phrase, "remembering" implies something forgotten, i.e. of the past. Both these examples show that the account of the union has shifted from the present, i.e. something that is constant, to the past, i.e. something that is sporadic. In short, the author is saying that union occurred in the past, and he assumes the task of calling back that past. Thus, this technique of manipulation of tenses in *Govinda* functions as a reminder of separation, which is similar to the technique of foreshadowing in *Layla.*

In the second instance, the extolment of Krishna immediately following the extolment of Jayadeva, refers to Krishna's roles as *avatara.* Each of the 10 verses (5-14), known as the *Dasavatara stotra,*[19] or hymn of the ten *avataras,* refers to a particular aspect and form of Krishna. Apart from the form, all of the *avataras* have an inward or esoteric interpretation. These roles are encapsulated and listed in verse 16, which constitutes an invocation, as indicated by lines such as "Homage to you, Krishna, In your ten incarnate forms!" (I:16).

All of these verses in homage to Krishna have an important relation to the account of the state of initial union. This is because each mention of the *avatara*'s descent (referring to union) has direct reference to man's salvation in the event of chaos (referring to separation). This notion of chaos and salvation is expressed as (I:5):

> In seas that rage as the aeon of chaos collapses
> You keep the holy Veda like a ship straight on course.

and further as (I:10):

> You wash evil from the world in a flood of warriors' blood,
> And the pain of existence is eased.

and, in a final example, as (I:14):

> You raise your sword like a fiery meteor
> Slashing barbarian hordes to death.

These examples indicate the metaphysical view of union and separation, referring to the descent that occurs as a direct result of disruption in the cosmic principle of *dharma.* In this manner, the effect of these verses in *Govinda* is similar to the effect of the expressions of fore-

[19] The ten epithets of Krishna in this hymn in the original Sanskrit version are *Minasarira* (Fish form), *Kacchaparupa* (Tortoise form), *Sukararupa* (Boar form), *Naraharirupa* (Man-lion form), *Vamanarupa* (Dwarf form), *Parasurama* (Priest), *Ramasarira* (Perfect Man), *Balarama* (plowman), *Buddhasarira* (Buddha), and *Kalkisarira* (the form of the final *avatara*). Cf. Miller (1984, 19-20), and "Dasavatara Stotra, Gita Govinda by Sri Jayadeva" (2000).

shadowing in *Layla*. In *Layla*, the impending separation is indicated by constant reminders or foreshadowing. In *Govinda*, by interspersing the verses on union with verses on the *avatara*, the reader is reminded of the past occurrences of the separation of man from his divine state, and his reinstatement to it through Divine intervention.

From the above discussion, it may be seen that the element of separation is vital to the portrayal of initial union. Its importance may be ascribed to two main reasons. The first is that the initial stage of union is to be distinguished from the final stage of union by the quality of innocence and inexperience of the lovers. As has been discussed, the lovers are young and completely lack awareness of themselves and their surroundings. The esoteric interpretation of this has also been given, that this is a depiction of the soul in the primordial existential state of unity with the Divine Beloved.

The second reason that separation is considered vital to union in the initial stage is that, in the mystical view, it is the element required to propel, or move, the traveler forward. Without this element, the ultimate destination of final union cannot be reached. In other words, separation is the catalyst for spiritual development and expansion. For this reason, the separation has been portrayed in both texts as an integral part of initial union.

It is in this context that the title of the chapter refers to both union and separation as "blooms," though qualitatively varied, of love's gardens. The duality inhering in the initial union is also reflected in relevant expressions in the text of the works. In the case of *Layla*, the duality is implicit in the following extract (II:5):

> He was drowned in the ocean of love before he knew that there was such a thing. He had already given his heart to Layla before he understood what he was giving away…. And Layla? She fared no better.

As Qays gives his heart away to Layla, the word "drowned" implies the ignorance and innocence of his bliss, and its disastrous consequences. In *Govinda*, the following verse has a similar phenomenon (I:25):

> On the soft slope of her breast,

The saffroned chest of Madhu's killer
Is stained with red marks of passion
And sweat from fatigue of tumultuous loving.

A foreshadowing lies in the mention of Krishna as "Madhu's killer," again a reference to his avataric function, and relating to impending chaos. Furthermore the reference to the stain of "red marks of passion," suggest the condition of separation in which man's passionate nature, *rajas*, predominates. Thus, the paradigms of union and separation are inextricably linked, and constantly held in tension in both texts.

There is a marked difference in some of the ways in which the two mystical traditions of Sufism and Bhaktism portray the element of separation in initial union. The former employs foreshadowing, the latter, extolment. However, the similarity is that the reference to separation is oblique and covert in both texts. It should be mentioned that the initial stage of union is distinct from the final stage of union in that in the former there is the element of separation, whereas in the latter there is none, as the last chapter of analysis will demonstrate. The fact is that the all-important element of separation has been portrayed extensively in both texts. It represents the primary element in *Layla* and *Govinda*, as it does in the poetic expression of most mystical traditions. If, in the process of discussion in this chapter the blooms in the garden of love have been gathered from the initial stage of union, the following two chapters will endeavor to extricate the thorns from a subsequent stage, that of separation.

CHAPTER FOUR

THORNS OF LOVE'S GARDENS: LONGING AND PAIN OF SEPARATION

... another rider came to me and
drove a thorn right into my heart;
its point still lodges inside and
causes pain.

(*Layla*, XXXIX:124-25)

He pierced my heart with arrows
of love
Whom can I seek for refuge here?

(*Govinda*, VII:4)

In Chapter 2, the notion of the development of the human soul on the mystic path was introduced as a series of levels in relation to man's spiritual potentialities. To recapitulate, this involves three main processes, beginning from initial or primordial union, advancing to subsequent separation, and culminating in return or reunion. Accordingly, Chapter 3 dealt with the initial union of Layla-Majnun and Radha-Krishna as a literary expression of the first or initial level of the mystic process. It was observed that the depiction conveys both the simple and perfect state epitomized by the bliss of union, as well as the complex and imperfect state, indicated by the imminence of separation. In dealing with the subsequent stage of the mystic journey in this chapter, the discussion of the state of separation of the lovers will proceed on a similar pattern of development.

The State of Separation

The state of separation, as will be demonstrated, is one of fragmentation and disconnectedness. Yet, it also has elements of connectedness. This is a similar pattern of development as the initial state of union, shown to incorporate a hint of the two opposing elements of perfection and potential imperfection. In the state of separation, the element of disconnectedness manifests as pain and suffering endured by the lovers, whereas the occasional awareness of fusion and harmony represents connectedness. Both the experiences of "disconnectedness" and "connectedness" referred to go beyond the physical and outward spatio-temporal dimensions. This means that the experience of disconnectedness is not confined to being physically apart, just as connectedness does not necessarily mean being in physical contact.

As the title of this chapter, and the quotations from each text at the beginning of the chapter suggest, the longing and pain endured by the respective pairs of lovers are characteristics of the "thorns" or trials, in the individual "gardens" of love, understood as a reference to the spiritual path. Considering the great lengths of the authors' portrayal of this element, and with the intention of providing due attention to its importance, a relatively large space has been allotted to its understanding and comparison. Furthermore, as this stage exhibits the phenomenon of connectedness and disconnectedness combined, the state of separation will be dealt with in two individual chapters. The present chapter will be confined to a discussion of the element of disconnection in separation, whereas the following chapter will deal with the element of connection in separation. This division, however, is along somewhat artificial lines. This means that the two elements mentioned do not form apparently discrete conditions in *Layla* and *Govinda*, but on the contrary, are strung in a seamless fusion. The expressions of pain in separation are constantly and unexpectedly substituted and interspersed by expressions of pleasure, through the recollection and mention of union. In fact, this alternating feature plays a significant role in problematizing the concept of "separation."

The problem in the garden of "thorns" stems from the issue of "the real" and "illusory." This may be illustrated by the metaphor of the mirage: to a lone, thirsty desert traveler, an oasis, or water, is both real and illusory. He "sees" it, yet cannot be certain of its reality. In *Layla*, a similar illustration of the real and the illusory is evoked in an instance related to the search for the lost Majnun (IX:30-31):

> ... however anxiously they searched for him, he was not to be found.... "Who knows," they said, "perhaps ... wild animals have torn him to pieces, or even worse has happened to him." Whereupon the youth's kinsmen and companions raised wailings and lamentations *as if* they were mourning the dead.
> But Majnun was not dead. As before, he had gone to a hiding-place in the wilderness. There he was living alone, a hidden treasure;... yet his grief provided him with a free passage, liberating him from

> the fetters of selfishness.... After a time, a Bedouin ... (was) walking along the same path. When he saw the lonely figure crouching in solitude, he suspected a mirage.... (emphasis mine)

In this quotation, the issue centers on the attitude of "as if," italicized above. On one hand is negativity, constructed upon pain: of loss, death, wilderness, lamentation, loneliness. On the other, the positive, or pleasure, emerges almost concurrently: loss is compensated by discovery ("he saw the lonely figure"), death by life ("Majnun was not dead"), fetters with freedom ("grief provided him with a free passage"), wilderness with treasure ("he was living alone, a hidden treasure"), and so on. Thus gain is a reward of pain. However the questions remain: is the "lonely figure" real or illusory? Is the negative illusory? Is the positive real? Is Majnun absent or present? and so on.

Similarly the mirage, although occurring in a different context, may be illustrated with reference to *Govinda*. In a description of the lonely Radha (IV:21):

> Her heart suffers strange slow suffocation
> In mirages of sandalbalm, moonlight, lotus pools.

her pain is apparent in the first line. But precisely through pain, the "mirage" of pleasure emerges, in the second line. A painful encounter is readily endured simply because it has the presence of the beloved as its object. Thus the lover finds both pain and pleasure in a delightful mirage. But again, similar questions about what is real and illusory arise from this example: which is real, pain ("slow suffocation"), or pleasure ("sandalbalm, moonlight, lotus pools")?

These examples represent the marked ambivalence in *Layla* and *Govinda* in relation to the experience of "separation." Furthermore, from the comparison of the mirage image, there appear differences in context, but similarity in the subtext. The context of setting in *Layla* is related to aridness (the desert), whereas in *Govinda* it is plenitude (the forest). The subtext is that in both, the positive exists concurrently with the negative, the real with the illusory, absence with presence, pleasure with pain.

The Pain of Separation

Thus the condition of "separation" is problematized, through ambiguity and ambivalence of expression, and depending upon perspective or approach. This poses stimulating and challenging questions about the "real" nature of the state of separation. For this reason, selected expressions, questions, situations, and possibilities relevant to the opposing elements in the state of separation will be presented and clarified in the course of this chapter and the next. This chapter, therefore, deals with some "thorns" or phenomena of separation in the individual texts, namely motion, and madness.

The occurrence of motion or movement shows correspondences in *Layla* and *Govinda*. In the former, it is Majnun's frenzied, repeated passage towards, and away from, Layla. His numerous journeys are amply illustrated, especially at the onset of separation. For example, at one point (IV:11), his journeys are referred to repeatedly. They are "filled with a deadly pain,... each day, the ghosts of his vain hopes chased him out into the desert" (IV:11). In the same event it is repeated: "swift as the north wind he flew along, kissed Layla's threshold ... and returned" (IV:10). And again: "on his way to her he ran fast,... On the way back he crawled" (IV:11).

In the course of Majnun's attempts to see his beloved, he becomes increasingly desperate. In his desperation, caution is thrown to the winds, as "... so far he had only come by night,... but now he could bear it no longer ... he had to see her" (V:13). And so he appears this time in broad daylight, "near the tent of his beloved" (V:13). On one hand the intensity of his yearning to see Layla will not let him rest, and on the other, his attempts to see his beloved are "brief, and from afar" (V:15). In this, Majnun displays the "wild imprudence," which has been earlier defined as a condition of madness. And yet, each time he reaches her tent, "Majnun, afraid of guards and spies, ran away" (V:15). A natural consequence of his recklessness is that these "secret sorties" are soon discovered, and guards of Layla's tribe "block the way against the disturber of the peace" (V:15). In all of these instances, the poignancy of Majnun's utter frustration and the futility of his attempts cannot be missed.

These frantic oscillations of Majnun share a similar pattern with Radha's movements. In *Govinda* it takes the form of a search in which she goes back and forth from her former meeting places with Krishna, in which Radha is "seeking Krishna in his many haunts" (I:26). Like

Majnun, her search is equally futile, for she seeks but does not find. This she expresses repeatedly as, "Whom can I seek for refuge here?" (VII:5). The narrative also informs that this search for "The god of love increased her ordeal" (I:26). Besides, the ordeal of Radha's search is as equally desperate as Majnun's. In repeated laments of seeking and not finding Krishna, her desperation is expressed in a death-wish (VII:5):

> Death is better than living in my barren body.
> Why do I blankly endure love's desolating fire?

From the illustration of the back-and-forth movement in both the texts, this phenomenon may be seen as evidence of the fragmentation and imperfection of the lovers as a result of separation.

The search for the beloved in association with motion is a lone and futile endeavor at this point. Yet the great tenacity and persistence of the lover is notable in both *Layla* and *Govinda*. A parallel may be drawn with the spiritual fervor and intensity required of the seeker of the spiritual life. In *Layla*, Majnun "suffered because he could not find the treasure for which he was searching" (IX:31). And yet he does not relinquish the search. He declares: "My eyes search only for you" (XLI:134) and vows that "even if she were a spark, deep inside the rock, I would still find her" (XVI:51). Similarly, in *Govinda*, Radha's search too is relentless. Looking for "Krishna in his many haunts" (I:26), her "trembling eyes search for him" (II:11). However, at this point the search is equally futile in both cases. Consequently, just as Majnun retreats to the desert, she too retreats, although it is not to the same location. Radha goes "at night to depths of the forest" (VII:4), i.e. a different location appropriate to the setting of *Govinda*.

It is important to note that the search for Krishna is conveyed in the refrains of a song. In this context, Radha is portrayed as a frail and forsaken creature seeking the sanctuary of Krishna's presence. As long as she does not find the safe haven she seeks, she is so physically vulnerable that (VII:8):

> Even a garland strikes at the heart of my fragile body....
> *Whom can I seek for refuge here?* (italics mine)

The refrain (italicized above), repeated in eight out of the ten verses of "The Thirteenth Song" deserves special attention. As a literary device, the repetitive refrain (*dhruvapada*) provides a rhythmic effect. Based on the classical Indian tradition of music, the refrains in *Govinda* are part of a composite pattern (Miller 1984, 10). They are comprised, like all other refrains throughout the text, of three interdependent units serving different functions: the narrative (which conveys the message), the description (which fulfils the aesthetics), and the singer/poet's identification with the song (which portrays his affinity/participation). The role of the refrain is explained as (Miller 1984, 10):

> the stable unit of sound and meaning in the song. Its content provides a context for the descriptive details of the couplets and intensifies their meaning.... A refrain unifies a song.

Thus, all refrains in *Govinda* characterize the poem as a "cycle of songs" (*padavali, prabandha*). Of special concern to the study is that the refrain provides an interesting literary contrast, as well as similarity, with *Layla.*

The contrast, or difference, between the texts in the back-and-forth movement concerns form. In the case of *Layla* the movement is presented chronologically in a series of events occurring over a period of time. However in *Govinda*, the movement occurs in a refrain at a particular point in time. The basis for this contrasting expression may be generic, and is explained as follows: *Layla* is a prose work in which length of text is not a principal consideration.[1] Therefore, the fictional time-span and the form of expression is not restricted. Thus the course of events spans several years. In this span, Majnun's movements are effectively portrayed through many separate events. In contrast, *Govinda* is a song, and appropriate to the economics of expression of the poetic genre, it necessarily involves brevity of expression and of time setting. Thus, the time setting of *Govinda* involves a span of several hours, or the course of one day. An effective portrayal of Radha's movements is therefore dependent upon intensity of expression. In

[1] In the original version, the genre of *mathnawi* is also practically unrestricted, one poem often comprising thousands of verses.

this case, an equal effect to that in *Layla* is achieved through refrains, rather than through repetition of events, or form.

While there is a difference between these texts with regard to form, there is also similarity of content, or substance, The similarity lies firstly with the repetitive quality. Just as in *Layla* there is repeated movement towards and away from the beloved, so too is this element present in *Govinda.* Secondly, similarity lies with the pattern of motion, in this case referring to the linear or cyclic movement present in both texts.

This phenomenon of cyclic process is readily associated with the symbolic and spiritual viewpoint. The movement demonstrated by the examples may be seen as generating spirals, or circles within circles, of development. These circles, which symbolize the struggles endured in the lovers' journeys, suggest "lower" levels of consciousness/awareness (Wilber 1996, 83). As the examples demonstrate, the "lower" stages of development are, in psychological terms, "instinctual, impulsive, libidinous, animal-like" (Wilber 1996, 84), and so on. These "lower," "downward," and "outward" tendencies are associated with the body, or the ego, or the self (*jism*, *sarira*). Only when there is a break from these tendencies can the spiritual journey progress in the "higher," the "upward" or the "inward" direction.

In Sufism, progress comes from renunciation of attachments (*zuhd*), at all levels of being, including "everything that distracts the heart from God, even to renounce the thought of renunciation. That includes of course, giving up the hope for heavenly reward or the fear of Hell" (Schimmel 1975, 110). Similarly in *Bhakti-yoga*, the renunciate (*tyagi*) who achieves detachment from all desire is the pure Bhakta. In this context, the Bhakta does not desire promotion to heavenly realms, nor does he seek salvation or liberation from material entanglement. A pure devotee "does not desire anything ... he only wants to please the Supreme Lord" (Prabhupada 1971, 424). This is confirmed by the verse in the *Bhagavad Gita* (8:14), which says: "For one who remembers Me without deviation, I am easy to obtain, O son of Prtha, because of his constant engagement in devotional service".

Although the stage of separation is beset with struggles, in spiritual terms it is seen as a positive, important, and necessary stage in the process of development. Thus, the frenzied movement, qualifying as a symptom of madness in both the lovers, is a step in this direction. The basis of this understanding is that this mad struggle is "not a *loss* of consciousness, but an intensification of consciousness" (Wilber 1996, 95). Thus madness is a seed, or beginning of growth, and the "madness" of Majnun and Radha are an intensification of consciousness directed at the object of devotion, the beloved. The beloved forms a magnetic center, and the most important factor in the seeker's life. Thus, the fragmentation of the lovers is not only a destructive process, but equally a constructive one. There has to be a breaking down before there can be a building up.

The desolation and isolation of the setting in which such a process takes place in the texts is an important aspect of the search for the beloved. Appropriate to the desert setting of *Layla*, Majnun retreats to the wilderness, the mountains, and the cave. The isolation is so overwhelming that "one would not wish anybody to find himself ... so deserted, so bleak and harrowing that it made the heart quail" (XXX:94). In this setting, Majnun's loneliness is poignantly expressed by diverse references, for example, "He crept into a cave groaning like a lizard which has been bitten by a serpent, and scattered the pearls of his tears into the tresses of darkness" (XXII:71). In other words, Majnun is alone, and lonely.

As if to set the seal on his anguish, Majnun retreats into a cave described as "A terrible spot, a place of anguish, a cave in the desert like a tomb, right in the flames of Hell" (XXX:93). In this place, Majnun degenerates not only physically but in the level of his humanity. When Nawfal, the warrior who later helps Majnun, first finds him, he is crouching among wild beasts, appearing to be hardly human (XVI:48):

> (Nawfal) ... stared towards the grotto, where he noticed a living being such as he had never encountered before.... The creature was crouching against the side of the rock, naked, wasted, arms and legs severely scratched by thorns, long strands of hair falling over the shoulders and the hollow cheeks. Was it an animal or a human being, a savage or one of the dead maybe a demon?

In this picture of Majnun, it is obvious that the state of separation is quite comprehensive, for it includes many dimensions of life, such as the human, the social, and the worldly. Furthermore the animal images in the above examples show a descension of Majnun into a sub-human state, associated with the body, or lower state, associated with the psyche.

From the above examples, it may be seen that at the microcosmic level, or at the level of Majnun's person, the retreat has two elements: darkness and isolation. These elements are reflected in the location, and echoed by nature (XXIII:73):

> Foaming like the waters of the Nile, the Milky Way seemed to flow across this celestial Egypt while Majnun, left alone, looked up to the sky like a bird with clipped wings.

and again, as Majnun himself utters (XXIV:75):

> Dying from thirst, I search the sky in vain
> Too late the cloud that brings the saving rain.

In the first expression, the reference to "the Milky Way" conjures up the vast firmament at night. Similarly, in the second expression, there is an association with "the sky" which he searches "in vain." This presents a relationship between the microcosm and the macrocosm, which is both a parallel and a contrast. The parallel relates to the quality of remoteness, both of Majnun and the sky. The contrast is between Majnun symbolizing finitude, and the sky symbolizing infinitude. Furthermore, the contrast suggests that discord and disharmony prevail at both the micro- and macrocosmic levels.

In a similar vein, darkness and isolation occur at the microcosmic and macrocosmic scales in *Govinda*. In the first case, in a general forest setting, Radha goes to a specific location, namely that of the "bower" or "thicket." Each of these terms refers to an enclosed, secluded place of foliage, an arbor (NSOED). However, her search here is fruitless, for Krishna is not in these places. This is conveyed in the expressions, "Why does barren disgust haunt my bower of branches, ... ?" (VII:28) and similar expressions (e.g. VII:[illegible]) quoted elsewhere. In these examples, there is a stark contrast between what Radha hopes to find, and what she encounters. Her great expectations are marked by her "barren disgust." Besides, similar to *Layla*, the desolation is reflected in elemental forces, as if nature too participates in Radha's solitude. For example, "The lonely moon (is) ... wan in love's desolation" (VII:21), and "The sweet spring night torments (her) loneliness" (VII:6).

A final parallel may be drawn between the texts from the following verse (IV:10):

Suffering your desertion,
She takes form as a whining doe
And turns Love into Death
Disguised as a tiger hunting prey.

From this example it may be seen that just as Majnun degenerates into a "creature" and an "animal," so too Radha "takes form as a whining doe," and disguises "as a tiger hunting prey." Thus the elements of zoanthropy and lycanthropy mentioned are present in both the lovers.

There is contrast as well as similarity between Radha's search for seclusion in *Govinda*, and Majnun's retreat into the dark cave in *Layla*. On the one hand, the contrast is that in *Govinda* the location is sylvan and fertile, whereas in *Layla* it is dry and arid. On the other hand, the similarity is firstly the factor of withdrawal in both; and secondly that both the bower and the cave represent places of seclusion, darkness, and desolation. Thirdly, the descriptions of Majnun and Radha are parallel in demonstrating elements of the animal-like condition mentioned in relation to the psychological state. Finally, the withdrawal is not only microcosmic, but also macrocosmic in both texts.

These conditions in the search of the individual lovers may be associated with man's lower nature, or base faculties. The constant fight of the "seeker of the path of God," involves not just "the relentless fight against man's lower nature, but a subtle psychological analysis of every thought as well as uninterrupted spiritual training" of even the secret motions of the soul and the heart (Schimmel 1975, 54). This training is associated with, and indicative of, the process of purification and transformation. In general therefore, it may be said that all of the foregoing examples from *Layla* and *Govinda* are phenomenally different but similar in principle.

The element of seclusion and retreat, prominently featured both in *Layla* and in *Govinda*, represents an important universal symbol, namely the symbol of the cave. Although there is no cave as understood literally in *Govinda*, the thicket is interpreted as an appropriate substitute, for it has all the relevant constituent elements as has been explained. The ensuing discussion will highlight and compare some points of this symbol, and explain its spiritual significance according to the relevant mystical traditions.

The presentation of the withdrawal or retreat shows obvious points of correspondence between *Layla* and *Govinda* in terms of setting, location, and effect. These may be represented schematically as in Figure 4 below:

In *Layla*	In *Govinda*	Significance
mountain	forest	the setting for retreat
cave	thicket	the location of retreat
heart	heart	the effect of separation: disconnection, fragmentation, and defeat

Figure 4: Elements of Correspondence in the Retreat

For discussion and comparison of the symbolic and spiritual significance of the above correspondences, only the term "mountain" will be applied to refer to both mountain and forest. In the same light, only the term "cave" will mean both cave and thicket; the term "lover" will designate both Radha and Majnun; and "heart" will refer to the effect of separation on the lovers. The symbol of the mountain, the cave, and the heart are closely interrelated and overlapping. However, this chapter will deal with the symbolism only to the extent of its relevance to the portrayal of the state of separation, namely the aspects of isolation and disconnectedness.

The mountain setting of the cave is expressed, for example, in *Layla* as "the mountains echoed his mourning songs" (LI:171), whereas in *Govinda*, Radha grapples with "The wondrous mystery of Kṛishna's sexual play in Brindaban forest" (I:45). In symbolic terms, on the one hand, the verticality of the mountain is representative of the interconnectedness of divinity and humanity, of movement upwards, and of the *axis mundi*, or spiritual center of the world. But, on the other hand, like every other important symbol, it is a meeting of opposites.[2] An inverse and complementary aspect of these representations

[2] Incidentally, particularly in the Hindu culture, the forest is looked upon in a similar way, i.e. nature as the source of life and vitality. Thus the forest is both a symbol of

is that the mountain is also a reminder of disconnectedness and downward movement, and of inaccessibility and isolation. In the context of separation, the mountain as the setting of the cave highlights and emphasizes the downward spiral, the isolation, and the ascetic state of the lovers in separation. This is because, as commonly acknowledged in the spiritual life, development "at first brings great suffering to the aspirant, not happiness" (Yatiswarananda 1989, 7).

The relationship of the mountain to the cave corresponds to the relationship of the setting to the location of the retreat. Thus, in contrast with the mountain (the setting) which is visible, the cave (the location) "is ... a place that is essentially hidden and closed off" (Guénon 1995, 148). In this connection, the Sanskrit term for "cave" provides a basis to illustrate the symbolic and spiritual meaning of the cave. From the root *guh*, the term *guha*, meaning "cave" may be extended to *guh-yam*, "confidential subject," and *gu-udha*, "secret," "mysterious." It is also found in reference to Guha, a child symbol in Hindu mythology. In the myth, Guha signifies "making visible the invisible," and "born of the secret place" (Sahi 1980, 103). This meaning may be applied to the idea that the Truth is revealed to the elect, in secrecy of initiation. In similar vein, the root *gup* means "to guard" or "hide," and from this, *gup-ta*,[3] meaning "secret." Thus *gupta* relates to everything which is of a secret character, and which is not externally manifested (Guénon 1995, 148). The above aspects of the cave characterize it as a spiritual center.

The prominence of the cave in the period of separation may also be seen in a different but related context, namely, the idea of transformation. As has been discussed, separation is necessary for transformation. Thus, in the spiritual realities, "apparent destruction is really a transformation" (Guénon 1995, 145). Mysticism symbolizes this transformation in terms of alchemy, the science of transmuting

asceticism (isolation) and eroticism (wild nature/growth). Besides, the typical Indian image of the *yogi* in lotus posture, in deep meditation, is physically evocative of both the mountain and the cave. Cf. Sahi (1980). Generally, in mystical traditions, the trees of the forest, with the branches turning upwards and the roots downwards, represent verticality and upward/downward movement.

[3] Equivalent with the Greek, *kruptos*, and the English, "crypt," synonymous with "cave" and "burial place." Cf. Guénon (1995, 145).

base metals into gold. Burckhardt has explained this as follows (1987, 180):

> For true alchemy, the lead or other base metal that was to be transmuted into gold was only a symbol—a very adequate one—of the human soul sunk in the darkness and chaos of the passions, while gold represented the original nature of man, in which even the body is ennobled and transfigured by the life of the spirit.

Besides being a symbol of transformation to the divine state, the cave also represents an image of the world, or the garden of earthly life. This is displayed in the texts, where both Majnun and Radha retreat into, emerge, and re-enter the cave, in alternating moods of pleasure and pain in the duration of separation from the beloved. This may be likened to moving between the lower or higher human states. Entering the cave means purification (by seclusion), or pain (as a result of being disconnected from the lover). Emerging means suffering (away from protection), or pleasure (rejuvenated as a result of finding refuge). Thus, the cave is at once a forbidding, barren depth to which the seeker descends in the struggle with the worst ordeals, and at the same time a means of protection from pain and sorrow. It gives access, not only to subterranean or infernal regions, but also to super-terrestrial domains (Burckhardt 1987, 144). In this way, the symbolism of the cave corresponds both microcosmically (the mental and physical condition of the lovers) and macrocosmically (as reflected in the elements) to the portrayal of the cave in the texts.

It may be noted here that in the search for the beloved, the movement in and out of the cave is reminiscent of both an upward and downward spiral motion. This motion may be interpreted as indication of spiritual progression or regression, depending on perspective. In other words, the positivity and negativity of a particular incident or event is ambivalent. This is an indication that "the truth" is relative in the material realities. Thus, the symbol of the cave as an image of the world shows that adversity and advantage are two sides of the same coin in the material world. In connection with Majnun and Radha (as symbolizing the human soul), trials and struggles are blessings in disguise, because without them the beloved (the Divine Beloved) would not be attained.

The close relationship between the symbolism of the cave and the symbolism of the heart mentioned earlier, may now be taken up. The connection between the two is indicated by various linguistic terms to denote "heart." On this matter, Guénon's opinion is that (1995, 147):

> there is a point of language to be considered, the importance of which should not be overestimated, but which is curious nevertheless ... and more so in that in the different languages the similar roots which denote the heart are to be found.

According to Guénon, the similarity in different languages referred to above is that "heart" in English (Arabic *al-qalb*), has the same root as the Sanskrit *hrd* or *hrdaya*, and the German *herz*. Furthermore, it is *ker* or *kardion* in Greek, and *kor*, in Latin. In addition, there is further correspondence in the Semitic-Hamitic languages. For example, the Egyptian word *hor* means heart, and *Horus* refers to the "Heart of the World" or spiritual center. Finally, in Hebrew, the word *hor*, written with the letter *heth*, signifies cave, whereas written with the letter *he*, signifies mountain. The first linguistic group is of the Indo-Aryan source, the second, European, the third, Egyptian, the fourth Latin, and the final, Hebrew. In other words, Guénon points out that, firstly, the same root exists in related languages. Secondly, that there is a phonetic convergence between diverse linguistic origins for the words referring to a notion or principle of limit, enclosure, and envelopment. Furthermore, literally and symbolically, the words for heart correspond to the denotation of the cave as a place enclosed within the mountain (Guénon 1995, 147-48).

The heart is also parallel to the image of the cave as a point of spiritual beginning and development. The characteristics of secrecy in relation to the terms denoting "heart," evoke the mystic initiatic rites as "a truth only within the scope of the restricted/elite" (Guénon 1995, 147-48). In this sense, the principles of beginning and originating associated with initiation (Latin *initiato*), are related to the image of the womb. The beginning is associated with the primordial condition, or human origins, expressed as the Divine-human unity. Thus, the cave, which is at the center of the mountain and a spiritual center is an equivalent of the heart. The heart, which is a physical center of the body, is the organ of intuition, as well as a spiritual center in one's being. As a spiritual center, the yearning for a return to the primordial condition originates in the heart (Guénon 1995, 114). This is manifested in the texts as the lovers' intense yearning and quest for the beloved, and for refuge in the seclusion of the cave. In this context, the whole phenomenon of seclusion may be understood as a metaphor of primordiality.

Thus it may be seen that the relations between the symbolism of the mountain, the cave, and the heart in *Layla* and *Govinda* correspond to the textual equivalences of these words in the texts. In this regard, it is interesting that although the texts are from cultural traditions involving linguistic, geographical, and religious diversity, they exhibit a similar structure in the portrayal of retreat and seclusion.

Apart from the phenomenon of motion, the "thorns" suffered by separation from the beloved are also expressed by madness. There are a wealth of expressions conveying the most immediate, outward effect of separation on Majnun. Qays, the "moon" transforms into Majnun, "the madman." If the moon is seen as a mirror of perfection, then the madman may be seen as representative of imperfection. On a similar basis of understanding, it may be recalled that in *Govinda*, Radha's delirious folly in rushing to meet her beloved is witnessed by a moon with "cratered stains." Here the moon is the mirror of perfection, and the "cratered stains" on it indicate imperfection i.e. in the sense of imminent separation. It is interesting that a direct connection between the moon and madness has often been established: the lunar affects the lunatic. Thus the lunar association and the lunatic aspect of the lover are seen as two sides of the same coin.

Definitions of lunacy or madness include various aspects of mental illness, frenzy, imprudence or wild foolishness, uncontrollable rage, and even ecstasy (NSOED). From such definitions it is surmised that the condition may be identified by a wide range of indications or "symptoms," at the physical, emotional, mental, and spiritual levels. However, as will become apparent, it is difficult to extricate these aspects or levels of madness entirely from one another.

The phenomenon of transformation from sanity to madness may be interpreted at various levels. At the outward level, madness is associated with mental illness. In terms of the psyche, transformation involving madness may also be seen as a manifestation of variations of zoanthropy, a form of madness in which a person believes himself or herself to be an animal and behaves accordingly, and lycanthropy, the mythical transformation of a person into a wolf (Wilber 1996, 82-99). These phenomena may be understood at another level, i.e. as a metaphor of man's primordial purity, and symbolically as a shedding of all pretence and deception. At the same time, it relates to the animal-soul (*al-nafs al-hayawaniyyah*), or a negative or egocentric tendency of the soul (*al-nafs, jivan*), as opposed to the spirit (*ruh, atma*), or the intellect (*aql, buddhi*) (Burckhardt 1973, 150). Generally, they may be associated with man's degeneration.

At a deeper, spiritual level, it signifies transformation. A prerequisite of spiritual realization is transformation of the nature and substance of the aspirant. In mystical terms, this involves an alchemical change in the life of the mystic that is total and comprehensive. Consciousness of both the positive and the negative tendencies, however, are necessary for spiritual development, maturity, and ultimately, realization. Finally, as mentioned in the definition of madness, an aspect of the condition of madness is ecstasy, which may be associated with "divine madness." As will be demonstrated from specific examples in the ensuing discussion, each of these aspects of transformation mentioned are apparent in the portrayal of both Majnun and Radha in the state of separation.

In *Layla*, it is said of Majnun that "Suffering has broken him and his mind has become sick" (XXIV:125). It may be surmised from this statement that his suffering is so intense that he slips into the condition of "madness." This is implicitly conveyed in the expression, "the reins had slipped from the rider's hand" (IV:10). Thus, upon being separated or "forced apart" (XLVI:156) from Layla, Majnun literally falls apart. As for Radha, she is "Like dew from lotuses with broken stems ... Radhika suffers in your desertion" (IV:14). This image of being "broken" is illustrated by an expression further on in *Govinda*, that she is "Broken by her passion's intensity" (IX:1).

The phenomenon of the lover being "broken" or fragmented by separation may be seen as a manifestation of imperfection. This phenomenon may also be understood from a mystical viewpoint in two ways. Firstly, for transformation to occur, there has to be a complete "break" with the previous forms and ways of one's existence, i.e. from worldly considerations and constraints. Secondly, a total "break" or annihilation of the self, or ego is necessary as a prerequisite for spiritual reconstruction. Both forms of "breakage" involve a severance, or a separation. It requires a transformation so total that it resembles a "death" of the old self. This transformation may occur through an ongoing struggle, seen as a process of purification. In this context, the "thorns" encountered by the lovers' struggle are perceived as representing this process.

The deterioration of Majnun's condition is described as: "the bridge between the two banks had fallen in" (VI:15). The bridge "fallen in" may be understood both as physical access being denied, as well as an indication of sanity slipping away. At this point Majnun takes to the mountains all alone, roaming around "more and more often, and for ever lengthening spells ... wandering aimlessly" (VI:15). His beloved, his family, and his tribe are abandoned, as he runs on trackless wastes, "paying no attention to roads and directions" (VII:20). In these circumstances he moves away from all human interaction. As Majnun says (VII:21-22):

> An outcast I have become. Family and home, where are they? No path leads back to them and none to my beloved. Broken are my name, my reputation, like glass smashed on a rock; broken is the drum which once spread the good news, and my ears now hear only the drumbeat of separation.

It may be observed that in moving out of human interaction, Majnun also moves out of the norms of human behaviour. The loss of contact and loss of sanity is manifested by a corresponding loss of garments. When he "beat his head with his fists and rent his garment from top to bottom" (VII:20) the last vestiges of his sanity are also shed. Thus the naked Majnun completes the picture of a homeless, outcast madman, a Majnun stripped of all outer coverings. Generally in symbolism, nudity expresses, and virtually actualizes a return to the essence, the origin, the archetype, thus to the celestial state (Schuon 2003).

In being separated from Krishna, Radha too suffers, although she is not explicitly labelled as suffering from madness. However, it is useful to compare her condition with the physical "symptoms" of Majnun's madness. As mentioned earlier in relation to Majnun's degeneration, the expression "His hair fell unkempt about his face" (VII:21), depicts Majnun as being in a state of disarray. Similarly, the picture of dishevelment of Radha is painted in images of hair and flowers. Her hair is "a tangle of wilted flowers" (II:15), and "Tangles of flowers lie wilted in her loosened hair" (VII:13). This phenomenon of the tangled hair of the "mad lover" in both *Layla* and *Govinda* presents an interesting correspondence, cited as a classic example of the "dialectical suspension between likeness and disparity" (Chenu 1983, 114), as an obvious "veiling" element here.

At the superficial level, unkempt hair is a display of the chaotic and the disordered. To the rational eye, it is symptomatic of psychic disorder, but for the insightful eye, "it is a clarion call to be non-fragmented and holistic and an invitation for re-balancing of the masculine and feminine elements of life" (Mohanados 1997, 443). Although the last view is culturally specific to the Indian context, it may be said that both texts use the symbolism to display a state of mind of the lover as possessed by, or connected to, divine power. Thus this inner experience is given expression in the symbol of tangled hair (Mohanados 1997, 443).

The portrayal of Radha as the "mad" lover is made explicit by her own words, in which she fantasizes about making love to Krishna. In "The Sixth Song," Radha's longing and yearning is voiced as (II:11):

> I reach the lonely forest hut where he secretly lies at night.
> My trembling eyes search for him as he laughs in a mood of passion.
> *Friend, bring Kesi's sublime tormentor to revel with me!*
> *I've gone mad waiting for his fickle love to change.* (italics mine)

In the above verse, the first two lines represent a visualization of a secret rendezvous. In this imaginary meeting, Krishna is present in "the lonely forest hut." Here, according to her, "he lies secretly at night." His presence is made more real because she hears him laughing "in a mood of passion." In other words, for Radha, the experience is "real," because it is sensory: she senses (hears) his presence. However, in the couplet that follows (above, italicized) she pleads with her friend to bring Krishna to her. This establishes her experience of his presence as virtual.[4]

In the above instance, the implication of mental instability is powerfully conveyed in a number of ways through contradiction. Firstly, there is a direct contradiction in the substance or content of the first

[4] The metaphor of the mirage, and the dialectic of the real and the illusory, is directly relevant to this example.

and second couplets. In the first couplet, Krishna is "really," or "actually" present for Radha. However, in the second, it turns out that he is "really," or "actually" absent. This element of contradiction upsets the equilibrium between what is real and what is not, and reflects Radha's "unbalanced" state of mind.

Secondly, the reference to Krishna with the expression "sublime tormentor" is another form of contradiction. The juxtaposition of the semantically opposing words "sublime" and "tormentor" constitutes an oxymoron, which emphasizes the depth of her trauma, and reflects a mental imbalance. At the highest level, however, this points to Krishna as the supreme cause of Radha's transgression, and the supreme object of her love. Thus he is the sickness and the salve, the poison and the remedy. This brings us to an opposition in symbolic articulation, expressed in Hindu philosophy by the notion of *visha-amrita*. In Sanskrit, the word *visha*, "poison" or "draught of death," is considered as the antithesis of *amrita*, or "draught of immortality" (Guénon 1995, 228). Thus, though different in form of expression, a similarity in content or principle emerges between the Sanskrit notion of *visha-amrita* (mortality-immortality), and the Persian notion of *ganj-ranj* (treasure-pain), which may be applied to the earlier discussion of Majnun in the context of madness and sanity.

Finally, the reference to "Kesi" is a significant metaphor of contradiction.[5] Because the reference typifies disorder and confusion, it conveys a powerful effect of inconsistency, paradox, and conflict, all characteristic elements of mental instability. Apart from contradiction, the intensification is mounted by the second couplet which is a refrain, repeated eight times. Thus, Radha's plaintive cry rises to a crescendo in this refrain, as her experience of longing and unfulfilled yearning drives her to madness.

Closely related to the condition of mental instability is the condition of intoxication or inebriation. This condition involves the corruption of the moral or mental faculties, and includes making a person stupid, insensible, or disordered in intellect with a drug or alcoholic

[5] In the Hindu scriptures, the epithet is a reference to Kesin, the mythical "demon horse," also called the "meanest of horses." In the *Bhagavad Gita*, the body is referred to as a chariot, and the senses to wild horses. Thus, the spiritual wayfarer constantly battles to gain mastery over the senses, which pull him in all directions.

liquor (NSOED). However, it is interesting that the definition of "intoxication" also refers, in a figurative sense, to the action or power of exhilarating, or exciting, the mind (NSOED). This particular sense of the word may be positive in a specific context, as will be illustrated in a separate discussion. Basically, the outward condition is understood to be negative, as it amounts to being destabilized and decentered from "normality." In this context, there is an obvious aspect of negativity pertaining to the intoxication of Majnun in *Layla*. For example, he is a man who has taken leave of his senses as in the description, "like a man whom wine has driven to raving madness and then cut down, robbed of his senses" (XXXIX:126). Furthermore, he is "drunk with longing and confused by feverish hope" (V:13). In this condition, Majnun epitomizes the "wanderer who did not see where he was going, drunk with the wafting scent of love" (XXVIII:88). All of these aspects fulfill the negative sense of the definition of intoxication.

In *Govinda*, Radha too has her fair share of the malady of intoxication. This is seen in the lines describing her as "drunk on honey buzz soft tones!" (XI:18). Furthermore, there is also an association with wine in the instance when Krishna entreats her to drink the wine of love (X:2):

> Abandon your baseless pride!
> Love's fire burns my heart
> Bring wine in your lotus mouth!

The above instance is a refrain which occurs repeatedly in "The Nineteenth Song" when Krishna finally approaches Radha. This Song, in which the refrain occurs in 8 out of the 14 verses, ends on the same theme of intoxication, with the description of Radha's eyes as "lazy with wine, like Madalasa" (X:14).[6]

In comparing the expressions of intoxication in *Govinda* and *Layla*, there are similarities as well as differences. In terms of differences, firstly, the references to the concept of intoxication in *Govinda* are far more limited in quantity, compared to the vast number of

[6] The Sanskrit root *mada*, means intoxication, or any intoxicating liquid. This mythical reference originating from the Puranas is associated with the illustrious Queen Madalasa who cheated Death.

references in *Layla*.[7] This difference may be attributed to genre, as discussed previously. Secondly, whereas the references are negative as well as positive in *Layla*, there appears to be little negativity to the concept in *Govinda*. This difference may be explained from a cultural basis. In the Indian cultural background of *Govinda*, alcohol is not a taboo as it is in the case of *Layla*. In fact the intoxicating *soma* juice figures prominently in Vedic ritual sacrifices.[8]

On the other hand, the similarity in expression between the texts is the obvious emphasis given to the concept of intoxication. The repetition and intensification provided by the refrain in *Govinda* may be seen as a qualitative compensation for the large number of references in *Layla*. Here again, there is difference in form but similarity in substance.

As previously mentioned, apart from the apparent effects of wine, the definition of intoxication also refers to the exhilaration of the mind, and elation to excitement beyond the bounds of sobriety (NSOED). This aspect of the definition is concordant with the spiritual implications of madness, mental struggle, and intoxication. Whereas in the ordinary sense, the state of intoxication temporarily eliminates man's mental and rational capabilities, in the mystical sense it is "the loss of awareness of all but God" (Schimmel 1982, 9). Thus the esoteric understanding of intoxication is the ecstasy of attaining the Divine. The "madness" of man on the spiritual quest is a "divine madness," or a state of "God-intoxication." This is the inner significance of Majnun losing his mind. Through this loss, and through constant suffering and pain, love for God is proved and matured (Schimmel 1982, 127).

The above view of madness includes the unitive experience, in which the self is obliterated and displaced by the Self, or God. In other words, the real becomes annihilated and the Real becomes manifest. This experience points to *tawhid*, the central concept of Sufism, and of Islam in general, which is eventually understood as "the extinction of the ignorance of our essential identity with the only Real. It is no

[7] A total of 75 occurrences of words related to intoxication were identified in *Layla*. The words are: "drink(ing)," "drunk," "cup (-bearer)," "wine," and "intoxicated."

[8] *Soma* is defined as the plant which yielded the mystic wine for the Vedic sacrifice; the wine itself represents the intoxication of *ananda*, the divine delight of being; *Soma* is the Lord of this wine of delight and immortality, the representative deity of the beatitude. See "Glossary of Sanskrit Terms in Integral Yoga Literature" (2004).

longer a unity of will, but a lifting of the veils of ignorance" (Schimmel 1975, 282). Thus the human mind is able to transcend not only the limitations of the senses, but also the powers of reasoning. In this context, it is said that the self "comes face to face with facts which it could never have sensed, or reasoned out" (Vivekananda 2001a, 7).

More specifically, just as pure wine is obtained through the fermentation of grape juice, the soul, by constant "fermentation" through repeated tribulation, develops until it becomes purified. Thus, "the human soul can mature only through suffering" (Schimmel 1982, 137). The pain and privation of Majnun and Radha may be viewed in this context. In Sufi poetry, Junayd praised poverty, *faqr*, in this respect. According to him, *faqr* is "an ocean of affliction, yet its affliction is complete glory." In this way, constant purification, or "affliction is the fastest steed to bring man to perfection" (Schimmel 1982, 137).

In this regard, the extent of Radha's privation and affliction is graphically described in the following verse (IV:10):

Her house becomes a wild jungle,
Her band of loving friends a snare.
Sighs fan her burning pain
To flames that rage like forest fire.
Suffering your desertion,
She takes form as a whining doe
And turns Love into Death.

In every line of the above verse, it is apparent that she confronts pain, isolation, loneliness, and even association with death. Thus her privation is very much like Majnun's in destitution at all levels. Moreover, the condition of both these characters corresponds at the spiritual level. The Bhakti concept of *karpanya* corresponds to the condition of *faqr* in Sufism. *Karpanya* is firstly "a sense of total poverty or nothingness of oneself in relation to what one strives after" (in Sivaraman 1995, 427). Secondly it includes the idea of "self-naughting as a prelude to self-realization" (in Sivaraman 1995, 427). Thirdly it refers to the state of total identification and unity, in which "there is neither creation, nor created, nor creator ... where there is neither *I* nor *thou*, where there is neither subject, nor object, nor relation" (Vivekananda, 2001, 16-17). This is applicable to Radha in the context of her "nothingness" without Krishna, illustrated in the verse quoted. It is a state that can only be obtained through renunciation of sense attachments, worldly comforts, and material pleasures. As it occurs in *Govinda*, all these human needs of Radha's are subsequently burned up in "flames that rage like forest fire" (IV:10), the fire of her desire for Krishna.

In summarizing the focus of examination in this chapter, several points may be noted. There is correspondence and equivalence in the "thorns" of separation and the different aspects of "madness" and their symbolic and spiritual significance. There are parallels in the transformation or metamorphosis of the human lovers from the state of divine perfection to the state of human imperfection. Basically, both Qays and Radha have moved from perfection, bliss, and wholeness, to imperfection, agony, and fragmentation. This feature has been interpreted and understood in mystical terms as representing "the arc of descent." Yet, although imperfection is regarded as a "fall," it is also a vital and dynamic process. From the perspective of metaphysical and cosmological realities which are cyclic in nature, descent is a requisite for the possibility of ascent, or return, to the perfect state.

Having said that, however, it has also been pointed out that the state of separation does not solely involve or portray imperfection and fragmentation. Towards supporting this opinion, attention will be turned in the next chapter to aspects of the state of separation which constitute that vital, dynamic "ascent" mentioned. Expressed in the language of the garden, if this chapter has been concerned with the prick of thorns in the garden of love, the following chapter will have a taste of its flowers and fruits.

CHAPTER FIVE

THORNS OF LOVE'S GARDENS: FUSION AND CONFUSION IN SEPARATION

> Layla was trying to find comfort in the garden;... perhaps it could show her the way to that other garden,...?
>
> (*Layla*, XIV:43)

> Meeting me under a flowering tree, he calms my fear of dark time,...
>
> (*Govinda*, II:8)

It has been mentioned in chapter 4 that in *Layla* and *Govinda* there are two opposite and contrasting phenomena in the portrayal of "separation," namely the "negative" and the "positive" aspects. This renders separation as a state of flux, which is defined as "continuous succession of changes of condition, composition, or substance" (NSOED). To illustrate, this state of flux changes from pain and suffering to pleasure and delight, or from fear and loneliness to comfort and companionship. The "negative" aspect has been extensively illustrated and analyzed in the previous chapter as being a condition of fragmentation and disconnectedness between lover and beloved. This chapter resumes the discussion by focusing on the "positive" aspect, which is the condition of fusion and connectedness.

The phenomenon of intermittent change between connectedness and disconnectedness is amply incorporated into the portrayal of separation in both the texts under consideration. It is important to bear in mind, however, that the experience of connectedness essentially remains a condition of the state of separation. This is the paradox intimated in the title of this chapter, referring to separation as both "love's gardens" and "fusion," as well as "thorns" and "confusion." It suggests that fusion and pleasure is brought into being by confusion and pain. In other words, it is because of separation that union occurs. In the texts, "fusion" is effected through various means and measures which enable the lovers to extricate themselves briefly from spatio-temporal limitations. Stated differently, "confusion" is a blurring of boundaries by which connection with the beloved is actually or virtually effected.

Based on the above explanation, fusion and confusion may be expressed as a binary relationship between tranquility and turmoil. In garden terminology, it is between flowers and thorns. This involves an experience, firstly, of the thorns of the garden, then subsequently, of an occasional glimpse of the flowers, and finally, of the pain of thorns again. In spiritual terms, this process corresponds to an awakening to the turmoil of material realities followed by the tranquility of the awareness of that Eternal, "other garden," the *Firdaus* of the Sufi and the *Goloka* of the Bhakta, and finally sinking down to, or being immersed in, worldly concerns once again. This journey or path that is characteristic of the mystic process, is seen as an endless, seasonal, or cyclic, pattern. In fact, it represents the *raison d'etre* of mysticism, and the literary language of mystics always displays a focus on the process or "path," rather than on the purpose or "goal."

Fusion and Confusion

A point to be noted is the perspective of subjectivity adopted in dealing with symbols of pleasure and pain or fusion and confusion. Firstly, opposite and contrasting aspects inherent in mystical symbols are not necessarily seen as positive or negative qualities, but rather, as complementary aspects of a phenomenon. Furthermore, it is acknowledged that mystical symbols are by nature paradoxical. Finally, it is accepted that qualities are subjective, depending on the perspective from which a phenomenon is approached. Therefore, in order to represent the reality of the "garden of love" in a comprehensive and holistic manner, the "thorns" as well as the "flowers" should be considered. Thus, selected phenomena, viewed as "thorns" in chapter 4 will, in this chapter, be viewed as "flowers."

To illustrate the subjectivity assumed in this regard, the analogy of the thorn itself may be used: it takes a thorn (or any sharp point) to remove a thorn (another sharp point). The texts illustrate this truth. It takes the presence of pain to bring Majnun and Radha to a sharp consciousness of the absence of pleasure. Expressed symbolically, only the "thorns" of suffering and pain can remove the "thorns" of impurity and ignorance. In this sense, pain is necessary as a vital process of spiritual development. This is articulated in *Layla* as "... what today we mistake for a padlock, keeping us out, we may tomorrow find to be the key that lets us in" (I:2). That is to say, the mystical journey requires the faculty of discernment and discrimination involved in recognizing the difference between "the padlock" and "the key."

The extracts of corresponding passages from *Layla* and *Govinda* quoted at the beginning of this chapter may be referred to in illustrating the subjectivity of expression. The full passages are as follows:

In ***Layla***	In ***Govinda***
Layla was trying to find comfort in the garden; she looked at it as an ornament framing the image of the beloved; perhaps it could show her the way to that other garden, the garden of paradise? (*Layla*, XIV:43)	Meeting me under a flowering tree, he calms my fear of dark time, Delighting me deeply by quickly glancing looks at my heart. My heart recalls Hari here in his love dance.... (*Govinda*, II:8)

Figure 5.1: Transcending Limitations in the Garden

In these expressions the means, and the objective, of transcending spatial and temporal limitations are mentioned indirectly. In *Layla*, "the garden" is the means to "show her the way." The objective is to "find comfort" and to reach "the garden of paradise." In this context, the reference to "garden" and "the way" suggest spatial dimensions. In *Govinda*, the "meeting" "under a flowering tree" is the means. The objective is for "delighting me deeply" and to "calm my fear of dark time." In this verse, the reference to "time" and "quickly" refer to temporal dimensions. In both cases, the limitations are transcended in the mind. In *Layla*, it is through Layla's perception of the garden, narrated as "she looked at it as an ornament framing the image of the beloved." In *Govinda*, it is by recollection of "Hari here in his love dance." Thus, fusion refers to the end, i.e. union, whereas confusion refers to the means of transcending physical realities. In this context, "confusion" is seen essentially as "an operative means, for man, of reintegration in his Divine Origin" (Lings 1975, 127).

On the above understanding, this chapter will examine the means by which comfort and delight are experienced and expressed within the state of separation. Besides this, as has been done for all other phenomena in previous chapters, an attempt will be made to discover the nature and extent of similarity and contrast between *Layla* and

Govinda in this regard, as well as in the symbolic and spiritual significance of expressions. The discussion will comprise two major components, firstly, phenomena which were presented in the previous chapter, and secondly, phenomena which have not been previously discussed. In the first component the same phenomena of seclusion and madness previously presented as "thorns" of separation will now be presented as "flowers" of union. The next component delves into the phenomena of dance, music, and song as found in *Layla* and *Govinda*.

Pleasure in Separation

There are elements of nature as well as human elements in the texts which relate to the portrayal of seclusion. A pair of natural elements expressing the phenomenon of seclusion is the mountain in *Layla* and the forest in *Govinda*. Each represents the "wilderness" or location of isolation. These physically vast and strong elements of nature afford, and symbolize, protection and refuge. Another pair of natural elements is the cave and the thicket respectively. Located within the context of the wilderness, these elements fortify the seclusion as well as accentuate it. Further, there are pairs of human elements involved in the seclusion. The first pair is the lovers, Radha and Majnun respectively, representing the body or the self which is shattered by separation and seeking shelter inside this fortified seclusion. The second human element is the "heart" of the matter of seclusion, which is the psychological condition of the lover. The heart that is broken is seeking to be repaired and restored. It will be argued that each of these elements mentioned, besides expressing the phenomenon of seclusion, represents a means of fusion.

It is convenient to compare the portrayal of seclusion in *Layla* and *Govinda* according to, firstly, the two natural elements, and subsequently, the two human elements. The following table provides corresponding expressions associated with the first pair, namely elements of nature:

Element	In *Layla*	In *Govinda*
Mountain/ Forest	the wilderness became Majnun's only refuge. Restlessly he roamed through its gorges and climbed steep rocks which no human being had explored before. He appeared,... seemingly one with the rocks, like the wild basil clinging to them. (XXXIV:103)	...mango trees tremble from the embrace of rising vines. Brindaban forest is washed by meandering Jumna river waters.... When spring's mood is rich, Hari roams here To dance with young women, friend, A cruel time for deserted lovers. (I:27)
Cave/ Thicket	So Majnun lamented, tearing his heart asunder in wild desperation.... Only when a new day climbed the mountain-tops..., did Majnun leave..., returning, like a fleeting shadow, to the caves and ravines of Najd. (XXXIII:103)	Revel in wild luxury on the sweet thicket floor! Your laughing face begs ardently for his love. Radha, enter Madhava's intimate world! (XI:14)

Figure 5.2: Elements of Nature in the Portrayal of Seclusion

In the table, the first and second examples from *Layla* directly illustrate Majnun's identification with the "mountain" and the "cave." It is explicitly expressed that he "restlessly ... roamed" in the "wilderness," the "gorges," the "steep rocks," and "caves and ravines." Furthermore, the ruggedness of the terrain seems to echo Majnun's "wild desperation." This conveys that he is "seemingly one" with these elements. Thus he identifies with them, and repeatedly returns to them. There is a dual implication in this. On the one hand the wilderness spells danger and isolation. At the same time these elements represent places of refuge and hiding. It is as if the broken, fragmented Majnun is drawn to these places because they are the means to become whole again. By the same token, it is as if this is the only way of achieving connectedness with his beloved.

The mystical symbolism of the above phenomenon may be explained as follows. The cave to which Majnun retreats represents the spiritual retreat (*khalwa*) of the Sufi. In most Sufi orders, the *khalwa* is looked upon as an aid to achieving "a state of permanent inward retreat" (Bakhtiar 1976, 94). In adherence to the Traditions of the Prophet, who used to retreat to caves in the mountains, the Sufi retreats to an isolated cell or location of solitude in nature (Bakhtiar 1976, 94). The retreat is devoted to "the remembrance of God and the forgetting of the self," under the supervision of a living spiritual guide, or *shaykh* (Bakhtiar 1976, 95), and involves strict disciplines such as fasts and extended periods of invocation. Thus the spiritual retreat represents dual aspects: renunciation and acceptance. Renunciation applies to the self and the world, which is left behind, and acceptance relates to the authority of the *shaykh* and the remembrance of God. This state is struggled for, through practice of the difficult austerities mentioned.

In *Govinda*, however, the possibility of union between Radha and Krishna is portrayed in the repeated exhortations to Radha to "enter Madhava's (Krishna) intimate world," in "Blissful Krishna" (XI:1-21). This is supported by nature images which function as symbols of regeneration: "seeds of ripe pomegranate" (XI:19) and "tangles of new shoots" (XI:20) in "a bright retreat heaped with flowers" (XI:16) and "sandal-forest winds" (XI:17) beckon Radha to "revel in wild luxury on the sweet thicket floor" (XI:14). At the same time, a mood of solitude and darkness evokes a sense of separation . The site of the prospective union "in the thicket buried in darkness" (XI:10) of Brindaban forest conjures a place of dark seclusion, and "the night's cherished cloak," and "dark lotus wreaths" (XI:11) reflect this mood. The tone of separation is emphasized by the fact that Radha "begs ardently for his love" (XI:14) for she has "languished too long" (XI:20), without Krishna. This juxtaposition of union and separation is indicative of a paradoxical principle of renunciation and acceptance in Hindu mysticism, which may be explained as follows.

In the Hindu tradition the forest and the thicket, by their remoteness and isolation symbolize *sannyasa*, or the ascetic state, and *nivrtti dharma*, the path of the renunciate. On the other hand, the wildness of growth associated with the forest, or trees, is representative of spontaneity and regeneration in nature, and suggestive of the creative and sexual activity of *pravrtti dharma*, man-in-the-world. This is evident from the references to the richness of "spring's mood" (I:27) and the invitation to "revel in wild luxury" (XI:14). In this sense, nature symbolizes the source of life and vitality, and thus, the forest and thicket have erotic undertones. The symbolism is based on the notion of worldly experience as a necessary process of spiritual development. In this context, the central meaning of the tree is both birth and life, or rather, "a rebirth, which also requires a dying" (Sahi 1980, 153). Thus, asceticism or renunciation, and eroticism or vitality of growth, are one and the same in the process of being reborn (Sahi 1980, 145).

This becomes more obvious by reference to the Sanskrit root word *vrt*, and its etymological relation to the notion of *nivrtti* and *pravrtti*. *Nivrtti* means return, cessation, or abstinence from worldly acts, inactivity, rest, and repose. *Pravrtti* means moving onwards, advance, progress, coming forth, activity, active life (Mishra 1998, 44). In this understanding, the thicket in *Govinda*, similar to the cave in *Layla*, represents both a point of departure and return. Furthermore, the Sanskrit root *vrt*, meaning "to turn," is linguistically related to the Latin term *vertere*. In Mishra's explanation (1998, 44-45),

> we may legitimately conclude that the words are etymologically related to "extrovert" (literally "turning outwards") and "introvert" (literally "turning inwards"). Thus ... it would follow that the state of *nivrtti* is seen as a precondition for union with the "eternal Brahman," while *pravrtti* is part of the process of creation.

In this context, *pravrtti*, associated with the "real" or physical, worldly experience, is essential to *nivrtti* (Mishra 1998, 43), or the "Real," referring to the transcendence of material realities, or spiritual existence. Thus, the importance of the secular to the spiritual life is that the association with worldly life is to learn of the difference between that and the spiritual life. The Bhakta's view of the worldly and the spiritual life is that these represent two necessary and interrelated stages of God-realization.[1]

[1] This is divergent from the orthodox view in exoteric Hinduism, in which eroticism and ascetism are mutually exclusive categories. In religious terms, only renunciation and retreat from the world is valued because it signifies transcendence and otherworldliness. See Mishra (1998, 43).

This is one of the ways that the "anomaly" of erotic expression in spiritual texts may be resolved. This anomaly naturally exists in the text of *Govinda*, which is, after all, renowned as an expression of Vaishnava Bhaktism. In this connection, it must be remembered that Divine revelation and redemption is appropriate to its particular spatio-temporal context. Thus in the primordial, Vedic age when primordial man was true to his original nature, utmost importance was placed on transcendence and other-worldliness. Whereas Bhaktism, the religion of love and devotion, is appropriate to the present age of "decay," the *Kali Yuga* (meaning "dark time" or "age of darkness"). In this context, Indian scholars agree that the redeeming feature of this age is Bhakti.[2] This agent of redemption is Krishna, the particular *avatara* of "dark time" referred to in the quotation at the beginning of this chapter.

Aside from spiritual symbolism, the mountain in *Layla* and the forest (or more precisely, the trees that comprise the forest) in *Govinda* represent cosmological symbols. They may be viewed as "a ladder reaching from the ground to touch the sky" (Sahi 1980, 153). In this connection, they represent established axial symbols. Thus, their verticality acts as a reminder of the interconnectedness of the divine and the human, and also of upward movement (Guénon 1995, 221). In this regard, the mountain and the tree represent both a meeting point between heaven and earth and a center of the universe, or *axis mundi*. Besides, in relation to their splendor, permanence, and strength, the mountain and the forest are symbols of authority. And finally, both are associated with age and maturity, as well as with pristine innocence. In this context, these natural elements symbolize primordiality. Thus, the close connection of Majnun and Radha with nature points to the possibility of a return to man's primordial origins or union with the Divine.

The cave and the thicket within the mountain and the forest respectively, may also be related to the notion of transformation as a positive aspect of separation. As has been discussed, separation is necessary for transformation. Thus, in the spiritual realities, "apparent destruction is really a transformation" (Guénon 1995, 145). As has been illustrated in chapter 4 in relation to the withdrawal of the

[2] See Hazariprasad Dvedi's *Madhyakalin dharma sadhana*, in Mishra (1998, 208n).

characters from community and social norms, and the death-wish articulated by both Majnun and Radha, in the spiritual life the "call" of the highest ideals necessitates a parting of ways, i.e. a death of the worldly life and a birth into the spiritual life. Thus, parting involves a transformation in the nature of a movement from one existential plane into another higher existential plane.

In mysticism, transformation is symbolically expressed in terms of alchemy. Literally, the "touchstone" is a mineral used for testing the quality of gold and silver, and is closely associated with "alchemy," or the transmutation of baser metals into gold. Figuratively, the touchstone refers to a criterion that serves to test the genuineness or value of something. This association with the touchstone and its function of testing, is specifically expressed by the following verse in *Govinda* (XI:12):

> Night spreads darkness as dense
> As tamala leaves,
> Making a touchstone
> To test the gold of love.

In order to "test the gold of love" in the context of devotion (*bhakti*) as a means of spiritual development, Burckhardt has explained the notion of alchemy and transmutation as follows (1987, 180):

> For true alchemy, the lead or other base metal that was to be transmuted into gold was only a symbol—a very adequate one—of the human soul sunk in the darkness and chaos of the passions, while gold represented the original nature of man, in which even the body is ennobled and transfigured by the life of the spirit.

Besides transformation (to the divine state, according to Bhaktism) or return (to the primordial state, according to Sufism), the cave also represents an image of the world, or the garden of earthly life. The movement to and from the cave symbolizes a quest for the beloved. Apart from the inward and outward movement, it is also reminiscent of an upward, or downward, spiral motion. This motion may be interpreted as an indication of spiritual progression or regression, depending on perspective. In other words, in the material realities, the positivity or negativity of a particular incident or event is ambivalent. Thus, as an image of the world, the symbol of the cave shows that adversity and advantage are two sides of the same coin.

In connection with Majnun and Radha (or the human soul), trials and struggles are blessings in disguise because without these experiences the beloved (or the Divine Beloved) would not be attained. This is displayed in the texts, where both Majnun and Radha retreat into, emerge, and re-enter the cave, in alternating moods of pleasure and pain in the period of separation from the beloved. This may be likened to moving between the lower or higher existential states. Entering the cave means purification (obtaining refuge), or pain as a result of being fragmented. Emerging means suffering (torn out from protection), or pleasure (rejuvenation as a result of finding refuge). Thus, the cave is at once a forbidding, barren depth to which they descend in the struggle with their worst ordeals, and at the same time, a means of protection from pain and sorrow. In this context, the cave may be seen as a means of spiritualizing life. It gives access not only to subterranean or infernal regions, but also to super-terrestrial domains (Guénon 1995, 144). In this context, the cave is "the complete image of the world, reflecting all states without exception" (Guénon 1995, 144). On this basis, the portrayal of the cave in *Layla* corresponds to this symbolism in *Govinda*.

The foregoing discussion has illustrated different means employed by the writers to express a similar idea. The similarity of the idea is that in both texts, the natural elements represent a point of refuge and means of connection. By extension, the elements represent a point of movement from being disconnected, or decentered, to being connected, or centered. Firstly, different elements of nature are involved in each text, namely the mountain and the cave in *Layla* and the forest and the thicket in *Govinda*. Secondly, Majnun's connectedness with these elements is implied, whereas the connectedness between Radha and Krishna is explicit. In general, however, both texts express that fusion is obtained through seclusion.

In summary of this point, it may be said that the connection in *Layla* and *Govinda* between the natural elements and the lover corresponds to various spiritual realities. Firstly, each of the elements mentioned represent man's spiritual centers, and his connection with the divine. Secondly, the identification with the spiritual centers and the solace it offers, signify human pliancy, or submission to divine authority. Thirdly, such surrender obtains the possibility of, or qualification for, union with the divine. In essence, this is tantamount to a return to man's primordial state. Thus, the wilderness does not just signify that man is alone and lonely. As mentioned, fusion with the divine is conveyed by seclusion. Again, that which is sacred is secret.

While the discussion thus far has considered the elements of nature as cosmological symbols, the ensuing consideration focuses on the human element as psychological symbols. For this purpose, the following Figure 5.3 below shows corresponding quotations from each text to illustrate the psychological condition of the lover, and more specifically, the state of the heart of the lover.

Element	In *Layla*	In *Govinda*
Majnun/ Radha	Who do you think I am? A drunkard? A lovesick fool, a slave of my senses, made senseless by desire? Understand: ... I have risen above all that, I am the King of Love in majesty. My soul is purified from the darkness of lust, my longing purged of low desire, my mind freed from shame. I have broken up the teeming bazaar of the senses in my body. Love is the essence of my being.... You imagine that you see me, but I no longer exist: what remains, is the beloved. (XLVIII:161)	Night is putting black kohl on their eyes, Tamala-flower clusters on their ears, Dark lotus wreaths on their heads, Leaf designs of musk on their breasts. In every thicket, friend, The night's dark cherished cloak Embraces limbs of beautiful adulteresses Whose hearts rush to meet their lovers. (XI:11)

Figure 5.3: The Heart of the Lover

The quotations from *Layla* convey two opposing aspects of Majnun's condition. On the one hand, he has been "broken up" and "lost his heart." On the other, he has "risen above" to a higher station, as he has become "purified" from "desire" and "the teeming bazaar of the senses." In effect this is a shedding of the human, worldly "self." The references to these two aspects may be related to the metaphysical notions of *fana'*, annihilation of the self, and subsequently *baqa'*, subsistence in the Divine Beloved, or the Self. The former idea is also expressed as "I no longer exist" (XLVIII:161), and "he had lost

... himself" (XXI:69), whereas the latter is indicated by the expression, "what remains, is the beloved" (XLVIII:161), and the possibility of achieving this state may be discerned from the expression, "if he could only win her, he would find himself again" (VI:16). However, this possibility is only achievable through purification of the heart, expressed as "the fire scorching his heart" (IV:10). Thus, Majnun's progress, or path to spiritual maturity, is conveyed by complementary metaphors of rejection (associated with pain), and reception or acceptance (associated with pleasure).

In *Govinda*, however, the examples relating to the lover and the heart suggest physical and emotional fusion. The first example indicates physical fusion through descriptions of physical elements, and image upon image of darkness that symbolizes union. The wealth of poetic diction in this regard is apparent from recurring images of darkness, conveyed by words like "night," "black," "kohl,"[3] "eyes," "tamala," "cloak," and "dark." Furthermore, these images are consistent with the erotic and sexual overtones of lovers meeting, at night, in the forest, "in every thicket." The erotic images are reinforced implicitly by reference to musk,[4] an aromatic aphrodisiac that arouses sexual desire, and explicitly by mention of "breasts" and "limbs" of "adulteresses," applicable to Radha. It is against this setting and atmosphere that "hearts rush to meet their lovers." Again, this phrase strongly evokes fusion. These images have been aptly described as acquiring (Mishra 1998, 159):

> those very mystical elements that are essential for Indian devotional verse. In its patterned intensity—the triumphant heaping of image upon image, sensuousness compounded by lushness of phrase—the passage has the power to transcend what seems banal.

[3] Referring to a black, medicinal, and cosmetic application for the eyes. In Greek, *kollurion* and in Latin *collyrium* (NSOED). Its association with medicinal properties is that it is used for healing, and with the cosmetic function that it is used as ornamentation. Thus it enhances sight as well as beauty. It is also symbolic of a physical and mental healing, as well as rebuilding and rejuvenation.

[4] Sanskrit *muska*, meaning scrotum, associated with the shape of the musk-bag of the musk-deer. In Persian *misk*, Latin *muscus*.

In the next example related to the heart, this same mood is maintained, except that physical elements are reduced, and emotional conditions and behavioral traits involving the heart or feelings are introduced. In this verse, Radha may be viewed in metaphors of "breakage" and "repair." The former is illustrated through expressions like "laments," "collapses," "cries," "trembles," "utters her pain," and "lying dejected" and "fearing." At the same time, "She evokes you in deep meditation," and strives "to reach your distant form." Thus, in *Govinda* too, there are alternating conditions of rejection and acceptance in the heart of the lover.

The two examples from *Govinda*, which eloquently and powerfully demonstrate the human and psychological elements, convey the view of the spiritual quest in Hindu mysticism. This view relates to the complementarity of, first, pleasure and pain, and second, eroticism and asceticism. The first has been illustrated, whereas the second may be explained on the basis of the Hindu mystical doctrine of *cakras*.[5] This refers to the seven centers of psychic energy in the human body, and the means to control these energies (*pranayama*). Control achieves deliverance into the spiritual life (*jivanmukti*), and liberation (*moksha*) from the cycle of birth and death (*samsara*). The doctrine also refers to a hierarchy of existential states of man's inner being. The first, or most basic *cakra* (*muladhara*) is of a centrifugal, or outward directed, nature. It is the basis of instinctive, human, tendencies. This energy is associated with *kama*, instinctual, subconscious desire, which includes the sexual drive. The highest, or ultimate *cakra* (*sahasrara*) is of a centripetal, or inward directed, nature. It is the basis of intuitive, divine, tendencies. This energy is associated with *buddhi*, the faculty of the intellect, and "doorway" to super-consciousness.

Thus, a worldly person's energies that are directed to worldly desires (*kama*), cause him to remain within the physical realm. On the other hand, energies that are channeled into desire for the Divine (*prema*) belong to the realm of the ascetic. This involves sexual continence, or sexual energy withdrawn from the worldly drive and redirected to the divine energy center. This channeling is a means of transforming and spiritualizing human life. Furthermore, it is a means

[5] A method of liberating the soul according to an orthodox esoteric system of Indian philosophy expounded by Patanjali in the *Yoga Sutras*.

of achieving liberation.[6] In this light, the Bhakta views "sexuality (as) ... either sacred or subhuman" (Schuon 1976, 67). This view of transforming and spiritualizing the lower human tendencies to higher realms is another basis of reconciling the paradox of eroticism-asceticism.

The above implications are woven into the lines of the verses under consideration. The portrayal of fusion is through juxtaposition of sexual overtones and mental undertones. The nature of the fusion is not "actual" or physical, but "virtual" or psychological. To begin with, Krishna is not physically present. It may be noted that the "embraces" spoken of are not physical because this line is immediately followed by the information that it is the "hearts," and not the body, that "rush to meet their lovers." In this regard, the choice of the epithet "Hari" in reference to Krishna is significant. In the first place, *hari* means light or illumination. Furthermore, pronounced *hri*,[7] it has a close phonetic resemblance and semantic relation to *hrd* or heart. Apart from the name, it is mentioned that Radha "evokes" Krishna through "deep meditation." It is made explicit that Radha "clings" to him not literally, but "in fantasy."

Radha's moves and motivations correspond to the various *cakras* that relate to human or natural love (*prakrta*), and divine or supra-natural love (*aprakrta*). The example shows that her motivations originate from the physical "embraces," associated with *muladhara cakra*, and sexual activity. Subsequently "her pain" involves the emotions, associated with *anahata cakra*, and the heart. This escalates to the spiritual level of "deep meditation," associated with the *sahasrara cakra*, and super-consciousness, whereby she transcends distance and connects with the "distant form" of Krishna. In other words, she develops from motivations of the physical (*sarira*) to the emotional (*manas*) and ultimately to the intellect (*buddhi*). Thus, if there is union, it takes place in a sacred context. On this basis, it is argued that the fusion explicitly and implicitly conveyed in these examples refers to spiritual fusion, or Divine union. The sanctified nature of this union is unequivocally

[6] This is why chastity is a hallmark of the spiritual giants of Hindu mystical orders. The notion of chastity also extends to thought, word, and deed. See Swami Vivekananda (2002, 68).

[7] Also, as in *aashri*, to take shelter, and *Khrista*, referring to Christ the Savior.

confirmed, as it is chanted in subsequent verses that "Madhava still waits for you in Love's most sacred thicket" (V:7). Firstly, the word "Love" in capitals signifies that it is of a Divine nature, and secondly, the thicket is qualified by the adjective "most sacred."

It is interesting to note the different expressions of purification of the heart in the corresponding pair of examples quoted. In *Layla*, the lover undergoes "fire scorching his heart" (IV:10), whereas in *Govinda*, she is "washed by meandering Jumna river waters" (I:33). One is cleansed by fire, the other by water. In another pair of expressions elsewhere in the works, the elements are transposed. Majnun says, "I was earth, dark and heavy; your grace has changed me into pure water" (XXXVIII:117), whereas Radha is burned by "flames that rage like forest fire" (IV:9). If the first pair of expressions is "fire" in *Layla* as opposed to "water" in *Govinda*, the second is "water" in *Layla* and "fire" in *Govinda*. On the level of physical realities, these are different and opposite forms of expression, but at the essential level, they refer to one and the same idea, namely purification.

In ending the discussion, the phenomenon of seclusion may be viewed in terms of the Hindu *mandala* and the arabesque pattern of the Islamic artistic tradition. To illustrate the portrayals of seclusion as they occur in the individual texts, they are reconstructed in the following table:[8]

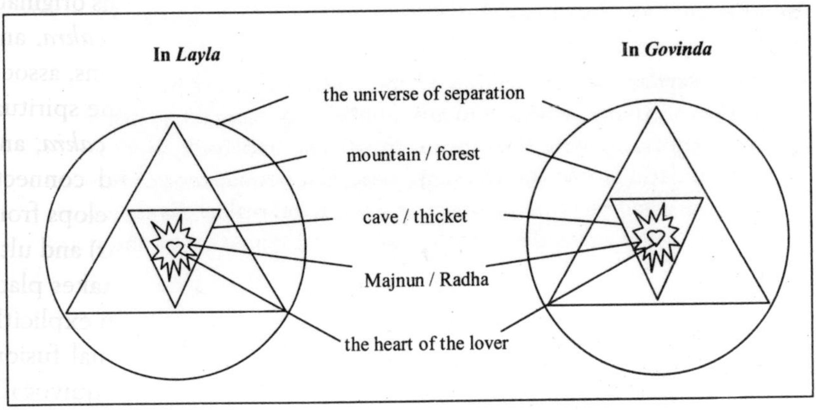

Figure 5.4: A Mandalic Perspective of Seclusion

[8] Adapted and modified from Guénon (1995, 149-50; see figures 13 and 14).

The diagram represents the portrayal of seclusion in terms of successive spatial and psychological elements corresponding to the positions and conditions of Majnun and Radha. Presented thus, the particular elements named in the diagram may be perceived as representing similar centripetal, or inward-bound, and centrifugal, or outward-bound, patterns in the individual texts.

The outermost element, represented by the circles, is the universe of the lovers in separation. Within it, represented by the triangles, are the mountain and forest respectively. Within these elements, the inverted triangles refer to the cave in *Layla* and the forest in *Govinda*. Within that, represented by the shape of explosions, are Majnun, and Radha, the fragmented human characters seeking wholeness. Finally, at the center is located the hidden heart of the individual characters undergoing the process of purification. Each of the elements expresses a symbolic significance of life, death, and spiritual rebirth, as has been explained. Thus the corresponding elements in *Layla* and *Govinda* represent the spatial and psychological journey traversed by Majnun and Radha. In turn, these elements correspond to the spiritual conditions of the mystic quest. In this sense, just as the mandalic symbol moves the seeker closer to the Beloved, which is the objective of the quest, so the individual portrayals of seclusion show the individual lover's progress in quest of the beloved. The following explanation of the *mandala* encapsulates this notion succinctly (Bakhtiar 1976:87):

> The mandala, as a reflection of the cosmos and cosmic processes within all things, works through numbers and geometry, beginning with Unity, moving through its theophany and back to Unity. It recapitulates at one and the same time, the permanence of Paradise as an idea and its impermanence as a temporal reality. To the mystic it evokes the surrender to Self, and the reintegration of the many into the One.

The foregoing discussion of the phenomenon of seclusion at both the literal and symbolic levels has revealed several factors. Briefly, it is obvious that there are convergences and divergences between *Layla* and *Govinda* in the individual portrayals of separation, both at the outward and inward levels of meaning. Furthermore, seclusion involves both pleasure and pain, depending on the ability of the lover to transcend limitations and boundaries. Thus pleasure and pain, which appear to be a relation of polarity, ultimately become identical. Thirdly, seclusion, or separation, works as a path of return to the original state, otherwise referred to as fusion or union. In other words, the "universe of separation" mentioned in the diagram is one and the same as the "universe of union." In this way, just as previously seclusion was viewed as part of a "descent," it has now been shown that it also belongs to "ascent."

The discussion in the remaining part of the chapter represents a focus on phenomena and symbols of ascent or union in separation that have not been presented in the previous chapter. As mentioned at the outset, this deals firstly with the phenomenon of "artistic" forms of expression which relate to forms of sacred art. Three elements that express the significance of the role of art in both texts are dance, music, and song. They are referred to as sacred art because, as the discussion will illustrate, they represent artistic and symbolic means of achieving union with the beloved. Characteristic of all other forms of symbolic expression, the three elements mentioned are conveyed in interrelated, and inextricably linked, expressions in the texts. However, they will be discussed individually to facilitate discussion.

The Persian word *darwish*, adapted in Turkish—in Malay, *darwis*, in English, dervish—literally means "the sill of the door." The term is commonly used to refer to the Sufi, as someone "who is at the door to enlightenment" (Friedlander 1975, 15). The dervish is closely identified, and implicitly linked, with the *sama'*, the gatherings of dervishes, and with the *shaykh*, the Sufi spiritual master.[9] In most Sufi orders, the *sama'* represents a spiritual gathering. The mystical ritual performance in the gathering is in some form of dance, led by the *shaykh* and accompanied by singing, recitation of the *silsila*, or retracing of the spiritual lineage, and *dhikr*, or measured recitation of the Divine Names. One of the most prominent elements which sets the mood for the performance of the dance is the *peshrev*, or musical prelude, played on the *ney*, a reed flute, which, as will be explained subsequently, has an important mystical significance. The rites create an atmosphere

[9] Specifically it is associated with the Whirling Dervishes of the Mevlevi Order, as the followers of Mawlana ("our master") Jalal al-Din Rumi are known. Rumi is one of the most outspoken Sufis on the importance of dance, and he is universally considered the whirling dervish *par excellence* (Schimmel 1979, 88).

which elevates the participant to a spiritual and ecstatic state, as well as symbolically expressing the connection of the soul with God.

In *Layla*, the dervish is associated with dance in the context of union, both implicitly and explicitly. The first reference to the dervish is introduced in the initial stage of the union of Layla and Majnun, which personifies the perfection of the primordial human state. In the expression, "Majnun was her slave and a dervish dancing before her" (V:14) certain inferences can be drawn about the nature of their relations. At one level, it points to a master-slave relationship in which Layla is the master and Majnun her willing slave. This is a common form of religious expression to describe the Creator-creature relationship. It also expresses the abject humility of the believer before the majesty of his Maker. However, in view of the context of union in which this expression occurs, the significance may be understood on a different level. The description of the "dancing" Majnun expresses his ecstasy in the presence of his beloved. The dancing movement symbolizes Divine Presence in that "the dancing which takes man out of himself, makes him die to his lower attributes, and grants him life in a higher sphere" (Schimmel 1979, 89). Incidentally, this view of dance supports the understanding of Majnun's madness and its effects in a positive light as presented earlier.

To understand better the significance of dance in this context, some points of the symbolism of the *sama'* may be noted. For the Sufi, the mystical dance represents a ritual of rebirth for it takes the lover into the Divine Presence. This has been explained by Schimmel as follows (1979, 88):

> Wherever God manifests Himself, the cosmic dance will begin. Mount Sinai, split asunder under the impact of overwhelming revelations, means for Rumi that it performed a dance of ecstasy during which the mountain unriveted itself and attained annihilation and was scattered piecemeal in the Divine Presence, just as man is annihilated in God as a result of his dance.

Thus dance is connected to the stations of *fana'* and *baqa'* of the spiritual aspirant. In this context, the nature of all mystical poetry is indicated in the statement that they are "born in the throes of rhythmical movement" (Schimmel 1979, 88). If the Sufi is regarded as being at "the sill of the door," his dance is compared to a "window that opens towards the heavens" (Schimmel 1979, 88).

The rites of the dance involve the arrangement of disciples in a circle around the *shaykh*, whose position in the center signifies his position of spiritual leader.[10] The spiritual master, who reflects the Divine Grace bestowed upon the Prophet, is to guide the initiate in the journey to God. In this sense, Majnun's dancing around Layla in the example quoted resembles the dance of the *sama'*. The dancers move in a horizontal spinning motion around the circle. This symbolizes the movement of the planets around the sun. This is the context in which the expression in *Layla*, "The seven planets, their hands linked, trod out the dance of fate," may be interpreted. Furthermore, the spinning is vertical. This symbolizes the point of contact between the worldly and the Divine realms, as well as the Divine Beloved. The hands are extended, the right palm upwards and the left downwards, symbolizing the dancer as a visible channel of *baraka*, Divine Grace, as well as the role of man as vicegerent of God on earth. Thus the dancer is an axial symbol. In the same connection, the *shaykh* represents the *qutb* or axis of his followers. These notions are conveyed in Majnun's reaction to a message from Layla (XXXIX:126):

> Without a word he kept staring at his hands, which held the sealed message.... Was it not a gift more precious to him than all the treasures of the world? Suddenly ... he began to dance, ever faster, ever wilder. He leapt high into the air, turning like a whirling top. Again and again, hundreds of times.

There are correspondences in this passage with the foregoing explanation of the dance. The sender of the message, Layla, symbolizes the Divine Beloved. The "sealed message" symbolizes contact from the Divine to the human, in the person of Muhammad, Seal of the Prophets. For Majnun, the "gift more precious than ... treasures" echoes the saying in the Prophetic Tradition, *kuntu kanzan makhfiyan...*, "I was a hidden treasure and wanted to be known, so I created the world."[11] This relates to manifestation and the Divine wish to

[10] The ensuing explanation of the symbolism of the rituals of the *sama'* is based on Bakhtiar (1976).

[11] This *hadith* is popular among the Sufis, but contested by others.

be known. Finally, Majnun's whirling represents the spirit's spiraling journey to Divine union. Spinning also signifies cosmic harmony, a part of which is "the dance of the dust particles, *dharra*, or as we may translate it into a modern concept, the atoms, which are attracted by the sun and dance around it" (Schimmel 1979, 88). Like the attraction of the dust to the sun, the lover is inexorably drawn to the Beloved, as echoed in Majnun's words, "I am but the whirling dust which envelops you.... Am I not famous as your slave?" (XLI:133).

The garments of the dervishes are part of the symbolism of the *sama'*. At the beginning, the *khirqa*, or long black coat is worn, representing "the dark earthly existence" (Schimmel 1979, 89), or tombs and worldly attachments. But during the dance, the coats are discarded and the whirling continues in white robes, "comparable to white moths whirling around the central candle," signifying the "dress of resurrection," the spiritual body (Schimmel 1979, 89). A semblance of this notion may be discerned from the following expression of Majnun's sentiments, which was quoted previously in relation to purification (XXXVIII:117-118):

> I was earth, dark and heavy; your grace has changed me into pure water. So I am dead to myself. Do not let me lose my way and perish,... only your grace can change my darkness to light and lift me out of the black night of my fate into your eternal day.

Here again, the metaphors of darkness and light echo the significance of black and white mentioned in relation to the dance. They are the archetypal symbols of Sufism for the stations of *fana'* and *baqa'*. In Bakhtiar's words, "Existence is light, and thus when light makes its full appearance, all things disappear" (1976, 90).

The greatest Muslim mystics have experienced the bliss of union through dance. Rumi says, in one of his poems, "Who knows Love's mazy circling, ever lives in God" (Bakhtiar 1976, 90). It is said that Mansur al-Hallaj, who was executed for his proclamations of identity with God, danced in his chains on the way to execution, for to him, "death in love meant union with the beloved" (Bakhtiar 1976, 88). This image has been mirrored in *Layla* in the episode of Majnun's encounter with the widow who was leading a dervish in chains. Majnun entreats her (XXV:77-78),

> Relieve this man of his chains and put them on me. I am one of those unhappy men with a disturbed mind.... Majnun recited his love poems, cried out "Layla ... Layla...," banged head and body against the stones, and, in spite of his chains, danced around like a drunken madman.

The reference to the circular dance of the God-intoxicated mystic is in the phrase "danced around like a drunken madman," whereas the relevance to Hallaj's dance is in Majnun voluntarily dancing in chains.

Furthermore, Hallaj's renowned allegory of the Moth and Candle, depicting the moth that circles the flame and is consumed by it, employs the dance as a mystical means. This allegory, ubiquitous in Sufi poetry, finds expression in *Layla* as part of Majnun's laments of separation from Layla, "Invisible candle of my soul, do not torture the night-moth fluttering around you" (IV:12), and "He hurried along ... like a butterfly rushing through the darkness towards the flame which it seeks to encircle" (XVV:76).

The whirling also symbolizes the attempt to return to one's center. In Islam, this is signified by the fifth tenet, the pilgrim's visit to the Holy Land of Mecca, the sacred center of the Muslim universe. Pilgrimage involves, among other acts, circumambulation around the Kaaba, representing the house of Allah. For mystics like Rumi and Hafiz the Kaaba is not a physical place but a spiritual plane representing the station of Union. Thus it is a symbolic representation of intimacy. It also symbolizes the Divine Essence, while the Black Stone within it represents the human spiritual essence (Bakhtiar 1976, 47).

In *Layla*, Majnun's pilgrimage is portrayed in an episode in which Majnun's father takes him to the Holy Land, in the hope that it would cure his "madness."

> ... their thoughts finally converged on the Caaba, God's sanctuary in Mecca,... Is not the Caaba the Altar of heaven and earth, where the whole world prays for God's blessing and help. Why not we?

However, standing before the Kaaba, instead of asking to be "cured" of his "madness," Majnun wishes for it to be intensified (VIII:27-28):

> I ask thee, my God, I beseech thee, in all the godliness of thy divine nature and all the perfection of thy kingdom: let my love grow stronger, let it endure, even if I perish.... My life shall be sacrificed

> for her beauty, my blood shall be spilled freely for her, and though I burn for her painfully, like a candle, none of my days shall ever be free of this pain. Let me love, oh my God, love for love's sake, and make my love a hundred times as great as it was and is!

Here Majnun speaks literally to the Divine about his relation with Layla. Rather than a cure, Majnun's prayer is to "perish," "be sacrificed," "burned," and so on. In effect, his wish is to be naughted. This may be understood as the Sufi's petition to merge with the Divine Essence. In this way, Majnun's circumambulation around the Kaaba, and his whirling around Layla, are echoed in the symbolism of the dance. Thus, "the planets rotating around the sun, the pilgrim's circumambulation around the Kaaba, the moth circling the flame, atoms circling their nuclei" (Schimmel 1979, 89), all evoke union with the Divine. From this perspective, the close connection between dance and the attainment of the Divine Beloved may be established.

It may be mentioned that the participation of the Sufi in the *sama'*, experienced entirely in terms of its esoteric significance, often meets with objection from the exoteric authorities in Islam, mainly in relation to music, and to what extent—if at all—it is permitted (Schimmel 1982, 220n). However, as commonly known, the basis of the divide in the approach to the connection with God lies between the exoteric and the esoteric observance, or between rituals and inner enlightenment.

In this regard, it is interesting that just as there is a difference in the *zahir* (outward) and *batin* (inward) aspects of Islam, so there is a difference in understanding the *rupam* (form, outward aspect) and the *swarupam* (essence, inward significance) of God in Hinduism. In Majnun's condition of separation in *Layla*, dance has been observed to be closely associated with the dervish and the master, renunciation and purification. These elements are inextricably linked to the motion of circling, rotating, and spinning, as ritual and as a discipline. In this connection it is interesting to enquire whether there are equivalent forms of expression in *Govinda* which may be understood on the basis of its essential significance.

The idea of dance as a medium of union with Krishna is conveyed in many instances in *Govinda*. The verse depicting commencement of separation, as Radha looks for Krishna, is immediately followed by mention of Krishna's dance. The fact that the reference to the dance occurs in the refrain, contextualizes dance within a ritualistic framework, specifically by its repetitive nature. The lines are (I:27):

> When spring's mood is rich, Hari roams here
> To dance with young women, friend,
> A cruel time for deserted lovers.

In this refrain, dance is associated both with union and with separation. Union is implied by the "rich mood" of "spring," a time of renewal and rejuvenation, as well as explicit mention of "Hari" coming "to dance with young women." Separation from Krishna, which he forces Radha to endure, has the effect of heightening her longing for him. This is suggested by the last line. The reference to dancing with Hari in this context implies that the dance is a means of overcoming separation. Similarly, in another song (II:3),

> A circle of peacock plumes caressed by moonlight crowns his hair.
> A rainbow colors the fine cloth on his cloud-dark body.
> My heart recalls Hari here in his love dance,
> Playing seductively, laughing, mocking me.

this notion is repeated, with both the elements of union and separation. The "playing" and "laughing" is juxtaposed with "mocking" as a means of heightening the experience. Besides, the image of the circle and the semi-circle, repeatedly introduced in this song in association with the "love dance," evokes the *mandala*. In the phrase, "a circle of peacock plumes," there are multiple references to the circle, illustrating the significance of the peacock in Hindu symbolism. Firstly, there is an explicit mention of "circle." Secondly, the peacock plumes are individually of a rounded shape, and collectively form a semi-circle. Thirdly, the motif on the peacock plumes resembles an eye, and is thus associated with the circle. Furthermore, the peacock, besides being Krishna's *vaahana*, or mount, is also a symbol of immortality, another association with the circle. The "plumes caressed by moonlight crowns his hair," which refers to the luminous corona surrounding the moon, is also associated with the circle.[12] Also, the cre-

[12] The reflective nature of the moon symbolizes the mind's faculty of reflection. Incidentally, the word "reflect" means both "think" and "mirror."

ative function of the moon is related to the cycle of nature (Sahi 1980, 94), which possesses a circular pattern. Besides, the words "crowns" and "hair" are related to the head, which is circular, and "rainbow" has a semi-circular form. The rainbow is generally considered as symbolizing the union of heaven and earth. In addition, the rainbow, from its close association with rain, relates to the symbolism of the descent of celestial influences into the terrestrial world (Guénon 1995, 263). Furthermore, the word "recalls" in the next line is associated with the circle semantically, by its meaning of calling back, and its association of return. Finally, the last two lines are repeated eight times as a refrain, which also suggests a circular motion. Thus all of the expressions mentioned associate the dance intimately with circles, or circles-within-circles. Implicit in this imagery is the notion of union and connection. Firstly, the circles express an enveloping and enfolding *mandala*, and secondly they imply the "inner circle" of devotees, or the elect, referring to the initiated spiritual aspirants.

The refrains from the two songs mentioned above may also be associated with the practice of *japa*, recollection, invocation, or repetition of the Divine Name. In this regard it may be observed that, firstly, Krishna is referred to by the epithet Hari, a specific form related to invocation. Secondly, the epithet is repeated in each verse to resemble a *mantra*. *Japa* is the Hindu mystical practice of inner concentration of the faculties upon the Ultimate Being or Reality, given paramount importance among devotees of the *swarupam*, in reference to the unqualified Supreme Being. This rite of concentration offers the possibility of a more abstract approach to the divine being, compared to the *rupam*-oriented worship of Krishna, which worships him as a deity, and through an image (McGregor 1973, 111-112n). From this explanation of *japa*, and its relation to the love dance of the *gopis*, it is apparent that there is an equivalence with the Sufi practice of *dhikr* mentioned in relation to the *sama'*.

A final example substantiates the association of the circle with the ritual of the love dance in *Govinda* (I:43).

> Hari praises a girl drunk from dancing in the rite of love,
> With beating palms and ringing bangles echoing his flute's low tone.
> Hari revels here as the crowd of charming girls
> Revels in seducing him to play.

In these lines, "dancing" is closely associated with "drunk," as it is in *Layla.* Images of circularity are evoked by Hari dancing, surrounded by "charming girls," "echoing" the tune of his flute. Besides, repetition is evoked by "beating palms" or clapping, and "ringing bangles" are semantically associated with the circle. Thus the verse comes alive with a circular rhythm, tempo, and cadence customarily associated with dance. All of the foregoing examples discussed display a common characteristic with the form of the *sama'*, namely its pattern of circularity. The "love dance" referred to in *Govinda* represents a specific circular dance called the *rasa krida*, or *raslila* in the mythology of Krishna. It reflects the divine joy, spontaneity, and play of Krishna, *lila.* There are three levels of understanding the symbology of this dance in relation to Krishna.

The first is its position at the level of *Goloka Vrndavana*, the Vaishnava term for the heavenly realm, or the Eternal Garden. The central motif of dance in this context, is cosmic creativity and activity, akin to the Dance of *Shiva Nataraja* (Coomaraswamy 1985, 59). Thus, Krishna is the embodiment of plenitude, grace, and joy. In the words of Coomaraswamy (1985, 64):

> the reason He dances lies in His own nature, all his gestures are ... spontaneous and purposeless—for His being is beyond the realm of. purposes.

In Vaishnava scriptures Krishna is described as "coming down from the top of the mountain dancing" (Rupa 1932, 48) to meet the *gopis.* In this context, the refrain just quoted reflects Krishna's joy in reveling with his creation, just "to play" (I:43):

> Hari revels here as the crowd of charming girls
> Revels in seducing him to play.

The second level of understanding the *raslila* is related to its setting, Brindaban. The earthly garden in which Vishnu manifests himself as the *avatara* of salvation, reflects the heavenly garden, *Vrndavana.* According to myth, Krishna danced collectively with the *gopis*, but multiplied himself so that each of the 16,108 *gopis* had a Krishna to herself. This has been expressed in *Govinda*, in another verse of the song mentioned in connection with the refrains, as "Vines of his great throbbing arms circle a thousand cowherdesses" (II:5). Transported to a state of ecstasy in the Divine presence, the *gopis* danced in a rotatory motion around Krishna. Thus the notion of "God's rhythmical dance of creation and his ongoing pulse in the preservation of the world" (Kinsely 1979, 7) is apparent at this level in *Govinda*. There are specific references to this aspect of salvation in association with the *raslila*, for example, as (II:5)

> Jewel rays from his hands and feet and chest break the dark night....
> Meeting me under a flowering tree, he calms my fear of dark time,
> My heart recalls Hari here in his love dance.

Salvation is referred to here by various means. Firstly, "jewel rays" or light, is juxtaposed with the "dark night," which he "breaks." Similarly, in the next line, "flowering tree," which is associated with spring and immortality, suggests renewal. It is juxtaposed with "dark time" or mortality, and Krishna "calms my fear" of this. Again, the words "recalls" and "dance" represent images of circularity. Thus the sense in which these expressions may be understood is that Krishna "dances to maintain the life of the cosmos and to give release to those who seek Him" (Kinsely 1979, 7).

The third level of understanding the *raslila* is its position as a mystical rite of the Bhakta in a re-enactment of the *raslila* with the *gopis* in Brindaban. To celebrate Krishna's play among the *gopis*, the Bhaktas of today participate in *bhajana*, a form of congregational worship (Singer 1966, 90). During the *bhajana*, a series of songs are sung, particularly the cantos of *Govinda*. Part of the ritual is the invocation of Krishna, and includes praise of the guru, traced back through his lineage to Krishna as the Godhead. It is a churning dance, in which the devotees dance in a circle around a lighted ritual lamp, symbolizing the presence of Hari (Singer 1966, 90). According to Norvin Hein (1993, 552) the dance has a "choreography" and "script," which tells the story of the *gopis'* infatuation with Krishna, of his "sporting" with them in the woods, of his separation from them, and of their final reunion. This practice, naturally, has a theological meaning, that is, the *gopis* represent the human soul in search of salvation. Through the *raslila* the devotees participate in the Divine Presence. The esoteric meaning of their constant and intense love for Krishna is that it is transformed into a spiritual and blissful devotion to a transcendent *Brahman*. Thus, the total passion with which the ideal devotee must surrender the self to God, may be likened to Radha, "the straying Hindu wife, who, love-mad, sacrifices reputation and home and security in her ruinous devotion to a paramour" (1993, 52).

The circular dance in which Krishna has multiplied himself symbolizes, firstly, the infinite capacity of Divine Love, secondly, His relation of *Istam* (sole, personal God) with each individual, and thirdly that devotees are related to one another through their relation in God. In Vaishnava doctrine there is also the belief that all souls are female and that Vishnu/Krishna is the only male (Hein 1993, 128-29). Thus just as the singular love of a woman for her lover is very much more intense and constant than any other sort of love in the world, "the love of the human soul for the Lord Supreme may only be that of the highest order" (Hein 1993, 130n). In other words, "the stages of human love reflect the stations of spiritual development ... illicit love becomes the very type of salvation" (Coomaraswamy 1985, 128).

In this connection, the portrayal of Radha in *Govinda* precisely mirrors the following precepts of Indian poetic expression. In relation to the woman involved in illicit love, Chandidas, a poet of 14th century India, has stipulated that (Coomaraswamy 1985, 131):

> The lovers must refuse each other nothing, yet never fall. Inwardly, ... the woman ... will sacrifice all for love, but outwardly she will appear indifferent. This secret love must find expression in secret: but she must not yield to desire. She must cast herself freely into the sea of contempt, and yet she must never actually drink of forbidden waters: she must not be shaken by pleasure or pain .... In this restraint, ... lies salvation.

Realistically, considering the extent of struggle involved to observe and achieve such "restraint," it is not surprising that "one such is hardly to be found in a million" (Coomaraswamy 1985, 131). It indicates that the mystic path may be traveled only by those of extraordinary mettle. Thus only the right disposition, endurance, and spirit of the seeker qualifies him as the "elect" or the "adept" as the spiritual aspirant is referred to.

The foregoing arguments have established dance as a mystical rite, symbolizing union with the Divine. In the comparison between the Sufi and Bhakti doctrines and rites there are correlations and correspondences in terms of both outward practice and inner principles.

This has found literary expression in *Layla* and *Govinda*, the most outstanding shared characteristic being the motif of circularity, resembling a *mandala*. In this context, the dance represents the creation of a sacred space within which the dancer is able to achieve a sense of wholeness. Thus dance has an ontological function. The associations with both the forms of dance mentioned show that they represent a means for the lover to connect with the beloved. Coomaraswamy's words in this regard, end this discussion on the mystical significance of dance in *Layla* and *Govinda* (Coomaraswamy 1985, 72):

> This is His dance. Its deepest significance is felt when it is realized that it takes place within the heart and the self. Everywhere is God: that Everywhere is the heart.

Thus dance is not only a means of unification, but also of identification, of the self to the Self.

Another artistic form of expression, or rather, form of "sacred art" that is closely related to the dance in terms of mystical significance, is music. The ensuing discussion will focus on one form of music in the texts, namely, the flute, as a specific means of expressing the human connection with God. The flute in its various forms, whether fashioned from the reed or the bamboo, has come to be universally recognized in mysticism, whether of organized or shamanic religious traditions, as a particularly apt medium for expressing the lament of the soul in pain of separation. Basically, "the simplicity of the flute evokes spiritual simplicity and primordiality, states of divine being (Maertens, 2003). Pan, the Greek god of the forest, who is worshipped as the symbol of cosmic vitality, plays the magical reed-pipe that stirs an echo in all things. The Japanese Zen pipe, or *shakuhachi*, is a tool of meditation and symbol of peace and tranquility that is dedicated to forge the body-mind. It is no surprise then, that the Persian *ney*, and the Indian *vamsam* or flute figures prominently in both Sufism and Bhaktism, and manifests in the poetic expression of these traditions.

There is a paradoxical aspect of the flute that makes it an extraordinary instrument, and enhances its relevance to mystical symbolism.[13]

[13] The explanation in this paragraph draws largely from an article entitled "The Paradox of the *Shakuhachi*" (2003) by an unnamed author.

Although its form is utterly simple, yet in the hands of a master musician it can produce an inconceivably broad range of musical sounds. It can move from pure, simple notes, to complex and expressive tones. In this regard it is interesting to note that according to authorities on flute music, at certain notes it is difficult to identify the difference between the flute sound and the human voice. Besides, the music of the flute can be both intensely melancholic and plaintive, and sprightly and enchanting. In these respects, the flute lends itself readily to mystical symbolism.

In Sufi literature, the poet's identification with nature in relation to the flute is apparent. In this connection the *ney*, or reed flute, being crafted of natural material, from a mere hollow stick "with minimum adulteration" (Kinsley 1979, 95), is an apt form of expressing identification with nature. Furthermore, the process of the reed being cut from its reed-bed and crafted to produce music has a symbolism of great depth. It expresses the reed as the self or the soul. The severing of the reed from its bed represents the separation of the soul from its real, eternal home, which is the presence of God. The haunting music of the flute reflects the awareness of this separation enveloping the self, and expressing its plaintive cry of pain. Thus Rumi's classic poem, the *Mathnawi*, mentioned in the first chapter, starts with the lament of the reed complaining of being "shred and shred" by the pain of separation from the Beloved.

In *Layla*, too, the reed is mentioned in a similar context. Expressions such as "the swaying reed has become a flute of sadness" (XXXIX:122), and "a reed sounding the melody of lost love" (XLV:150), convey loss, pain, and separation. However, as the paradox of separation has been repeatedly been shown to be, separation and union are indivisible. Thus besides expressing loss and pain, the *ney* also symbolizes a message from the beloved (Nurbakhsh 1984, 171). Specifically, it represents a call to the beloved. This idea is discernible in Majnun's message to Layla (XXIV:75):

> Do not delay, lest you should find me dead.
> Caught by the wolf, the lamb hears all too late
> The shepherd's flute lament its cruel fate.

In this context, the message may be interpreted as a call of help for Divine guidance and salvation. Thus, this example portrays not separation, but the prospect and possibility of union.

The dual symbolism of the *ney* has been well-explained by an authority (Nurbakhsh 1984, 171):

> This term symbolizes the human heart and soul, which has two sides, one facing the world of divine unity and the love of divine essence, and the other facing the world of multiplicity and the domain of sensory experience. In the first case, the supersensory lights of the divine realm are conducted through the windows of the senses and the psychological faculties to the visible world. Thence, the spiritual longing and restless love hidden in the synthesis of body and spirit stirs to motion, drawing the heart away from its natural inclinations, back to its original realm, beckoning with plaintive strains....

In the above quotation, a difference is maintained between "natural" and "original" inclinations of the heart, the former referring to bodily or worldly tendencies, as opposed to spiritual and divine tendencies. Thus the *ney* is seen as the instrument of remembrance, sounding a clarion call to the soul for return to its real origins. In the context of the "two sides" mentioned, the awareness of sadness, loss, and separation is the other side of joy, gain, and union. Such an awareness leads the soul towards an awakening of "the real," or Divine Essence, and away from "the unreal," or sensory experience. As was mentioned in passing with regard to the *sama'*, it is in this connection that the significance of the *ney* with dance is understood. In the dance of death and rebirth, the music of the *ney* symbolizes both a death to the sensory world and a rebirth into the supersensory realm. As Majnun cries, "My memory is blank, the gale has blown away all I possessed.... I am no longer the man I was, ... !" (XXXI:98).

The symbolism of the *ney* has another context related to union. The method of producing sound from this instrument is by blowing into it. However, in playing the flute, blowing requires great powers of breath control to obtain the subtle differences in note, pitch, and tone.[14] In mysticism, breath and its control is important to spiritual practice in attaining superconscious states. The expression "the *gale*

14 "The Paradox of the *Shakuhachi*" (2003).

has *blown* away" (emphasis mine) in the example just quoted in the above paragraph indicates this relation. Besides, there are numerous other expressions in *Layla* which represent the relevance of breath and blowing. The examples below speak of breath as a means of transcending separation. Of Layla it is said that her eyes (XXVII:87):

> ... looked only for Majnun, or for a sign from him. Might not a breath of wind bring a speck of dust from his mountain cave?

Whereas of Majnun it is said (IV:12):

> He is seeking your breath in the blowing of the wind and tells his grief to the earth. Send him a breath of air as a sign that you are thinking of him.

These expressions evidence a reciprocation and mutuality in the communication of the lovers. In the first instance, it is Layla relying on "a breath of wind" to connect with Majnun. In the second however, it is Majnun, "seeking your breath." Further, in the following example (XXXIX:119),

> It was ... one of those mornings which waft a scent of paradise over the world, as if its breeze were the breath of the Messiah awakening the dead.

breath is associated with life, salvation, and return. In each of the three foregoing examples, "breath" may be associated with the sound from the flute. The esoteric interpretation of breath blown into the flute expresses the Divine act of creation. It is said that in creating from Himself all creatures, God blew His own soul only to humans. Thus, the *ney* symbolizes "the body of man, the breath blown into it, the Spirit, and the sound that issues from it, the voice of God."[15]

Moreover, like the flute, the human is also an instrument. Man becomes God's voice, God's mirror, and ascends and reunites with God (2003). This relates to the story of creation that starts with the command of the Almighty Spirit, *Kun faya Kun*, "Be! and so it is!" To be, and being, or existence, is the start of the circle of descent, and

[15] "The First Eighteen Verses of Rumi's Masnevi" (2003).

subsequently the ascent towards becoming perfected man, which the Whirling Dance ceremony represents. The general rule is that everything in the universe tends towards its origin. Man, "in the vicinity of his Beloved, was watered with His spiritual light, as was the reed of the *ney* once watered by a stream or a lake" (2003). Thus, when he succeeds in obtaining spiritual water, he can be green and fresh, i.e. attain eternal joy. This association between breath and renewal or eternal life is reflected in many expressions in *Layla.* The following are examples:

> You are my soul's life-giving breath. (XXXI:97)

> ... and now with every breath, with every sigh, (he) feels the stream of life slowly returning. (XXV:76)

> What is human life ... take it as a breath of air merging into eternity. (XLIV:148)

These lines, evoking life, recreation, and time, express the Sufi view that the universe is being re-created at every moment. In the words of Bakhtiar, "At every moment what appears to be a time-connected universe returns to God. There is continuous, instantaneous expansion and contraction" (1976, 117). And further, as Toshihiko Izutsu expresses it, people who do not perceive this are in confusion because they do not know the constant renewal of things with each Divine Breath (Bakhtiar 1976, 117).

From the above accounts and examples it is evident that together, both the instrument and its music are a medium by which the human soul can approach the Divine. From the simple, rudimentary form in its bed of rushes, to the complex, accomplished music of the flute, the reed-flute is associated on many levels with steps that lead from separation to return, from an "immature," material man to an awakening for spiritual food, to salvation, or unification with God. Thus, the flute represents the paradox of the two sides of the coin. In this connection, the word "cleave" may be cited as expressing this paradox particularly well, because it means both "to join together" and "to break apart" (NSOED).

The references to the flute in *Govinda* are apparently different from their occurrence in *Layla* in that they are associated solely with

Krishna and the bliss of his sport, and speak primarily of joy and union. Thus, Krishna's flute makes sprightly music. For example, the following verse (V:9),

> He plays your name to call you on his sweet reed flute.
> He cherishes breeze-blown pollen that touched your fragile body.
> In woods on the wind-swept Jumna bank,
> Krishna waits in wildflower garlands.

in association with the "sweet reed flute," conveys an idyllic lovers' tryst. The flute is conspicuous as an instrument of alliance. Krishna does not call Radha by name, rather he "plays your name" on the flute, implying that the sound of the flute will be recognized and identified by Radha as a "call" from Krishna. Besides, the mention of "pollen" on "your fragile body" is suggestive of fusion and fruition, and the last two lines explicitly related to Krishna as bedecked with "wildflower garlands" and awaiting Radha on the banks of the Jumna, represent overtones of union.

There are several elements of correspondence in this verse with the esoteric interpretation of expressions in *Layla* in relation to the flute. The first is associated with water, in the reference to "Jumna" in *Govinda*, which is sacred to the Hindu. It represents water, symbolizing sanctification. This element corresponds with the Sufi association of the reed with streams and the fact that it flourishes in its home. Thus the flute is associated with the spiritual stream that is instrumental in the achievement of eternal joy, as mentioned in the explanation in relation to the expressions in *Layla*. The second element of correspondence is that the sound of the flute is representative of a "call." Krishna, or God, calls the name of Radha, or the human soul, by blowing on the flute. In this respect, the expressions "breeze-blown" and "wind-swept" reinforce the relation to breath. The meaning here is parallel to the Sufi interpretation that the sound of the flute represents the voice of the human soul. The contexts are different in that, in *Layla* the call is from the human to the Divine whereas in *Govinda* it is from the Divine to the human. But in both cases the flute is the medium of the call and instrumental in establishing connection between the lovers, be they Divine or human. The third corresponding element is that of hope and salvation associated with the flute. In the example, Krishna "plays," he "cherishes," he "waits," and he ornaments himself. All of these suggest that he anticipates union, and illustrate Divine receptivity and reciprocation. By extension, this indicates the prospect of Divine redemption, associated with Krishna's role of *avatara.*

The final correspondence is that, in both cases, the event or episode of union is conveyed not as actual, but potential. Because the possibility of union originates from the context of separation, it may be concluded that the essential meaning conveyed in the examples of both texts is that without separation there cannot be union, just as without descent there cannot be ascent. The one is always latent in the other (Dimock 1991, 4).

In Vaishnava symbolism, the sound of Krishna's flute is particularly associated with the Divine "call." This has been expressed by Kinsley as (1979, 95),

> Krsna's flute is an extension of his beauty. Not only is it the most beautiful sound imaginable, it imparts the essence of Krsna's intoxicating nature ... it ... echoes throughout Vrndavana, beckoning all to join him in the forest.

The beckoning of the "enchanting flute" is so irresistible that the *gopis* are mesmerized into leaving not only their homes and husbands, but morals and conventions, rules and regulations, in answer to it. The esoteric interpretation is that it symbolizes the irresistible call of the souls of men back to their Creator (Kinsley 1979, 95). The *gopis* are the chosen ones who hear this call, "the hearts that are ready to vibrate and leap up at his call" (Maertens 2003). It has been explained in this regard that the *gopis* are not ordinary people, but embodiments of a spiritual passion, extraordinary by their extremeness of love, personal devotion, and unreserved self-giving (Maertens 2003).

In another example from *Govinda*, the lure of Krishna's flute is expressed as (II:2):

> Sweet notes from his alluring flute echo nectar from his lips.
> His restless eyes glance, his head sways, earrings play at his cheeks.
> My heart recalls Hari here in his love dance,
> Playing seductively, laughing, mocking me.

On the one hand, Krishna is "sweet" and "alluring," on the other he is "laughing" and "mocking." It beckons, by its association with "nectar," the symbol of immortality. And, as in *Layla*, this immortality is an extension of God's lips and breath. Yet at the same time it "plays," to break down all resistance of the ego, of the self. The effect of Krishna's flute is that the cowherdesses are powerless to resist, as may be seen in the following verse (I:46):

> And beautiful cowherd girls wildly
> Wind him in their bodies.
> Friend, in spring young Hari plays
> Like erotic mood incarnate.

Thus, the music is capable of exciting desire, and the "cowherd girls" are driven to distraction, forgetting all but Krishna. And, as the previous examples have shown, they dance in abandon. In fact, when Krishna comes to dance with them, even nature laughs at their frenzy (I:3):

> When spring's mood is rich, Hari roams here
> To dance with young women, friend,...
> Tender buds bloom into laughter as creatures abandon modesty.

Thus it may be seen that music has the power to transcend bounds, laws, restrictions, even modesty. "It is the love of the human soul for the divine in a mystical relationship unsullied by institutions and authorities, unsullied even by language" (Maertens 2003). Kinsley has described this power as follows (1979, 103):

> It is time, it proclaims, to join his symphony of joy, to frolic in the forest, to scamper in play, to realize every dream that one has ever dreamed in his world of infinite possibility. Krishna's flute incites the world to dance.... It asks nothing but surrender ... and participation in its magic world. Krisna is the master magician ... and his wand is his flute.

In the myth of Krishna the flute breaks through all the propriety and reserve of the *gopis*. It is important to note that the *gopis* are not loose, but virtuous women, "jarred loose from their self-control" (Maertens 2003).

If the *flute* is associated with Krishna, love trysts, and the possibility of union with him, it is interesting to observe that the references to "*reeds*" are often associated with Radha, unfulfilled trysts, and lingering in separation. Radha waits (VII:9):

> ... among countless forest reeds;
> Madhu's killer does not recall me, even in his heart.
> Whom can I seek for refuge here?

as she suffers the pangs of loneliness without Krishna. Here the diction reinforces her suffering. The reference to him by the epithet "Madhu's killer" seems to indicate that the waiting in vain is killing her. She is lost, as she laments that he does not "recall" her, "even in his heart." Alas, the call of Krishna's flute does not reach Radha's heart. As her source of "refuge" is lost, she is lost. In another example, she vacillates, unwilling to take responsibility for the loss (VII:11):

> Or does my lover's anguished mind so tangle the path
> That he cannot come into this thicket of vines
> And sweet swamp reeds where we promised to meet?

In asking herself what the reason for his absence could be, she deludes herself that it is Krishna, and not her, who is "anguished" and Krishna whose path is "so tangled." She does not admit that he will not, rather than "cannot," come to meet her. This shows she is still in a state of ignorance, through her denial and self-delusion.

Two elements are noticeable here, the first being that the reeds are associated with both union and separation. The love tryst is to take place among the "forest reeds" and the "sweet swamp reeds" and thus the reeds are associated with union. However, the images of "forest," "tangled path," and "swamp," evoke the obscuration and obstacles that stand in the way. Thus the reeds are associated with separation. Based on this understanding, the esoteric interpretation is that union is only possible when the "tangles" of the ego have been unwound. This leads to the second element in these examples, Radha's ignorance, caused by her ego. Due to her ignorance, she is unable to understand that the cause lies with her, and not him. It *is* possible to reach Krishna, as evident from his erotic dalliances with other *gopis* among the reeds (I:42):

Eager for the art of his love on the Jumna riverbank, a girl
Pulls his silk cloth toward a thicket of reeds with her hand.

In fact it is also evident that it is not only possible to "pull" him, but that he waits in great expectation among the reeds (VI:1):

In a clump of reeds on the Jumna riverbank
Where Madhava waited helplessly,
Reeling under the burden of ardent love,...

The esoteric interpretation is that Divine help is available, but man has to avail himself of it. If Krishna is not there in the reeds, it is because he is everywhere. The world is *maya*, the illusion of ignorance, which covers the Divine. This indicates what has been mentioned earlier, in relation to spiritual development and preparedness for the Divine vision: It is not that God is far from man, but that man, due to ignorance, is unconscious of God's presence, as illustrated by Radha.

Finally, it may be observed that on the whole, the reeds are more closely associated with the human characters, compared to the flute-music, which is seen as an extension of the Divine Player. In this regard, the reed may be related to the idea of "raw material," whereas the flute is related to the "finished product." Only when the reed has "matured" does it become the music. Thus, only the *gopi* who loves Krishna selflessly, attains him. Only when the time is "ripe" does the lover meet the Beloved. In becoming matured and perfected, the divine spark of the human soul finds realization.

The study and comparison of the portrayal of "the arts" in the texts has shown a high degree of correspondence between *Layla* and *Govinda*. As a means of transcending separation, the correspondence is firstly at the level of different categories of art. This means that the categories discussed function integrally as different points of a spectrum in taking the lover beyond his or her material realities and bounds. Secondly, the correspondence is at the level of quality. All the categories mentioned in both texts express the spiritual dimension in equal measure as well as serve as a medium for expressing the connection of the lover with that spiritual dimension while in the state of "disconnection" from it. Thus, "the arts" in both the texts qualify to be deemed as "sacred art."

This chapter has addressed the issue of union in separation, or the means of connection with the beloved in the state of disconnection. However, it must be noted that from a spiritual viewpoint, the means *is* the end. In the previous chapters, it has been shown that the lovers have, to use garden terminology, been intoxicated by the flowers of the garden of love, pierced by its bitter thorns, and tasted the sweetness of its fruits. However, these have been fleeting glimpses of the garden from behind the veil of *maya.* Therefore, the next chapter will attempt to lift the veil in order to reveal the eternal perfumes of "that other Garden" portrayed in *Layla* and *Govinda.*

CHAPTER SIX

THE GARDENER AND THE GARDEN: RETURN AND UNION REGAINED

The garden was greener than an emerald, and shone with infinite light.

(*Layla*, LIV:175)

Revel in a bright retreat heaped with flowers!
Your tender body is flowering.

(*Govinda*, XI:16)

From the discussion in previous chapters, the journey of the lovers and the path they have traveled lend themselves easily to the analogy of the circle or wheel. From the starting point of initial union, the wheel turned a subsequent downward curve into despondence and disconnection, and a consequent and simultaneous upward curve of joy and connection. The delineation of these processes was presented schematically in chapter 2 as being both linear and cyclical in nature. As was explained, they are linear in terms of being successive in a spatio-temporal context, and cyclical in terms of their repetitive and recursive character. On the point of cyclic nature, however, it is to be noted that the ultimate or final goal of the entire process is both a point of return and a point of no return. In this context, this final chapter of analysis and comparison will witness the wheel coming full circle, or a return to the state of union, in terms of the "end."

Return and the End

Before embarking on an analysis of the final stage, a disclaimer is necessary as to what is considered as "the end." As has been demonstrated, the division between the "actual" separation and "actual" union is significantly blurred. Previously, the parameters of the physical or corporeal connection of the lovers have been expanded by incorporeal means, or by the emotional, mental, psychological, and spiritual faculties. Consequently, in both works the evocation of the lover's presence is so strong that it is often difficult to ascertain as to when, and whether, the beloved is, in fact, absent or present. This phenomenon is reminiscent of Rumi's classic expression of the Absolute, as a Presence that is Absent, or an Absence that is Present.

In light of such a phenomenon, the discussion of union and separation has been so far based on artificial divisions merely to facilitate the consideration and illustration of selected events and expressions, which more often than not belong to both separation and union. As such, the parameters of what constitutes the reunion or "ending," as far as the discussion in this chapter is concerned, should be established. In general it is based on the final point of transition from the corporeal to the incorporeal, the worldly to the spiritual, or the mundane to the supra-mundane realm.

Death and Transition

In the case of *Layla*, the last two chapters of the text, which are an account of Majnun's final moments before death, and subsequently, the depiction of the lovers in the dream of the character referred to as Zayd, will be considered as the "ending." In *Govinda*, it is considered from the last two verses of the "Twentieth Song" to the end of the work, "The Twenty-Fourth Song," when Radha literally stands before Krishna at the entrance of the thicket, and subsequently, the overt expression of their sexual union in the closing verses. The justification for considering these points as marking the ending is guided by the substance of the narration, as well as principles of the respective mystico-religious traditions. These will become apparent in the course of the discussion in this chapter.

A notable feature about the "ending" is its marked brevity. Statistically, in *Layla* the extract being considered represents slightly less than 3% of the whole text, whereas in *Govinda*, it is higher, constituting about 15%. However, as will be illustrated, the diction in the "ending" in both cases is dense with symbolic significance relating to a Return. In this regard, it is relevant to consider the portrayal in the texts in the usual way, namely, the content or substance of the depiction of reunion, the spiritual implications, and thirdly the similarities and differences between the expressions in the texts.

To facilitate discussion of the ending, the saga of love in both *Layla* and *Govinda* is dealt with in different sections, namely as the "prelude," the "reunion," the "core," and the "center." "Prelude" is taken to mean "preliminary performance, action. or condition, preceding and introducing one that is more important" (NSOED). In this context, the prelude is considered as contributory to the "ending" or Return. By "reunion" is meant the depiction of the lovers' reunification, while the "core" refers to a particular quality of this reunion. Finally, "center" refers to a specific point of the core that represents a key element to the whole ending. Again, it should be borne in mind that such divisions are entirely artificial, and in fact there is no clear textual demarcation as to the precise point that one ends and the other begins.

Prelude: At the Sill of the Door

There are several features in the prelude which will be discussed individually. In *Layla*, the first feature of the prelude is the account of Majnun's last journey to Layla's tomb. The following passage (LII:172):

> Once more he dragged his body to Layla's tomb. When he arrived evening had fallen, darkening the ocean of the sky. Soon Majnun's boat was to weigh anchor for his journey into the night. He resembled an ant exhausted unto death, twitching for the last time, a serpent writhing in its death-throes.

represents an introduction to Majnun's death. From this passage it may be seen that the journey to Layla's tomb is the prelude to his ultimate journey: death. A noteworthy feature of the passage is the highly figurative and analogical language. The juxtaposition of the phrases "dragged his body" and "to Layla's tomb" in the first sentence constitutes an analogy between the living and the dead. In other words, there is a correspondence between the state of Majnun and Layla. He is no longer pictured as a person, or a living man, but a "body," a term commonly used to refer to a corpse. In the next sentence, the death-like image of Majnun is reflected in the elements of nature. The words "evening," "fallen," and "darkening" conjure images of darkness and death. The association of his arrival at the tomb with the "ocean of the sky" expresses the microcosm of his body on a macrocosmic scale. It is as if he is dispersed into, and merged with, the elements. The images of darkness and death continue in the same vein in the sentence that follows, in the metaphor of the boat on a "journey into the night." In the final sentence, the likeness of Majnun to "an ant exhausted unto death" and "a serpent writhing in its death-throes" again conveys strong overtures of death. This sentence particularly expresses the notion of transition at two levels, firstly by the association of the human with the animal world, and secondly, from the association of the world of the living with the world of the dead. Generally, at the outward level, the whole passage demarcates Majnun's transition in corporeal terms from life to death.

At the inward level of interpretation, the passage is heavily laden with symbolic and anagogic significance. In the prelude, the fact that there is still life in Majnun, and that he is practically dead, has strong mystical overtones. It is reminiscent of the *hadith* often quoted by the Sufis, *mutu qabla an tamutu*, "die before ye die" (Schimmel 1982, 132), referring to the idea of spiritual death and return, in which the orientation is towards emptiness and total receptivity. This idea is echoed in the two Divine names which complement each other, *al-Mumit*, "He who kills," and *al-Muhyi*, "He who bestows life" (Schimmel 1982, 132), in which death is viewed as the passage to union with the Beloved. Thus, the prelude, in which Majnun is "alive" but also "dead," evokes this notion which involves a death in life, or in the Manifest, and a rebirth into the Hidden (Bakhtiar 1976, 84). That is to say, a death to the worldly, transitory life, and a deliverance into the spiritual, eternal life. Thus Majnun's presence and his condition at Layla's tomb at the last point before death indicates this orientation.

As has been explained previously, in the esoteric view the symbol of the tomb, or death, is the complement of the womb, or life. Furthermore, as the tomb is that of Layla, representing the Divine Essence, it may be asserted that for Majnun, or the human soul, it is the Divine or spiritual life that is the destination of the journey. Finally, it may be said that the site of the tomb of Layla is, for Majnun, a sacred space. It represents the place of his "hidden treasure." In this respect there is another analogy between Layla and Majnun. Just as her body is enclosed in the tomb, so Majnun's soul is enclosed in his body. However, the point is that Layla's soul is not there, but returned to its original Home. Thus, so long as Majnun's body is alive, his soul is trapped within the "tomb" of the body, and cannot be united with hers. In this context, death for Majnun means freedom and rejuvenation. This expresses the Sufi awareness of the truth "that death in love means union with the beloved" (Schimmel 1979, 89), and the doctrine of annihilation and resurrection.

The depiction of Majnun's condition in life as parallel to Layla's state of death reflects the human soul at the point of identification with the Divine Essence. Stated differently, the depiction shows that the physical dimension of his being merges into the metaphysical dimension. This may be substantiated by several expressions in the passage. The reference to the "ocean of the sky," directly evokes the heavens, or the incorporeal, metaphysical "beyond." The ocean is a well-known mystical symbol, signifying the extensiveness and inclusiveness of Divinity, as well as the transforming power of water (Schimmel 1982, 61). Besides, the related symbolism of water, the drop, representing the human soul, and the ocean, representing the Divine Essence, also emerge in this reference. Furthermore, the ocean is associated with the "boat," which is the body. The body is the vessel, or vehicle of the soul, by which it will cross the ocean of life. Thus the "boat" is a bridge between worlds. As the word "night" is synonymous with "Layla," the "journey into the night" may be understood as a journey into the Divine. This suggests the personal *mi'raj* of the Sufi that is inspired by the famous *mi'raj* of the Prophet, the night journey of heavenly ascension. Further, the Prophet's journey occurred on the Night of Ascent, *laylat al-mi'raj*, when according to the Koran, the Prophet was taken by the archangel Gabriel from Mecca to Jerusalem and from there ascended to the highest heaven and drew nigh to the Divine Presence Itself (Nasr 1991, 418). Thus the journey referred to in this passage may be understood as reflecting the journey of the spiritual traveler, expressed by Schimmel (1982, 79), as follows:

> ... the journey of the soul, which might take him, in imitation of the Prophet's *mi'raj*, to the heights of the transcendent God, or lead him finally into the depths of the ocean of his own soul, to find the beloved there.

On this basis, it may be assumed that this "night" prefigures Majnun's ultimate sight of his beloved. The word "anchor" in relation to the "boat" is also significant, in the sense of moorings. Figuratively "anchor" refers to "a firm hold, a point clung to, a ground of confidence, security, etc." (NSOED). This understanding establishes the Divine as the point of departure and return, and all else between. In the context of this statement, the reference to God by His Beautiful Names, *al-Awwal* or origin, *al-Akhir*, or return, *al-Zahir*, the Outward or Manifest, and *al-Batin*, the Inward or Hidden, are particularly relevant.

Thus, as the wheel turns, this prelude to the "end" may be more appropriately referred to as the "beginning of the end." In fact, if at the outward level of meaning the representation of Majnun's transition is from life to death, at the inner level it is from death to eternal life. Thus, it is "the beginning." In this nomenclature, the inverse relation between the physical and metaphysical realities is apparent. Also, it represents another mystical paradox. In the mundane sense, life is temporary, and death is permanent. But spiritually, in the understanding that "death" refers to body, and "life" to the soul or spirit, death is temporary, and life is permanent.

If at this point it is affirmed that Majnun is at the "sill of the door" of illumination, it is interesting to compare how Radha fares at this stage of her journey's end. Radha's point of contact with Krishna begins with her arrival at the entrance to the thicket within which Krishna dwells. This event represents the first aspect of the prelude to ultimate union in *Govinda.* The point of contact referred to begins as follows (XI:13):

> Seeing Hari light the deep thicket
> With brilliant jewel necklaces, a pendant,
> A golden rope belt, armlets, and wrist bands,
> Radha modestly stopped at the entrance....

Various phenomena about this verse that may be observed, first from the outward level and subsequently at the inward level. An apparent element is that Radha actually "sees" Hari. Contrary to her previous "incorporeal" experiences of his presence, he is at this point bodily or physically present before her. Besides, she "modestly" stops short at the "entrance," as stated in the last line. Her present action is considered contrary to her character, because prior to this event she has been constantly depicted as relentlessly "preying," "haunting," and "hunting," her "quarry," Hari. Thus, the present development of the sighting of Krishna, and her sudden modesty, contrasts with her character in the past. In this context, these developments are indications of change, or transition, in Radha.

Incidentally, an interesting cross-cultural parallel may be drawn, in relation to the phenomenon of Radha momentarily stopping short at the entrance. Whereas in the miracle of the *mi'raj*, the Prophet Muhammad alone entered the Divine Presence, Sufi poets stop at the threshold of Love. They are like Gabriel, symbol of the Intellect.[1] In this context, Radha resembles the Sufis. Her action of stopping at the entrance to the thicket within which Krishna dwells symbolizes that in the presence of the Beloved, the old Radha, the Intellect or *buddhi*, is left behind. Furthermore, this interpretation may be confirmed by the expression, "Graced by arrows of Love, even Radha's modesty left in shame" (XI:33). This loss of modesty is ontological, symbolizing that there is nothing left of the old Radha or consciousness of the body-self. She is able to see the Divinity shining through the human body complex. This condition exemplifies the feeling that "the goal of love is loss of awareness of all but God" (Schimmel 1982, 9). All that Radha knows, and sees, is the Divine Presence within.

The next obvious point about the verse are the apparent images of light and illumination. In the first line, "Seeing Hari light the deep thicket," Krishna is the source of that light which emanates from the "thicket." In this line, light and darkness are juxtaposed. The collocation of the epithet "Hari" (illumination) and "light," contrasts with darkness, evoked by the collocation of "deep" and "thicket." In the couplet that follows, Hari is depicted as bedecked with ornaments, "With brilliant jewel necklaces, a pendant, a golden rope belt, armlets, and wrist bands." From the inventory of his numerous jewelry, the form of Hari is in correspondence with the attribute of his name. Thus, Radha's first sight or vision of her beloved after the long night of separation is a glittering, dazzling Hari materialized in all his splendor and majesty. Finally, it should be noted from the lines quoted that this event, as prelude or introduction to ultimate union, takes place in the thicket. As mentioned, the thicket is associated with darkness, and described as "deep," conjuring an atmosphere of mystery and secrecy. In this context, the thicket in which Krishna dwells, and where Radha sees him, represents a sacred space to Radha, just as Layla's tomb represents sacred space to Majnun. In physical terms, it

[1] In the words of Schimmel, "Muhammad entered the Divine Presence alone, while Gabriel had to remain outside,... or (his) wings would get burnt.... That is why he becomes, for later Sufi poets like Rumi, the symbol of the Intellect which must stop at the threshold of Love" (1982, 184).

may be said that Hari within the thicket symbolizes the heart within the body. In seeking all over Brindaban forest, Radha finds him within her own heart.

In Indian religio-poetic expression, the spiritual significance of ornamentation and decoration is that it indicates beauty. And in mysticism the synonymy between Beauty and Truth is universal. Thus, ornamentation symbolizes the connection with Truth. In other words, ornamentation symbolizes mystical union. Sure enough, in the opening lines of the final sequence in *Govinda*, "The Eleventh Part," it is stated that "Kesava dressed elaborately" and "Radha dressed in gleaming ornaments" (XI:1). The choice of the epithet, Kesava ("long-haired one"), underscores the role of ornamentation. Krishna's long hair is associated with his irresistible beauty and charm. Besides, in epic and Puranic literature Kesava is the killer of Kesin, the horse-demon. Esoterically this is the removal of the ego or self, and its replacement with the Self. When Radha's ego is completely effaced, she attains oneness with the Beloved. Thus the lines foreshadow the reunion by reference to both the beautiful and awesome aspects of Krishna. Schimmel's words, expressing the connection between beauty and truth, are particularly applicable in this regard (1975, 295):

> The eternal theme of the interaction of love and beauty forms the continuum beneath the delicate melodies.... Each time one reads (the words) they disclose a new aspect, as if veils were taken off the meaning and again replaced by new veils of different color.

Thus it is assumed that Krishna's ornamentation displays his willingness for the ultimate union, or *yoga*, with Radha. For her, it expresses "the sudden unveiling of what is, for man, the truth of truths" (Lings 1981, 32). Thus the passage indicates that in beholding Krishna in the thicket, Radha beholds Truth itself. As the veil of *maya* is lifted, she gazes at Ultimate Reality.

An interesting connection may be established between Krishna's willingness and Radha's hesitation. At the outward level, and based on the portrayal of her character and personality, so far it is questionable that Radha is actually overcome by "modesty" as stated. Instead, it is likely that she is fulfilling a poetic convention: the requirement that the woman-in-love rush to meet her paramour with all incumbent constraints. This is something that can be accomplished only by an adept. As pointed out in the Coomaraswamy quotation in chapter 5 in this regard, the requirement is that she should not, under any circumstances, display the turmoil and tempest of her real emotions.

At an inward level, although it is true that the prospect of *yoga*, or union, is evoked by Krishna's readiness, it is particularly *hatha yoga* that prevails upon Radha in this instance. *Hatha yoga* is defined as "union with the Supreme *via discipline*" (emphasis mine).[2] Thus, in holding back, Radha displays this discipline. This means that she has become an adept, and by extension, an elect. Therefore, at both the outward and inward levels, Radha is in a state of preparedness for ultimate union with her Beloved. In fact, both Krishna and Radha are ready for union with each other, but the difference between them is that, Krishna's preparedness is manifest, whereas hers is concealed. In any case, the lines portend that she has reached a point of transition.

The possibility of alchemical transformation is noticeable in *Govinda* in a previous sequence on the state of Radha in separation. In conveying her agony over Krishna's dalliance with other *gopis*, the poet Jayadeva sings (VII:35):

> His color deepens like rain-heavy thunderheads.
> Long desertion won't tear at her heart.
> Wildflower-garlanded Krishna
> Caresses her, friend.
> His bright cloth shines gold on black touchstone....

Contrary to what Radha fears, it is pointed out here that the "long desertion *won't* tear at her heart." Instead, Krishna "caresses her." In these lines it is significant that Krishna's color is likened to "rain-heavy thunderheads" and "black touchstone." Both expressions evoke darkness and the mystery of the unmanifest aspect of Krishna. It suggests that though seemingly absent he is not only present, but omnipresent. This awareness is the key to alchemical transformation, of which he is the "black touchstone." Thus, the verse immediately preceding the account of the prelude in *Govinda* may be seen as the final point of Radha's transition and transformation. It closely corresponds with

[2] Omkarananda Ashram (2003).

the alchemical transformation of Majnun, illustrated earlier in this chapter.

In this respect, it is necessary to digress briefly, in order to observe the Hindu mystical paradigm of *kaaca-pakka*, or "raw and ripe," and its illustration. The Sanskrit term, *kacca*, meaning "raw," phonetically resembles the word *kaaca*, for the substance "glass." The "raw" soul, tied to the world, flashes like glass, whereas the "ripe" soul has the brilliance of a jewel. A sentence in *Layla* echoes this precise notion: "Our hero desired the jewel" (I:2), and not the glass. Furthermore, the term *pakka*, meaning ripe or cooked, refers to the expert or spiritual adept, represented by the expression "like seeds of ripe pomegranate" (XI:19) in reference to Radha at the ending of *Govinda*. The physical likeness of "ripe pomegranate" seeds to the ruby is obvious here. But beyond the apparent similarity, the quality of this jewel is interesting. The English definition, as "a rare and valuable precious stone," may also refer figuratively to "a person (esp. a woman) of great worth or beauty" (NSOED). Both these aspects of the ruby are consonant with the Sanskrit usage and associations. Even more interesting, in terms of alchemy, it represents "the red form of the philosopher's stone" (NSOED). Thus, the present association of the ripe pomegranate with Radha represents the complementary aspect of the previous, *kacca* Radha. At this point, as Krishna says, she "has come far," and thus is now *pakka*, i.e. she has transformed alchemically into the "desired" "jewel."

Returning to the verse of the "sighting" of Krishna, and the one referring to alchemy just considered, it is observed that there is juxtaposition and contrast as well as contradiction and paradox in the images conveyed: light and darkness, readiness and hesitation, the hidden and the manifest. However, as has been demonstrated repeatedly, in the esoteric understanding these phenomena are characteristic of mystical symbolism, and therefore, are complementary and not contrastive. Hari represents both darkness and light because he is the unmanifest, transcendent *Brahman*, as well as the immanent, Divine descent, both majesty and beauty, embodied in the dazzling, bejeweled *avatara* who enticingly awaits Radha. Thus, by allowing Radha to "see" him, Hari reveals Himself as the supreme Personality, *Purushottama*, in all His mystic opulence. In the presence of the supreme Alchemist, Radha is transmuted from base, worldly "metal" into spiritual "gold." The seeker becomes the seer.

The dazzling depiction of Krishna is strongly suggestive of the episode in the *Bhagavad Gita* where Arjuna experiences the *Visvarupa Darsana*, or the revealing of Krishna's Universal Form.[3] In the case of Arjuna, as nothing in the created world can be found parallel to the Divine Essence, Arjuna cannot "behold" what is revealed with ordinary sight, unless he has the gift of Cosmic Vision, or in Hindu terminology, the faculty of the Third Eye. Thus, this gift is acquired by human perfection through yogic practice and bestowed through Divine Grace. Stated differently, first the human deserves, then the Divine serves. In this context, human effort and Divine Grace are mutual. As Krishna says in the *Bhagavad Gita*, "But you cannot see Me with these eyes of yours; I give you Divine sight; behold My Supreme Yoga" (11.8). It is only Cosmic Vision granted by Krishna that enables Arjuna to see Him. The philosophical principle behind Krishna's revelation of his Universal Form is the Omnipotence, or rather the "Aumnipotence" and the "Aumnipresence" of the Brahman. Thus, the *Visvarupa Darsana* episode in the *Bhagavad Gita* is a prefiguration of the phenomenon of Radha's sighting of Krishna, of her yogic prowess, and of his resplendence in the prelude to ultimate *yoga* in *Govinda*.

The foregoing discussion on the "sighting" of Krishna in the prelude in *Govinda* has shown Radha's direct, immediate, experience of the Divine Presence. This depiction of Radha has a corresponding depiction in the experience of Majnun, though in different circumstances. In *Layla*, it is represented by the phenomenon of Majnun's death, which is set apart from ordinary death in various ways. One is that the physical condition of his body does not deteriorate, as ordinarily happens. The account of the event conveys that "for a long time no one knew" that he was dead, perhaps for "as much as a year." The second is that, "wild animals surrounded the grave" as "guardians" "protecting" it. Furthermore, "even beasts which feed on carrion did not touch him," and only when his remains become dust, and are "returned to earth," do the animals depart. Thus in light of these circumstances of his death, it is referred to as "the riddle" and described as, "Death had completed his work so well that no one felt fear or disgust. The white shell, its pearl vanished, was washed clean"

[3] See *Bhagavad Gita*, 11.10-12.

(LIII:174). Finally, it must be recalled that the narrative of Majnun in death is ended by the poem and has already been discussed in relation to the depiction of the resurrection and reunion of the lovers, "in the world above," which constitutes a transition.

At the surface level, there appears to be no likeness in this depiction of Majnun to Radha's experience of proximity with God. However, the inward level of interpretation yields a different understanding. Each one of the aspects mentioned in relation to Majnun's death is extraordinary, and even miraculous. This indicates Majnun's death as a manifestation of the work of the Divine Hand. The final sentence of the description is an indication of Majnun's proximity with the Divine Presence. At one level, the reference to the "shell," suggesting the body, and "the pearl," suggesting the soul, points to the close connection between the two aspects of the self. Thus death has "washed clean" the worldly existence of self, and the original, divine Self has emerged. At another level, this sentence is strongly reminiscent of the *hadith* of the hidden treasure. Thus it may be interpreted as expressing the mutuality of the human-Divine connection, realized in Majnun. In this context, the "shell" refers to Majnun, or the human aspect, whereas the "pearl" refers to Layla, or the Divine aspect.

The foregoing arguments show that the experience of proximity with the Divine corresponds, as well as differs, in the two texts. It corresponds essentially, in terms of the experience, and differs outwardly in terms of the setting and mode of expression. In *Layla*, the setting is at Layla's tomb, whereas in *Govinda* it is in the thicket. The former conveys the experience implicitly, whereas in the latter, it is made explicit.

Reunion: Celestial and Sexual Encounters

In *Layla*, the setting of the reunion is portrayed as a garden. The lovers, referred to as "that pair of unsated souls," are reunited in "a many-splendored garden" (LIV:175). The description directly and indirectly conveys that the garden referred to is none other than the Eternal Garden. The "fabled garden of Iram" refers to the Persian *Bagh-e-Iram*, or *Gulistan-i-Iram*, meaning Garden of Paradise. Further, reference is made to "the houris of paradise." Besides, in "this spiritual abode" there is, "to the seeing eye, a blue empyrean in every meadow" (LIV:175). It is interesting that all this is visible only to the "seeing eye." In this context, the common adage, "seeing is believing" may be transposed to "believing is seeing." In other words, only if there is capacity can one see. Besides, "the empyrean," referring to the highest heaven, the sky, cosmic space, and figuratively meaning an exalted region, realm, or group (NSOED), leaves no doubt that the reunion takes place at a higher level of reality, namely, Paradise.

In consideration of such circumstances, a closer examination of some of the prominent features of the reunion is important. The first feature is that it is conveyed in the dream of a character referred to as "Zayd." There are two significant elements in this fact. Firstly, in Sufism, mystical dreams, or *ru'ya*, visions, and inspiration, are part of a spiritual ethos, and specifically found within the prophetic tradition (Bakhtiar 1976, 116). Thus the mystical dream points to the *alam al-mithal*, "the world of symbols and similitudes, which exists between the sensible, phenomenal world and the world of intelligible noumena" (Bakhtiar 1976, 116). In other words, the "seen" as well as the "unseen" are part of the spiritual reality. Therefore, Zayd's dream of the lovers in Paradise is real at a different, but higher level of reality. Accordingly, the lovers, initially referred to as "the unsated souls" (LIV:175) in the prelude, are consequently referred to as "the twin fountains of light" in the reunion. In this phrase, the reference to "twin" indicates intimacy and inseparability. Further, the reference to "light" no longer applies to the separate, gross substance, or personality of Layla and Majnun, but the fused, subtle, spiritual essence of the characters. Thus, "seen" in this "light," Majnun has arrived at his ultimate destination.The second important feature about the dream is that it is "seen" by Zayd. From the following passage, it may be observed that Zayd is no ordinary man (LIV:174-175):

> Sweet, gallant Zayd never abandoned the grave of our twin fountains of light. Stringing together their candid verses with sensitivity, he exposed Layla and Majnun's *affaire de coeur* to the admiration of the world.... In his sleep an angel revealed to Zayd....

Firstly, Zayd's exalted personality and his actions at the service of the lovers is extolled. Secondly, indication of his extraordinary poetic capacity conveys the spiritual position of the bard[4] as a point of con-

[4] The term is associated with primordial cultures and oral traditions. It is derived from the Gaelic/Celtic *bard*, referring to "an ancient Celtic order of minstrel-poets,

tact between the human and divine realities. Thirdly, in being the only witness to, and transmitter of, the reunion to the world, he is of a rare capacity. Fourthly, his account is not just of any event, but an "*affaire de couer*," an affair of the heart. And finally, the dream is "revealed" to him by an "angel." All these points, besides setting him apart from the ordinary man, also associate Zayd with the religious context of Islam.

Furthermore, the position of Zayd in the Islamic tradition, as well as its semantic implications, reinforce this contention. In the first instance, Zayd is a historical figure within the Prophet's circle. In the second, the name is phonetically related to *zahid*, or *shahid*, literally meaning "witness." Thus, it is associated with the Koranic reference to the Prophet as a Messenger of God, in the verse, "O *Nabi* we have sent you as a witness" (XXXIII:45). Finally, the character of Zayd in *Layla* may be associated with Sufism in specific reference to the *Mathnawi* of Rumi. In this reference, Rumi refers to a "Zaid" in exalted terms in Story XV, "Counsels of Reserve given by the Prophet to his Freedman Zaid." As illustrated by the following extract, the vision of Zaid in the *Mathnavi* occurs in a context that is remarkably similar to Zayd's celestial vision of the Garden in *Layla*: [5]

> At dawn the Prophet said to Zaid,
> "How is it with thee this morning, O pure disciple?"
> He replied, "Thy faithful slave am I." Again he said,
> "If the garden of faith has bloomed, show a token of it."
> The Prophet again urged Zaid to deliver to him a present from that celestial region, as a token that he had really been there in the spirit. Zaid answered that he had seen the eight heavens and the seven hells, and the destinies of all men, whether bound to heaven or hell.... As, on the day of judgment *it will be manifest to all men* whether a soul belongs to the saved or to the lost, *so now it was plain and manifest to him*. He went on to ask the Prophet if he should publish this secret knowledge of his to all men....

The italicized words have similar implications as "the seeing eye" discussed earlier in relation to Zayd's extraordinary stature, as well as the

who composed and sang verses celebrating the achievements of chiefs and warriors, recording historical evens, traditional lore, etc." (NSOED).

[5] See "Book I. Story XV. Counsels of Reserve given by the Prophet to his Freedman Zaid" (2003).

latent capacity of all men to "see" at the level of super-consciousness. Thus, as the foregoing arguments have tried to establish, the dream of Zayd possesses reality, authenticity, and credibility in the spiritual viewpoint.

Apart from the circumstances of the dream, some features of the description of the setting of the reunion may be examined in terms of their metaphysical content. A major feature is the rich, sensual imagery employed in reference to the "many-splendored garden" (LIV:175), similar to the promise of Heaven in the *Sura* al-Fajr of the Koran (89:30). Thus, essential Koranic themes are evoked by the descriptions of the garden in *Layla*, such as the four rivers of paradise (47:15), gardens with fruits of all kinds (36:57), with running springs (88:12), peace and security (15:46), and pleasant shades (36:55).[6] The passage in *Layla*,

> ... in his sleep an angel revealed to Zayd a *luminous*, many-splendored garden. There was ... a *shining lamp* in every flower petal,... The garden was greener that (sic) an *emerald*, and *shone* with *infinite light*.... In the shade of a *solar* rose,... two angelic beauties were seated in this place of pleasure,... in *raiments of light*.

conveys multiple images of radiance and brightness. Firstly, there is repetition of the same image by a variety of different words and phrases associated with light, as italicized. Secondly, the repetition occurs within phrases, in terms of quantity as well as quality. To illustrate: in the phrase "a shining lamp in every flower petal," a multitude of lamps is evoked. There are not only many flowers, but also many petals in each flower. The multiples are escalated in the phrase, "shone with infinite light," making it innumerable and immeasurable. Thus in these two cases, the repetition is in terms of quantity. Besides, the light of the "emerald" is also dual. Like all gemstones, it not only reflects, but also emits its own light (Brians 2001). Incidentally, the line in which the emerald is mentioned evokes the *Laylat al-Qadr*, Night of Power, referring to the night of the Revelation of the Koran. It is said that on this occasion, the pious were blessed with the vision of the divine light in the night sky (Schimmel 1975, 179), which shone with

[6] Quoted in Barakat (2003, 14).

a luminous, emerald light. In reference to the "solar rose," the association is with the light of the sun, which is unparalleled in its brightness. Thus, this pair of examples conveys multiplicity in terms of quality.

Apart from visual images, there are olfactory images, conveyed in metaphors of perfume: "night opened its pouch and scattered musk over the day," and auditory images, as in "Minstrels plucked their strings as doves cooed the melody of Zand."[7] In this connection, "music is seen as the resonance of eternal harmony" (Schimmel 1975, 77). Finally, there are taste and tactile images, as in the phrase "pressing their lips to their wine cups, and then joining in a kiss." This form of varied repetition is a particular technique of Persian writing. All of these images of the senses, piled one upon the other in describing "this place of pleasure," construct an image of unbounded pleasure and matchless enjoyment. In terms of its lyrical quality, the description resembles the arabesque pattern in Islamic art, in which repeated patterns and rhythms construct elaborate designs on an object of decoration. This elevates the words and associations of light in the description to the level of sacred art. Thus the words of description are reminiscent of the call of return, through the Word, which is the essence of the Koran. This call has been represented in many art forms which function as the source of remembrance and evocation (Bakhtiar 1976, 52). The allusion to doves in the phrase "as doves cooed" indicates return. This reference may be seen as a litany, in accordance with the Sufi perspective of the language of the birds. Farid ad-Din 'Attar gave classical form to the ancient idea of the "soul bird" in his *Mantiq at-Tair.* In this epic, thirty birds, guided by the hoopoe or *hudhud*, perform the difficult journey to Mount Qaf, where the *Simurg*, or king of birds lives (Schimmel 1982, 75). In this context, the dove is always asking the way towards the Friend by calling *ku ku*, "Where? Where?" (Schimmel 1982, 75), as if seeking the Way of Return.

[7] The association with "Zand" emphasizes the supremacy of music in the Persian context. After a long period of dormancy during the Safavid dynasty, Persian music was revitalized during the Zand dynasty. Classical Persian music is inspired by songs recorded in the memories of experts, passed on from generation to generation, and based on technical milestones which recognize the beauty of its repertoire. See Zahed Sheikholeslami (1997).

Apart from the sensual images in the description, there is also treasure imagery. Symbolic expressions in this regard are plentiful, conveyed repeatedly in related words such as "fortune," "filigree," "ornamenting," "emerald," "cups," "rubies," "treasured," "gem." Thus the passage conveys the "hidden Treasure" of the Divine phrase, which Majnun has not only found, but also "known." This illustrates the paradigm of *ganj-ranj*, relating to the human-Divine connection mentioned previously. As anticipated, pain has ultimately turned into gain. In this respect, it is clear that at this point of Majnun's existence, the Hidden is also the Manifest.

It has been mentioned, and maintained, that the correspondence between cultures in expressing the human-Divine encounter exists at the esoteric or essential level. In this regard, the circumstances featured and discussed so far in relation to the reunion in *Layla* may be compared with that of *Govinda*, initially to find out if they correspond, and if so, subsequently to determine the nature and extent of the correspondence.

The question may be asked, which phenomenon in the portrayal of "the end" in *Govinda* can possibly be regarded as equivalent to the celestial vision of Zayd confirming the reunion of the lovers in Paradise? As there is no trace of such a dream in *Govinda*, one might turn in the direction of a qualitative equivalent for a possible answer. In other words, the answer may lie in a noumenal, rather than a phenomenal, correspondence in expression. Thus, as the extraordinary, the supra-mundane, and the metaphysical elements of the portrayal of reunion in *Layla* have been illustrated, these aspects may be sought in the portrayal in *Govinda*.

In terms of an extraordinary experience, it may be argued that the sexual union explicitly portrayed in *Govinda* is equivalent to the dream in *Layla*. In several religious traditions of the world, mysticism has turned to human sexual images and metaphors to convey symbolically the connection with the Divine. In this respect, however, the depiction in *Govinda* is both real and symbolic. However, the forms of expression utilized in conveying this connection are appropriate for the purpose of establishing that the celestial vision and the sexual encounter are equivalent experiences, totally different as they may be in appearance.

One prominent point of correspondence deals with "sight." The dream or vision involves seeing and perception at a higher level of reality just as does the sexual encounter. In fact, the notion of sight, dwelt upon a great deal in the closing episode, lends itself readily to this idea.[8] The effect of Radha's "look" and the role of the "glance" is of particular interest in this regard. The Hindu notion of *darshan*, involving vision, applies to any aesthetic or artistic experience. But in this case it also involves mental and auditive perceptions. Krishna is described as "a slave bought with Sri's flashing glance," illustrating the exceptional nature of the "glance." The expression, implying that the feminine, darting look seldom fails to hit its mark, seems to encapsulate woman at her most artful, and thus most powerful. On the part of Radha, the effect of seeing Krishna is (XI:23):

> Her restless eyes were on Govinda
> With mixed alarm and bliss
> As she entered his place....

Thus the "meeting" of eyes may be considered as part of the "foreplay," which sets the tone for the bodily encounter of the lovers. In Hindu thought, the eye expresses a myriad of symbolic meanings. Particularly, there is a curious link between feminine sexual power and the power of seeing (Sahi 1980, 176):

> We find that in the sex-play between feminine nature (*prakrti*) and masculine (*purusa*) the play of eyes is essential. Repeatedly in Hindu love poetry the meeting of the eyes is spoken of as a sort of sexual contact. Thus the downcast eyes of the woman stress the form of the *yoni*, while the open eyes of the man represents the *lingam*.[9]

In folklore, the eye has a magical correspondence with the sun in its power to burn or pierce what it gazes at (Sahi 1980, 178). In this context, the relation between the eye and the sun represents "a natural attraction between corresponding forms. An eye is attracted to another eye" (Sahi 1980, 178). Besides (Sahi 1980, 178):

[8] Using the MonoConc Program, a concordance of words related to "see" was generated. There is a high ratio of occurrences. In about 4 pages of the ending, there is a total of 27 occurrences. The words included are "see," "eyes," and "glance," and their variants and inflections.

[9] The italicized terms refer to the female and male genitals respectively.

> The eye represents evolved consciousness, emergence ... the dividing power in man to distinguish vision through division, and this power is absorbed back into the unitive experience of being.

Thus, the moments of eye contact between the lovers proceed to have the ultimate, desired effect. The unitive experience referred to in the above quotation may be directly illustrated in this regard. The following verse in relation to sight is pregnant with undertones of union, and correlation (XII:1):

> Seeing the mood in Radha's heart,
> Hari spoke to his love;
> Her eyes were fixed
> On his bed of buds and tender shoots.

At one level, it is possible to identify correlates. One pair is that of sight, related to Krishna's "seeing" and "her eyes." Another pair is of response, related to action. Being Divine, Krishna can "see" "the mood in Radha's heart." Incidentally, this expression echoes the Koranic verse, "and We know what his soul whispers within him, and We are nearer to him than the jugular vein" (50:16). The human complement to the Divine seeing is Radha's "eyes," "fixed on his bed of buds and tender shoots."

At a deeper level, "sight" is instrumental to change. At the moment of sight, "Hari spoke" whereas all this time he did not. Furthermore, the words in reference to Radha, "Your tender body is flowering" (XI:16), speak of the change: the spiritual bud has blossomed. Thus sight constitutes a dynamic force in the transformational process of Radha, taking her beyond her physical self to "see" the Reality of Krishna's "intimate world." This precise notion is suggested by the verse (XI:32):

> Her eyes transgressed their bounds,
> Straining to reach beyond her ears,
> They fell on him with trembling pupils.
> When Radha's eyes met her lover,
> Heavy tears of joy
> Fell like streaming sweat.

In this respect, it may be said that both the sight and the experience of Radha "reach beyond" and "transgress" the ordinary level of human existence. The "joy" in this example, and the "bliss" in a previous one, both resulting from "sight," suggest that Radha has arrived at the level of *Sat-Chit-Ananda*, Truth-Consciousness-Bliss. The sexual consummation in reunion may thus be understood in this context. As Jayadeva sings: "Worship Hari in your heart and consummate his favor!"

Apart from "sight" in relation to the characters, there are various other elements confirming a correspondence between the texts in this regard. One relates to the role and personality of the bard or poet, or the "seer" in traditional culture. The character of Zayd in *Layla* was amply demonstrated to be extraordinary in this respect. Again, an equivalence may be drawn in *Govinda* with the participation of Jayadeva in the encounter of reunion. The expressions of the active participation of Jayadeva in the prelude are cast in the same vein, in the reunion. The following verse occurs as part of the aftermath, or "after-play" of sexual union (XII:19):

> Make your heart sympathetic to Jayadeva's splendid speech!
> Recalling Hari's feet is elixir against fevers of this dark time.
> She told the joyful Yadu hero, playing to delight her heart.

On the possibility of a dual reference to "Jayadeva," two interpretations have been given (Miller 1984, 23). The first is that it refers to Krishna, since in the literal sense, *jaya* means "victory" or "triumph," and *deva*, "the shining one," refers to God. The epithet occurs in this context elsewhere in a chant as "Triumph, God of Triumph, Hari!" (I:17). The second interpretation is that it refers to the author of *Govinda*. In this reference, the poet assumes tremendous importance. Firstly, his name and thus, participation, is implicitly inscribed into the climax of the text. Secondly, this importance is explicitly spelt out in the lines. They convey that the poet is instrumental in effecting a pliancy in the heart of the lover.

Expressions of the condition of pliancy abound elsewhere. For example in the following expressions,

> Your tender body is flowering. (XI:16)

Let my place be ravaged by your tender feet! (XII:2)

"tender" is used in the sense of fragile, and needing protection. Yet, concurrently there is a developmental or progressive aspect in these references, as if implying that the tender quality is the path to both "flowering" and "ravaging." The flowering of the spiritual potentialities ravages and naughts the earthly, human needs. And this is echoed in the poignant, tender plea of Krishna (X:4):,

Be yielding to me forever,
My heart fervently pleads!

Krishna, the Supreme Teacher, himself demonstrates this important quality of "yielding" and surrender for the spiritual traveler. As mentioned before, it is a prerequisite of reaching the spiritual destination.

Another illustration of equivalence in expression is that in the vision *Layla*, the love relation is described as an affair of the heart, entailing a purification and "polish" of the heart. In this respect, so too does *Govinda*. Parts of a concluding verse of *Govinda* relating to "vision" once again confirm a correspondence (XII:21):

His musical skill, his meditation on Vishnu,
His vision of reality in the erotic mood,
His graceful play in these poems,
All show that master-poet Jayadeva's soul
Is in perfect tune with Krishna,
Let blissful men of wisdom purify the world
By singing his Gitagovinda.

Here again, as in the prelude, the hyperbolic and anagogic elements of the poet's role are present. Particularly, in pointing out the power of "His musical skill" and "graceful play in these poems," the poet implies that his song can lift the veil of mystery concealing the connection between sight and "vision," "erotic" and mystic, "reality" and Reality, human and Divine. In other words, the sexual encounter is spiritualized and Radha is divinized. As explained earlier, this is possible in the Hindu context where the material and the spirit are not dichotomized. Accordingly, in *Govinda*, the story deals with a humanized *avatar* and a divinized human being. In this regard, the poet's role in the verse is particularized as that of the mystic-seer.

Based on the above discussion, the role of Jayadeva may be seen as equivalent to that of Zayd in *Layla* in many respects. Both Jayadeva and Zayd are witnesses to the reunion of the lovers, and to the transmission of knowledge. Just as the angel reveals the vision of reunion to Zayd, Jayadeva's "skill," etc. attains the "vision of reality." Thus Jayadeva assumes the role of seer in much the same context as that ascribed to the saint, Zayd. Whereas Zayd's vision is associated with the *alam al-mithal*, Jayadeva's "meditation on Vishnu" associates him with the spiritual sky, *devaloka*, literally "realm of the gods," and ultimately the supreme realm, *Brahmaloka*. Being "in perfect tune with Krishna," his "soul" can reach the transcendent world of Brahman to which "blissful men of wisdom" can go, "by singing his Gitagovinda." Thus, although Jayadeva sets the final encounter in the material world he conveys that to all intents and purposes the material world is a shadow or reflection of the spiritual world and its Divine archetypes. Furthermore, in the context of its primordial setting, the encounter is entirely natural, *sahaja*, which is the original, primordial state of man. In this connection, it is interesting to note that, similar to Jayadeva's exhortation in *Govinda*, "Let blissful men of wisdom *purify* the world," it is narrated in *Layla* that with the death of Majnun, there were "strangers of *pure* heart mourning the lovers." The lovers are in different circumstances in the individual texts, the former, in life and this world, and the latter in death and "the world above." Yet both involve purification of the heart by man, effected through undying Love.

A further point of correspondence relates to the sensual imagery in *Layla*, presented in relation to the portrayal of reunion. The visual images, relating to sight and light have been dealt with at length. It is interesting to find that, besides being similar in form, the images of the sense are also similar in nature. For example, the following verses, quoted here in the sequence they appear in *Govinda*, share the attributes of repetition and recurrence, through chants (italicized), and through varied erotic imagery and symbolism (highlighted). Furthermore, the expressions share the association with the various senses and levels of being, which have been pointed out in relation to the discussion on *Layla*:

Verse	sense	level
Revel in **wild** luxury on the sweet thicket floor! Your laughing face begs **ardently** for his love. *Radha, enter Madhava's* ***intimate*** *world!*	taste tactile	emotional
Revel in a thick **bed** of red petals plucked as offerings! Strings of pearls are **quivering** on your **rounded breasts**. *Radha, enter Madhava's* ***intimate*** *world!*	visual tactile	physical
Revel in a bright retreat **heaped** with flowers! Your tender **body** is flowering. *Radha, enter Madhava's* ***intimate*** *world!*	visual	physical
Revel in the fragrant chill of **gusting sandal-forest** winds! Your **sensual** singing captures the mood. *Radha, enter Madhava's* ***intimate*** *world!*	olfactory auditory	physical emotional
Revel where swarming bees **drunk** on honey buzz soft tones! Your emotion is rich in the **mood of love**. *Radha, enter Madhava's* ***intimate*** *world!*	auditory	emotional

Figure 6.1: Relation of Expressions to Human Senses and Levels

The verses do not need individual explication as they are self-evident in the case of correspondence. However, particular mention may be made concerning one phrase that combines duplication with eroticism, "gusting sandal-forest" (XI:17). This expression is pregnant with poetic and mystic possibilities. Although the word "gusting" is generally associated with wind, another sense is of "sudden bursts of feeling or action" (NSOED). In this sense, the word may be associated with the discharge of semen. Next, "sandal" refers to the aromatic sandalwood, which has aphrodisiac properties, and in the Indian tradition is associated with sexual stimulation. Besides, the association of the forest with eroticism is well established. Finally, in the expression, reference is made not just to a piece of sandalwood, but an entire "forest" of it. Thus the phrase is brimming with the quality of bounty.

The foregoing explanation of this phrase deals with literary technique and symbolism. However, in examining further the sentence in which the phrase occurs, the mystical aspect may be revealed. The words "Revel in the fragrant chill of gusting sandal-forest winds!" express firstly, the notion of "revel," relating it to the celebration of the joy of reunion. Secondly, "fragrance" evokes a heavenly aura, as perfume is a well-known mystical symbol. Thirdly, the undertones of sexual congress in the phrase "gusting sandal-forest" relate to union with the divine. Finally, the "winds" are associated with the breath of God, in the context pointed out in chapter 5. Thus at a deeper level, the quantity, suggested by abundance at the literal level, expresses the union in qualitatively elevated terms.

Contextualized within the religious, mythical, and poetical framework, and raised to the level of a mystical connection, it may be seen that the portrayal of reunion corresponds in the individual texts on several points. And in the search for an equivalent of the dream of Zayd, the physical encounter of sexual union in *Govinda* may—seen in the above light—be equated to the metaphysical encounter of celestial vision in *Layla*.

Core and Center: The Original State

Two different elements which crown the ending episodes of *Layla* and *Govinda* are referred to as "core" and "center." They will be discussed in reference to a particular extract from each of the texts. Thus "core" refers to an extract or passage of verse being considered, and "center" to a particular expression in each of the extracts. The analogy of the circle and the point may be applied to describe the difference between the core the center. Both constitute elements of Return to the "original state." The extract in *Layla* is as follows (LIV:176):

> These two friends are one, eternal companions. He is Majnun, the king of the world in right action. And she is Layla, the moon among idols in compassion. In the world, like unpierced rubies they treasured their fidelity affectionately, but found no rest and could not attain their heart's desire. Here they suffer grief no more. So it will be until eternity....

There are several points in this extract worth observing. The first is that the lovers "are one," as anticipated in the prelude. This is the metaphor of the drop merged into the ocean. Secondly, in this "oneness" is "right action" on the one hand, and "compassion" on the other. That is, there are attributes of mutuality and complementarity in the reunion. Thirdly, there is movement from "the world" to "here," which is from a lower to a higher existential plane. Fourthly, there is contrast between "the world," in which the lovers had "no rest" and "could not attain" what they desired, and "here," where "grief (is) no more." Finally, this state just described "will be until eternity." This last expression is the point of the reunion which is perfect, eternal, and infinite, the point of no return.

These observations constitute an explicit confirmation that in *Layla*, Majnun has proceeded, or returned, to the original state in the Garden of Paradise. However, it should be noted that there is a specific difference between this depiction of re-union, and the depiction of union discussed in Chapter 3. Whereas the "union" was riddled with undertones and forebodings of "separation," the "reunion" has no such reference or association. Therefore, the state of "oneness" that Majnun returns to, is seen as the ultimate or supreme station of the Sufi.

It is interesting to find out if there is an equivalent crowning episode in *Govinda*. In this regard, the verse on the sexual union of Radha and Krishna may be regarded as the "core" of the reunion. The following lines of the verse in question substantiate this observation (XII:10):

> Displaying her passion
> In loveplay as the battle began,
> She launched a bold offensive
> Above him
> And triumphed over her lover.
> Her hips were still,
> Her vine-like arm was slack,
> Her chest was heaving,
> Her eyes were closed.
> Why does a mood of manly force
> Succeed for women in love?

In these lines, firstly, the act of sexual congress is regarded as the ultimate act of physical union. Thus it constitutes a representation of the "mystic embrace" or *Unio Mystica*. In the mystical perspective, the act of procreation is symbolic in emulating the original act of Creation. Thus the lovers in *Govinda* are one in terms of body, or substance, whereas the lovers in *Layla* are "one" in terms of spirit, or essence. The depiction in the former is corporeal, whereas in the latter it is incorporeal. However, both convey the same notion of "one-ness," or merging. Secondly, the nature of the interaction between the lovers in *Layla* appears to differ for the present case. Whereas in *Layla* there is mutuality and complementarity, it appears that the union in *Govinda* is depicted in metaphors of opposition and confrontation. This is conveyed by images of war, in reference to Radha's "battle," her "bold offensive," her "triumph," and "manly force" over Krishna. However, what is also apparent about "battle" is that it is in fact a "battle" of love, and "loveplay." In this sense, beyond the literal level of interpretation, it corresponds to the principle of complementarity and mutuality expressed in *Layla*.

The element of movement from one state to another, which is the third point noted in *Layla*, is also present in *Govinda*. From the passive Radha, hesitating at the entrance of the thicket, the move is in becoming the active party, "displaying her passion" and taking the lead or initiative "above him" in the "battle" of love. The movement may also be seen in terms of change, from the employment of feminine guile to an assumption of "manly force" in the masculine role. The spiritual significance of the expressions "succeed" and "triumph" is that Radha moves from *kacca* or raw to *pakka* or ripe. The spiritual novice ultimately becomes the accomplished expert, and the transformation is complete.

The contrast pointed out in *Layla* in relation to "the world" and "here" has an equivalent in *Govinda*. However, the contrast is not between worlds in *Govinda*, but between Radha's active state and state of stillness, conveyed in the expressions, "her hips were still, Her ... arm was slack.... Her eyes were closed." Moreover, the contrast between "grief" and "eternity" in *Layla* is matched by the contrast between "bold offensive" and "stillness" in *Govinda*. On these points, the state of "eternity" of the lovers is considered as the "center" in *Layla*, whereas the "stillness" represents the "center" in *Govinda*. The word "still" is possibly etymologically related with the Sanskrit root *sthir*, meaning "situated" and "steady." Furthermore, the Sanskrit phoneme *sthi-* represents the ultimate goal in Hindu mysticism, expressed by the notions of *sthira buddhi* and *brahmani sthitah*. The former term refers to the person of steadied wisdom, or intellect, which is comparable to attaining *Brahman*-hood (Sivaraman 1995, 435). The latter, meaning "established in the Transcendent," refers to the Perfected Man. Thus Radha's stillness in the bliss of sexual union with Krishna goes beyond mere sense pleasure, essentially corresponding to Supreme Bliss, or the attainment of the Bliss of Brahman. Thus, the expressions of *Govinda* quoted above echo confirmation of the verse of *brahmani sthitah* in the *Bhagavad Gita* (V:20), which means:

> Established in Brahman, with firm understanding and with no delusion, the knower of Brahman rejoices not, getting what is pleasant and grieves not, getting what is unpleasant.

In this understanding, beyond the phenomenal reality of the active, masculine quality of Radha's "bold offensive," "triumph," and "manly force," lies the noumenal Reality of Perfected Man, the Supreme Man, the Cosmic Person, *Purushottama* (Sivaraman 1995, 433),[10]

> pure sentience, changeless, eternal, and omniscient, nonactive recipient or enjoyer ... pervading the world with only a fourth of himself, whereas the remaining three parts transcend to a region beyond.

In this context, Radha is essentially the same Supreme Soul that Krishna manifests in his Universal Form. Thus she is more than "man" and "human," and what appears to be a depiction of the corporeal, sensual, and sexual self is essentially the incorporeal, super-sensory, and spiritual Self.

A final point of equivalence between the expression of the "center" in the individual texts concludes the comparison. It is noticeable that there is no speech or any form of articulation by the lovers in either *Layla* or *Govinda*. There is articulation before, and in the case of *Govinda*, after, this point, but during this episode none of the characters speak. Instead, at the center, the element of "eternity" predominates in *Layla*, and the element of "stillness" predominates in *Govinda*. Both these elements have an underlying similarity in that they evoke the idea of no movement or change. At the outward level, the former encompasses the notion of time standing still, whereas in

10 Combined form of *purusha*, "male," and *uttama*, "supreme."

the latter, it denotes physical stillness. Thus, the absence of speech and the presence of timelessness, common motifs of mystical union, are consistent with the notion of the "Center." The phenomenon of silence is indicative of a pivotal, and universal, aspect of the mystic experience, namely, its ineffability. In the Traditionalist perspective, this experience is expressed as one that "cannot be situated in time or space" (Schuon 1984, 21), and "defies visualization or even consistent description" (Smith 1984, xiii). The lover is eloquent in quest of love, but in the Presence of Love becomes silent. Another aspect of the silence is that, only in total and absolute stillness can the silent, inner voice be heard. This voice is none other than the voice of the Self.

This chapter, dealing with "the end," which involves the transition of the lover to the ultimate stage of mystical union, has demonstrated the wheel of spiritual progress come full circle. It has also shown that "progress" is none other than "return" to the Garden of Love, and subsistence in the immediate presence of the Gardener. The return is like an arc curving backwards to its point of departure. The fundamental nature of the account of the reunion of Layla and Majnun in the "fabled garden" in Zayd's account of his "dream," is of much the same essence as Jayadeva's account of Radha "seeing" Krishna in the thicket in "Brindaban forest." The difference lies in the modes of portrayal and levels of reality of each case. The former, being a dream encounter, belongs to the non-physical reality, whereas the latter is a physical encounter. The similarity between them originates from an esoteric understanding, and the inherent metaphysical aspects in both. In each portrayal, the lover has undergone the ultimate alchemy, from the existential plane of the body to that of the soul, from the human to the divine, from the circle to the center. The course of this change has been dealt with in the context of various elements, namely, the prelude, the reunion, the core, and the center, although this classification is characteristically a fluid one.

The Wheels Come Full Circle

The ending of the *affaire de couer*, or affair of the heart, when related to developments in the period of separation, lends itself to the motif of the *mandala*. The elements discussed in relation to the episode of "the end" in the narrative correspond roughly to Patanjali's philosophical system of Yoga. As has been explained previously, this system relates to the different dimensions and levels of being, involving the physical body (*sarira*), the senses (*indriya*), the mind (*manas*), the intellect (*citta*), and the Self (*atman*). These levels are in consonance with to the seven *cakras* of the human microcosm, conceived as centers or spheres, each representing a higher or deeper point in the centripetal progress to the point of identification with the Center. Beginning with the stage of separation from the Beloved, these mandalic levels of spiritual development correspond to different points of the ending in both *Layla* and *Govinda.* This may be represented diagrammatically as follows:

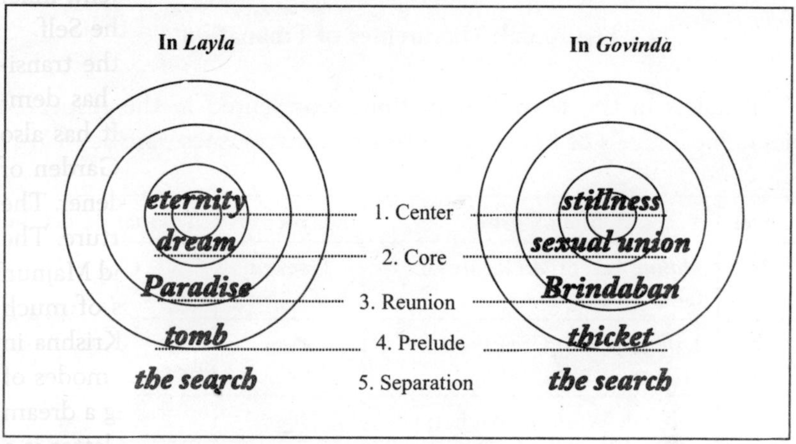

Figure 6.2: Levels of Spiritual Development

The above representation of the textual depiction of the ending, which has been mentioned above in the Hindu context of the *mandala*, may be also seen in light of the Islamic doctrine of Divine emanation. According to the Sufi understanding, Divine emanation is a two-fold process, the intelligible and the sensible (Bakhtiar 1976, 13). The universe or macrocosm, and the human being or microcosm, contain hierarchically both the intelligible and sensible existences. These levels of existence are reflections of the Archetypes, which are possibilities contained within the Absolute or Divine Essence, and actualized in the sensible, phenomenal world (Bakhtiar 1976, 13). In this context, the textual depiction corresponds essentially with the hierarchy of emanation. The following representation has been adapted from Bakhtiar (1976, 13), to illustrate this correspondence:

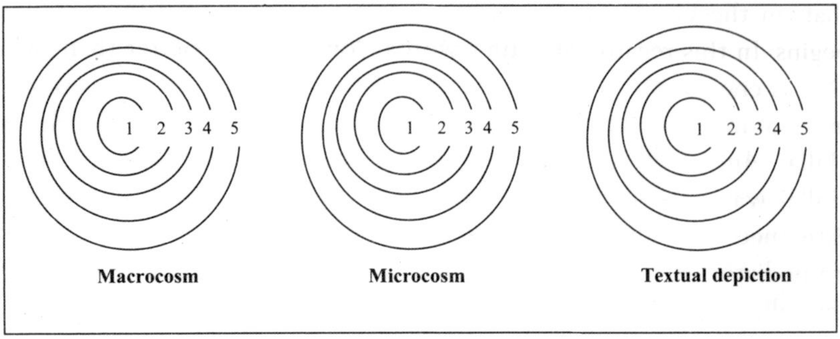

Figure 6.3: Hierarchies of Emanation

Parallels in the textual depiction, represented in the respective hierarchical levels of being or centers of consciousness, are as follows:

Level	Macrocosm	Microcosm	Textual depiction
1.	*Hahut*: Essential Nature of God	Essence	Center
2.	*Lahut*: Divine Creative Nature	Spirit	Core
3.	*Jabarut*: World of Archetypes	Heart	Reunion
4.	*Malakut*: World of Symbols	Soul	Prelude
5.	*Nasut*: Human Nature	Body	Journey

Figure 6.4: Hierarchies of Being

At the level of the macrocosm, "the Garden of Eden is both center and summit of the earthly state" (Lings 1981, 50). From the textual depiction, the "Center" is analogous to the "Essence" of the microcosm.

Where Gardens Congregate

Based on the foregoing discussion and comparison, it may be concluded that in the episodes of the ending of *Layla* and *Govinda*, outward and textual differences and divergences in the individual depictions increasingly lead to equivalences and correspondences at the inward level of understanding. Thus, one finds ample evidence that, in the Garden of Love, the saga of *two* ends, and that of *One* begins. In this regard, Majnun's words, "one name is better than two. One is enough for both" (XXXIV:104), reflect the Sufi secret of the unity of man and God. They echo the famous *shathiyyat* of Mansur al-Hallaj, *Ana'l-Haqq*, "I am the Absolute Truth" (Schimmel 1982, 30). Hallaj was put to death for the apparently heretical ferment of this utterance, but in fact the words point out, as Majnun's words do, his immediate consciousness of the complete annihilation and negation of the self, and the subsistence in, and affirmation of, none but God. An identical phenomenon, reflecting the Hindu mystical utterance, *aham Brahmasmi*, "I am Brahman," is mirrored in Radha's words, "I am Krishna, Madhu's foe" (VI:5). In both cases, the drop, in surrendering its identity, becomes the ocean. This formulation has been expressed by mystics of both traditions. Abu Bakr Siraj ad-Din, a contemporary Sufi Master and eminent Traditionalist, says that "Universal Man realizes eternally in the Truth that he is nothing and yet that He is Everything" (1982, 19). The words of Swami Vivekananda, 20th century Bhakta and carrier of the message of ancient Vedanta to the modern world, echoes this refrain: "When thou hast naught, thou hast all. When thou art naught, thou art all" (1926, 294).

In no small measure, the popular forms of reference to the archetypal lovers in their individual spiritual traditions attest to the formulation of oneness. In the Sufi tradition, the lovers are remembered as "Layla Majnun," rather than "Layla *and* Majnun." Whereas in the Bhakti tradition, the myths of the lovers in Brindaban are always referred to as the "Radha Krishna myths," and not the "Radha *and* Krishna myths." In fact, these forms of reference reflect the extent of integration and assimilation of the two into one.[11] These forms of reference have, through the ages, and in diverse cultures, come to be synonymous with Love, and their mention is immediately associated with the fragrance of the Garden of Love.

In this chapter on the ending in the individual texts, the exposition has dealt with the depiction of ultimate union, or the Return. The high degree of correspondence in literary phenomena that has emerged

[11] Hindu names/surnames like Radhakrishnan and Lakshminarayan thus epitomize the archetypal integration, and the complete balance and harmony of opposites, male and female, human and divine, etc.

suggests parallels at the esoteric level between the two different mystico-religious traditions. The close correspondence of the ending in the texts is not astonishing in light of the Traditionalist perspective of the "transcendent unity of religions" formulated by Schuon. The nearer one gets to the Center the less are the differences. This perspective does not at all point to a sentimental idea of humanity as an "amorphous agglomerate," in which the world's peoples are only "superficially" and "accidentally" different (Oldmeadow 2000, 69). Rather, humankind is "divided into several distinct branches, each with its own peculiar traits, which determine its receptivities to truth and shape its apprehensions of reality" (Oldmeadow 2000, 69). This idea has been expressed by Schuon as (1969, 66-67):

> Essentially all religions include decisive truths and mediators and miracles, but the disposition of these elements, the play of their proportions, can vary according to the conditions of the revelation and of the human receptacles of the revelation.

In closing, it is relevant to recall here the cyclic or cosmic relationship of Hinduism with Islam. The *sanatana dharma* of Hinduism, as a Primordial Tradition, appears to have correspondences with the *al-hikmah al-khalidah* of Islam, as the Last Revelation (Schuon 1984, 89). The etymological implications of the Latin word *religare*, "to bind," and its English derivative "religion" are significant in this context. In verbal variants, the English prefix "re-" denotes repetition, often with the added sense of a return to an earlier state (NSOED), e.g. "re-build" or "re-establish." Furthermore, the root "lig-" refers to a bond or something that holds two things together, as seen in derivative nouns like "ligament" and "ligation" (NSOED). Thus, more than being a belief system or pious attachment, the word "religion" is primarily a bind that obtains renewal or return, and further, that holds man to God (NSOED). This sense of the English word is in remarkable consonance with the Sanskrit word *dharma*, in the term *sanatana dharma*, which is the equivalent of "Hinduism" in English. The accord lies in the root *dhar* which means to bind or hold to something that returns harmony or union with the Supreme Brahman (Sriddharanandaji 1997). These words in different languages, referring to the same end, are in concordance with the Traditional view of religion. In this context, it may be said that that the Persian gardens of *Layla* and the

Indian forests of *Govinda* converge and congregate at the "heart" of the "gardens of love." As Sri Ramakrishna, the 19th century Bengali mystic-Bhakta *par excellence* sang in ecstasy, *mann karo na desa-desi*, "The heart speaks not of nation, nor nationality."

CHAPTER SEVEN

THE GARDEN UNVEILED: PRESERVING DIVERSITY, OBSERVING UNITY

> You tell us different names,
> but it is He whom you mean
>
> —A. Schimmel

In the contemporary context, the teachings of a tradition are considered authentic and authoritative only if they are verified by, and cited from, recorded or historical texts. However, it should be remembered that tradition also represents ahistorical realities because it originates from beyond recorded history. Thus, a great part of mystical teaching is oral and even anonymous (Abu Bakr 1988, 9). Sourced from living traditions, their truths have been passed down from Master to disciple, through generations (Abu Bakr 1988, 9). The same principle of transmission applies to traditional art, including literature. In the case of *Layla* and *Govinda*, in the Persian tradition, thousands of *ghazels* are credited to Nizami and the legend of Layla-Majnun (Gelpke 1997, xi); similarly Jayadeva's songs and verses on the Radha-Krishna myths have been a source of religious inspiration in the Indian tradition (Miller 1984, ix).

While the traditional view adheres to the power of the spoken word, in the modern context, power has transferred to the written or printed word. Whatever the case, words possess inherent meaning and power. Therefore, this work has been directed at unveiling the power inherent in "the words" of the English translations of *Layla* and *Govinda*. Regardless of whether they are reductions or amplifications, or are removed in time and space from their original milieus, it is possible to discover what spiritual truths lie beyond literary expression. This objective has been enabled by a hermeneutical approach in the search for "orginary actions and their purposes" (Md. Salleh 1995, 11).

Correspondence and Convergence

This work has presented something not attempted before, namely a comparative study of symbolic expressions of the spiritual quest of the Sufi and the Bhakta, as understood in *Layla* and *Govinda*. This has been done with the basic objective of discovering equivalences of expression at both the literary and the mystical levels. Beyond the comparison of the substance of the texts, the nature and extent of the similarities and differences have never been inquired into before. The conclusions which have emerged in this regard are summed up in the ensuing paragraphs.

Firstly, there is equivalence and correspondence at the level of literary phenomena, between the texts in question. This correspondence involves both form and substance. Form includes language, through which both works yield "jewels" of great beauty and profundity, each from its own distinct "garden." The diction employed by both poets is largely primordial, elemental, and enigmatic, and thus has a mythical and archetypal quality. They are diverse forms, yet share symbolic significance. Tracing the stories of love through its treatment in two different literary traditions of the same period offers insights into the common literary heritage of these traditions. Besides, in comparing elements pertaining to the depiction of human love, it is found that both *Layla* and *Govinda* adhere faithfully to their respective underlying socio-cultural norms and literary conventions. In this respect, each represents its own tradition and spatio-temporal milieu, while at the same time exhibiting common values.

Secondly, apart from literary phenomena, there is a relatively high degree of correspondence in the mystical significance of expressions. The inherent spiritual dimensions and essential truths that are veiled and concealed by literary expression have been unveiled and revealed in the light of underlying spiritual principles of two different mystico-religious traditions of the 12th century. That is, *Layla* has been understood on the basis of the Islamic-Sufi tradition of Persia, and *Govinda* according to the Hindu-Bhakti tradition of India. The stories also offer insights into several ways in which two different mystical traditions have sought to define and interpret reality. Common motifs in the love stories allow an understanding of them as parables of the spiritual journey. Some motifs which have been dealt with, such as being lost and found again, the overwhelming beauty of characters and setting, of pain and betrayal, of dream and vision, seem to be equally important in both the mystical traditions from the way they recur, unify the story, and illustrate the station of the spiritual wayfarer (Stokes 2004). In relation to the principle of cyclical progression, both present an account of principles of "ascension" which are at the same time in consonance with principles of "descension." In the context of such correspondences, the texts are seen as reaffirmations of perennial principles.

Finally, there is an interesting convergence that emerges from consideration of textual elements, *vis-a-vis* meta-textual elements. The phenomenal likenesses in the texts refer to "textual elements" while the diversity in origin and religious traditions refer to the "meta-textual elements" in them. The convergence may be illustrated axiomatically as follows:

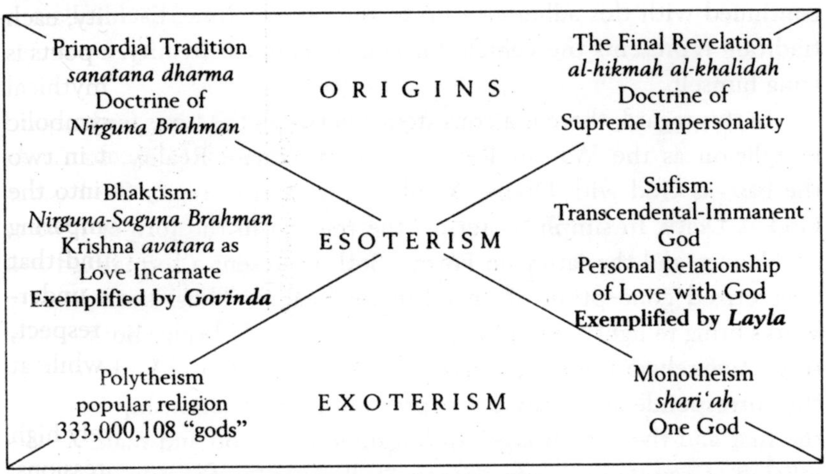

Figure 7.1: Convergence of Textual and Meta-textual Elements

In the diagram, the distinction occurs at the level of origins and the exoteric dimension, which has a diversity of forms, or belief and practice. While the chronological and geographical origins are diverse, an intersection occurs at the level of mysticism. This esoteric dimension shares a unity of principles, as propounded by the Traditionalists. In Schuon's words, "The Divinity manifests Its Personal aspect through each particular Revelation and its supreme Impersonality through the diversity of the forms of Its Word" (1984, 26), whereas Lings expresses this as, "There is only one water, but no two Revelations are outwardly the same" (1981, 12). Both *Layla* and *Govinda* attest to this inward unity and outward diversity.

In the context of the above understanding, the last finding, which is tangential to the objective of the research, is the textual indication of the emphasis of mysticism upon formal religion. As Schuon has fittingly remarked, "spiritual realization is inconceivable ... (unless) one is in conformity with the religious ambiance of the spiritual means in question" (1984, 60n). In this sense, the texts tend to confirm that mysticism is *not* "free from the shackles of religion," as has often been erroneously expressed about mysticism (Lings 1981, 15). Rather, both tacitly convey a deeply ingrained and strict adherence to revealed Truths incorporating methods, doctrines, and disciplines. In this sense, both Hinduism and Islam are "living" traditions which have continued with this adherence up to the present time. Each religious tradition represents the vehicle for man to contact divinity, by divinizing himself.

In this regard, there is a consistency between the texts with regard to religion as the Way of Return to an Ultimate Reality. In *Layla* the basis is God with Divine Attributes, and in *Govinda* the basis is God as Deity. In simplistic terms, the religion in the former centers on Names, and the latter on Forms. Both represent a formalized and concretized conception of an Ultimate Reality. Thus, both literary works bring to light the bridge to ultimate Union, a bridge built on the respective religious foundations of Hinduism and Islam.[1] Embedded in the correspondence of textual expression is the relationship between the first and the last "bridge" or "ligament" of God and man. As the religion of *sanatana dharma* comes "full circle" in the religion of the last Revelation, the Primordial Tradition returns to its pristine perfection.

[1] This phenomenon about traditional literary expression may be accounted for by the symbiotic connection of art, religion, and the sacred language. As elucidated by Braginsky (1993, 74-76): "The central position and the role of the structuring principle both in the ancient and in medieval ideological milieu belonged to religion.... The religious Canon not only determined the principal elements of ... literatures, it also provided the latter which (*sic*) a means of expression—the language of the Canon.... The language itself was often considered sacred, which served to confirm its authority."

The Way Forward

On the basis of the findings derived, the present study suggests avenues for further study in various directions. Though originating from medieval times and exhibiting a traditional worldview, these literary works have stood the test of time in their applicability and pertinence. In this light, the present study suggests that other comparative studies on antiquated works may be useful in uncovering the treasure inherent in the wisdom of the past. The current tide of accepting all that is modern and technology-based, and rejecting as obsolete all that is ancient and spiritual, may be stemmed by a revitalized interest and awareness that has almost vanished, of man's true nature and origins. There is a huge potential for reclaiming this awareness through the discovery of traditions in relation to their artistic expression. The ancient epics, legends, and myths like the Indian *Ramayana* and *Mahabharata* and the Greek *Odyssey* and *Iliad*, each a treasure trove of its own cultural tradition, are possible pairs for comparison. Besides, works of great writers from the East and the West like Basho and Blake, Kalidasa and Shakespeare, may be studied and compared in terms of potential mystical content. Especially in the context of current global conflicts of identity based on religion, an awareness of "the other" through the study of literary expression would bring to light the bedrock of shared values and principles of diverse peoples of the world.

The present study has pointed out equivalences and correspondences in literary and mystical symbolism in a horizontal manner. This means that the exposition of the "lover" has been of a generalized nature, covering of a wide variety of symbols. Many specific and significant features and phenomena in the texts remain to be studied in a vertical manner, or in depth. These are, to name a few, the role of the "friend" or "companion," the connection with wild animals or feral nature, the spiritual symbolism of elemental motifs like earth, water, and light, or the diverse nature of reciprocation of the "beloved." These phenomena offer infinite, challenging, and fascinating prospects for study and comparison as spiritual symbols. Ultimately, the perfume of words in symbolic gardens draws one to that which lies beyond words, the That which should not be forsaken.

Epilogue

There is no love
but for the First Beloved
You tell us different names,
But it is He whom you mean

Annemarie Schimmel, *Nightingales Under the Snow*, 1997

GLOSSARY OF PERSIAN/ARABIC AND SANSKRIT TERMS

Persian/Arabic Terms

'alam al-mithal: the world of similitudes and symbols. 167, 176
'aql: the intellect. 49,108
baqa': subsistence in the Divine. 49, 127, 134, 136
batin: inward, esoteric, essence. 59, 138, 160
darwish: one who is at the door to Enlightenment. 133
dhikr: measured recitation of Divine Names. 133, 140
fana': annihilation of the self. 49, 66, 127, 134, 136
faqr: spiritual poverty. 114
firdaus: paradise. 24, 25, 44, 118
ghazel: Persian ode, love poem. 189
hadith: saying of the Prophet. 33, 35, 39, 135, 158, 166
ishq: divine love. 42, 48, 84
jism: body, self. 48, 99
khirqa: long black coat worn by the dervish. 136
laila: night. 24, 25
Laylat al-qadr: the "Night of Power" or "Night of Descent," referring to the night of the revelation of the Koran. 169
Laylat al-mi'raj: the "Night of Ascent," when the Prophet was taken by the archangel Gabriel from Mecca to Jerusalem and from there ascended to the highest heaven and drew nigh to the Divine Presence Itself. 159
malaikat: angels. 38
mathnawi: rhymed poems, usually consisting of hundreds of lines, employed for heroic, romantic, or narrative verse. Also the name of Rumi's famous poetical work. 15, 17, 23, 25, 27, 98, 145, 168
nafs: soul. 108,
nafs al-hayawaniyyah: the animal soul; the negative or egocentric tendency of the soul. 108
nazira: artistic revision or response to earlier poetic works. 24
ney: reed flute. 133, 144, 145, 146, 147, 148
peshrev: musical prelude. 133
ruh: spirit. 48, 108

sama': spiritual concert of the dervish/Sufi. 133, 134, 135, 136, 138, 140, 141, 146
Shahadah: divinely revealed testification; Islamic credo. 36, 64, 66
shaykh: honorific form of address for Sufi spiritual master. 27, 54, 122, 133, 135
Shari'ah: the Divine Law which is rooted in the Koran and *Hadith*. 191
tawhid: oneness of God. 113
ta'wil: to cause to return to origin (spiritual hermeneutics). 9
zahir: outward, manifest. 59, 138, 159
zuhd: renunciation of attachments. 99

Sanskrit Terms
advaita vedanta: Hindu doctrine of non-duality.
amrita: nectar, immortality. 111
atma: spirit. 78, 108
avatara: divine descent (embodiment of divine attributes). 30, 36, 37, 38, 40, 62, 69, 70, 72, 73, 89, 90, 124, 141, 150, 164, 191
bhajan: devotional song. 17, 142
bhakta: devotee. 33, 37, 38, 40, 41, 48, 49, 59, 70, 72, 73, 75, 86, 99, 118, 123, 130, 142, 185, 187, 190
bhakti: selfless devotion. 5, 7, 8, 18, 19, 21, 22, 34, 39, 40, 41, 49, 60, 62, 68, 73, 91, 99, 114, 124, 125, 143, 144, 185, 190, 191
Brahman: the Absolute. 36, 37, 38, 39, 49, 57, 67, 69, 70, 72, 73, 123, 142, 164, 165, 176, 180, 181, 185, 186, 191,
brahmavidya: supreme science (of interpretation). 9
darshan(a): vision. 172
deva: "the shining one,"deity. 38, 174
dharma: a divinely ordained natural law, order, and harmony. 35, 37, 72, 89, 122, 124, 186, 191, 192
gopi: cowherdess. 32, 39, 51, 54, 66, 67, 68, 77, 78, 86, 140, 141, 142, 150, 151, 152, 153, 163
Goloka: heavenly realm. 45, 55, 57, 62, 118, 141
govinda: divine cowherd, epithet of Krishna. passim
guha: cave. 104
guru: spiritual guide. 56, 142
Istam: personal loving God. 143
japa(m): measured recitation of the *mantra*. 140
jiva/jivan: soul. 38, 39, 57, 108
jnana: Divine knowledge. 49

Kali-Yuga: the Dark Age. 62, 69, 124
kama: profane or worldly love. 40, 41, 42, 129
karpanya: spiritual poverty. 114
lila: Krishna's sport, dalliance with the *gopis*. 28, 32, 39, 141
madhu: honey, springtime. 70, 91, 152, 185
mantra: chant or incantation of Holy Names. 56, 57, 58, 140
maya: the veil of ignorance. 39, 49, 153, 154, 162
moksha: liberation (in death). 49, 129
mukti: liberation (in life). 49, 57, 129
nirguna Brahman: the unmanifest, transcendent, and attributeless aspect of *Brahman*. 36, 38, 191
prakrti: the feminine aspect of divinity. 38, 76, 172
prema: sacred or divine love. 40, 41, 42, 48, 68, 86, 129
purusha: the masculine aspect of divinity. 38, 62, 76, 78, 181
raga: musical mode for evoking certain emotions and responses. 17
ragakavya: drama customarily performed to the accompaniment of song, dance, and music. 15, 17
raslila/rasa krida: Krishna's circular love dance with the *gopis*. 141
rupam: form, outward aspect. 138, 140
saguna Brahman: manifest, immanent attributes of *Brahman*. 36, 38, 191
sahaja: the middle or perfected spiritual path. 40, 41, 176
sahajjiya: a spiritual aspirant who has attained the middle or perfected state. 40, 41
sahrdaya: participant or kindred spirit. 22, 44
sarira: body, self. 48, 99, 130, 183
shakti: feminine principle/energy. 38, 41
smrti: intuitive knowledge. 35
sruti: revealed knowledge. 35
swarupam: essence, inward significance. 138, 140
tyagi: renunciate. 99
Vaishnava: worshipper of Vishnu/Krishna. 30, 32, 37, 38, 39, 40, 41, 65, 68, 70, 86, 124, 141, 143, 150
vamsam: flute. 144
yoga: to yoke, to join, to unite. 40, 99, 113, 129, 162, 163, 165, 182

For a glossary of all key foreign words used in books published by World Wisdom, including metaphysical terms in English, consult: www.DictionaryofSpiritualTerms.org.
This on-line Dictionary of Spiritual Terms provides extensive definitions, examples and related terms in other languages.

BIBLIOGRAPHY

1. TEXTS

The Story of Layla and Majnun. Translated from the Persian *Leili o Majnun* of Nizami (twelfth century) and edited by Rudolf Gelpke. Final chapter translated from the Persian by Zia Inayat Khan and Omid Safi. Revised edition New Lebanon, New York: Omega Publications, 1997.

The Gitagovinda of Jayadeva: Love Song of the Dark Lord. Translated from the Sanskrit *Gitagovinda* of Jayadeva (twelfth century) and edited by Barbara Stoler Miller. UNESCO Collection of Representative Works. Indian Series. New Delhi: Motilal Banarsidass, 1984.

2. WORKS ON THE TEXTS

"Analysis and Comparison of Gita Govinda and Song of Solomon." http://216.254.55.131/viewpaper.asp?papernum=7185 (21 March 2000).

"Black Peacock - Gita-Govinda: Thus Arose the Love of Radha and Krishna." http://www.goloka.com/docs/gita_govinda/gita_govinda_01.html (20 July 1999).

Brians, Paul. "Study Guide for Nizami." http://wwwlwebivore.com/sites/Nizami_Study_Guide_for_Layl.html (7 October 2001).

Chatterji, Suniti Kumar. 1981. *Makers of Indian Literature: Jayadeva.* New Delhi: Sahitya Akademi.

"Dasavatara Stotra, Gita Govinda by Sri Jayadeva." http://home.att.net/~s-prasad/dasavatara.htm (5 April 2000).

"Gita Govinda, Govinda's Song." http://www.carthage.edu/~lochtefe/gitagovinda.html (21 March 2000).

"Layla and Majnun: The Classic Love Story of Persian Literature": http://www.traveltajikstan.com/ books/layla_majnun.html (28 March 2002).

"Layli and Madjnun in Persian Literature." http://www.art-arena.com/perlm.htm (26 July 1999).

Mukherjee, Hemanta et al. *Songs of "Kavi Jayadeva's Gitagovinda."* Music by Sunil Satpathy. Cassette Recording by Sight and Sound Pvt Ltd. Bombay, 1989.

Siegel, Lee. 1978. *Sacred and Profane Dimensions of Love in Indian Traditions as Exemplified in* The Gitagovinda of Jayadeva. Delhi: Oxford University Press.

"The Original Legend In Arabic Literature." http://www.art-arena.com/aralm.htm#top (26 July 1999).

Vatsyayan, Kapila. 2001. "The Gita Govinda Project." http://ignca.nic.in/gita.htm (20 August, 2001.)

3. REFERENCES

A Treasury of Traditional Wisdom. 1981. Presented by Whitall N. Perry. 2nd edition. Bedfont, Middlesex: Perennial Books.

Abu Bakr Siraj ad-Din. 1988. *The Book of Certainty: The Sufi Doctrine of Faith, Vision, and Gnosis.* Lahore: Suhail Academy.

Ali Ahmad. 1992. "Karya Naratif Sufi: *Mantiq al-Tair* —Satu Pengenalan Ringkas (Sufi Narrative Works: *Mantiq al-Tair*—A Short Introduction." In *Sastera Sufi* (Sufi Literature). Baharudin Ahmad, ed. Kuala Lumpur: Dewan Bahasa & Pustaka, 12-23.

Arberry, A. J. 1958. *Classical Persian Literature.* London: Allen & Unwin Ltd.

———. 1972. *Sufism: An Account of the Mystics of Islam.* London: Georg Allen & Unwin Ltd.

———. 1977. *The Doctrine of the Sufis.* Translated from the Arabic, *Kitab al-Ta'arruf li-madhhab ahl al-tasawwuf* of Abu Bakr al-Kalabadhi (10th century). Cambridge: Cambridge University Press.

Ardalan, Nader and Laleh Bakhtiar. 1973. *The Sense of Unity: The Sufi Tradition in Persian Architecture.* Publication of the Center for Middle Eastern Studies, No. 9. Chicago: University of Chicago Press.

Ardalan, Nader. 1998. "The Paradise Garden Paradigm." In *Consciousness and Reality: Studies in Memory of Toshihiko Izutsu.* Ed. Sayyid Jalal al-Din Ashtiyani, et al. Tokyo: Iwanami Shoten Publishers, 97-127.

Baharudin Ahmad. 1992. *Sastera Sufi.* Kuala Lumpur: Dewan Bahasa & Pustaka.

Bakhtiar, Laleh. 1976. *Sufi: Expressions of the Mystic Quest.* New York: Thames & Hudson.

Barakat, Heba Nayel. 2003. *Between Eden and Earth: Gardens of the Islamic World.* Kuala Lumpur: Islamic Arts Museum Malaysia.

Bhagavad-Gita As It Is, The. 1971. Trans. His Divine Grace A.C. Bhaktivedanta Swami Prabhupada. Manila: The Bhaktivedanta Book Trust.

Bhagavad Gita, The. 2002. Trans.. Srimath Swami Chidbhavananda. Trichirapalli, India.

Blaikie, Norman. 1995. *Approaches to Social Enquiry.* Cambridge: Polity Press.

"Book I. Story XV. Counsels of Reserve given by the Prophet to his Freedman Zaid." http://www.intratext.com/IXT/ENG0134/_PG.HTM Masnavi I Ma'navi (2 August 2003).

Braginsky, V. I. 1993. "The Religious Canon as the Basis of Literary Traditions in Medieval Cultures of the East." *Alam Melayu* (Malay World), *Jurnal Akademi Pengajian Melayu* (Journal of the Academy of Malay Studies) 1, no. 1: 73-95.

———. 1998. "*Yang Indah, Berfaedah dan Kamal: Sejarah Sastra Melayu Dalam Abad 7 - 19* (The Beautiful, the Gainful and the Perfect: The History of Malay Literature of the 7-19 Centuries). Jakarta: *INIS*: 621-622, fn 90.

———. 2004. Examiner's Comments to PhD Thesis, p. 6.

Burckhardt, Titus. 1973. *An Introduction to Sufi Doctrine.* Trans.. D.M. Matheson. Lahore: Sh. Muhamad Ashraf.

———. 1976. *Art of Islam: Language and Meaning.* Trans.. J. Peter Hobson. Westerham, Kent, UK: World of Islam Festival Trust.

———. 1987. *Mirror of the Intellect: Essays on Traditional Science and Sacred Art.* Trans.. and ed. William Stoddart. Albany: SUNY Press.

Chenu, M.D. 1983. *Nature, Man and Society in the Twelfth Century.* Chicago and London: University of Chicago Press.

Coomaraswamy, Ananda K. 1981. *Figures of Speech or Figures of Thought: Collected Essays on the Traditional or "Normal" View of Art.* Second series. New Delhi: Munshiram Manoharlal Publishers.

———. 1985. *The Dance of Shiva: Fourteen Indian Essays.* New York: Dover.

———. *What is Civilisation? And other Essays.* 1989. Suffolk: Golgonooza Press.

Dasgupta, Shashi Bhushan. 1969. *Obscure Religious Cults.* Calcutta: Firma K.L.M Private.

Dimock, Edward C., Jr. 1991. *The Place of the Hidden Moon: Erotic Mysticism in the Vaisnava-sahajiya Cult of Bengal.* Delhi: Motilal Banarsidass.

"The First Eighteen Verses of Rumi's Masnevi." http://www.iran-shahr.com/ney.htm (March 2003).

Friedlander, Ira. 1975. *The Whirling Dervishes.* New York: Macmillan Publishing.

"The Fundamentals of Sufism."
http://www.qss.org/articles/sufism/sufi8.html (14 July 1999).

Gadamer, Hans-Georg. 1989. *Truth and Method.* Revised 2nd edition. New York: Crossroad.

Ghazi bin Muhammad. 2001. "The Traditional Doctrine of Symbolism." *Sophia: The Journal of Traditional Studies* 7, no. 1 (Summer): 85-108.

Greenblatt, Stephen. 1990. *Shakespearean Negotiations.* Oxford: Clarendon Press.

Guénon, René. 1991. *The Great Triad.* Trans. Peter Kingsley. Cambridge: Quinta Essentia.

———. 1995. *Fundamental Symbols: The Universal Language of Sacred Science.* Trans. Alvin Moore, Jr. Rev. and ed. Martin Lings. Oxford: Quinta Essentia.

Hahn, Lewis Edwin et al., eds. 2001. *The Philosophy of Seyyed Hossein Nasr.* The Library of Living Philosophers, XXVII. Chicago: Southern Illinois University.
http://216.122.238.174/soulculture/vol8_4/011v8_4killguru.htm (12 August 2003).

Hein, Norvin. 1993. *Religions of the World.* Bedford: St. Martins.

Herlihy, John A. 2003. "Recreating the First Man."
http://www.authorsden.com/visit/viewarticle.

asp?AuthorID=1363 (15 October 2003).

"Kavi Jayadeva's Gitagovinda." 1989. Songs by Hemanta Mukherjee et al., music by Sunil Satpathy. Bombay: Sight and Sound.

Kinsley, David. 1975. *The Sword and the Flute: Kali and Krsna, Dark Visions of the Terrible and the Sublime in Hindu Mythology.* Berkeley: University of California Press.

———. 1979. *The Divine Player: A Study of Krsna Lila.* Delhi: Motilal Banarsidass.

Levy, Reuben. 1969. *An Introduction to Persian Literature.* New York: Columbia University Press.

Lings, Martin. 1981. *What is Sufism?* London: Allen and Unwin.

———. 1987. *The Eleventh Hour.* Cambridge: Quinta Essentia.

———. 1991. *Symbol and Archetype: A Study of the Meaning of Existence.* Cambridge: Quinta Essentia.

———. 1999. "Frithjof Schoun and René Guénon." *Sophia: The Journal of Traditional Studies* 5, no.2: 9-24.

———. 2003 "René Guénon." Transcript of a lecture at the Prince of Wales Institute in London, and sponsored by the Temenos Academy. http://www.sophiajournal.com/Vol1Num1/Article02.html (30 June 2003).

Maertens, James W. "Krishna's Flute: The Pied Piper and Divine Ecstasy." http://www.bardwood.com/KRISHNA.HTML (4 August 2003).

Marcoulesco, Ileana. 1993. "Mystical Union." In *The Encyclopedia of Religion.* Ed. Mircea Eliade. New York: Macmillan Publishing Company.

McGregor, R. S. 1973. "*Raspancadhyayi*: The Round Dance of Krishna." In Nanddas, *The Round Dance of Krishna and Uddhav's Message.* Trans. McGregor. London: Luzac & Co.

Md. Salleh Yaapar. 1988. "A Pilgrimage into the Orient: *Ta'wil* as a Form of Islamic Hermeneutics." *Muslim Education Quarterly* 5, no. 3 (Spring):44-49.

———. 1995. *Mysticism and Poetry: A Hermeneutical Reading of the Poems of Amir Hamzah.* Kuala Lumpur: Dewan Bahasa & Pustaka.

Mishra, Vijay. 1998. *Devotional Poetics and the Indian Sublime.* Albany: State University of New York Press.

Muhammad Bukhari Lubis. 1990. *Bunga Rampai Sastera Parsi.* Kuala Lumpur: Dewan Bahasa dan Pustaka.

———. 1993. *The Ocean of Unity:* Wahdat Al-Wujud *in Persian, Turkish and Malay Poetry.* Kuala Lumpur: Dewan Bahasa & Pustaka.

Myers, Jack and Michael Simms. 1989. *The Longman Dictionary of Poetic Terms.* New York: Southern Methodist University.

Nasr, Seyyed Hossein. 1991. *Islamic Spirituality: Foundations.* New York: Herder & Herder.

"Nizami." http://www.omegapub.com/nizami.html (17 September 2001).

"Nizami Ganjavi." http://vwww.scf.usc.edu/~baguirov/nizami2.html (14 July 1999).

"Nizami Ganjavi: Thinker and Poet of Genius." (1141-1209). http://www.zerbaijan.com/nizami1.htm (14 July 1999).

Nurbakhsh, Javed. 1984. *Sufi Symbolism: The Nurbakhsh Encyclopedia of Sufi Terminology.* Vol. 1. Translated by Leonard Lewisohn and Terry Graham. London: Khaniqahi-Nimatullahi Publications.

Oldmeadow, Kenneth 2000. *Traditionalism: Religion in the Light of the Perennial Philosophy.* Colombo: Sri Lanka Institute of Traditional Studies.

Omkarananda Ashram. "Online Sanskrit Dictionary." http://sanskrit.bhaarat.com (21 August 2003).

Palmer, Richard E. 1969. *Hermeneutics.* Evanston: Northwestern University Press.

Prabhupada, Swami, trans. 1971. *The Bhagavad Gita As It Is.* Manila: The Bhaktivedanta Book Trust.

Preminger, A., and T.V. F. Brogan, eds. 1993. "Hermeneutics." In *The New Princeton Encyclopedia of Poetry and Poetics.* New Jersey: Princeton University Press.

Preminger, A., and T.V. F. Brogan, eds. 1993. "Symbolism." In *The New Princeton Encyclopedia of Poetry and Poetics.* New Jersey: Princeton University Press.

Quito, Emerita S. 1990. *The Philosophers of Hermeneutics.* Manila: De La Salle University Press.

Ricouer, Paul. 1972. "The Symbol Gives Rise to Thought." In *Ways of Understanding Religion.* Ed. Walter H. Capps. New York: The Macmillan Company.

———. 1981. *Hermeneutics and the Human Sciences*. Ed. and Trans. John B. Thompson. Cambridge: Cambridge University Press.

———. 1986. "Composition and Interpretation." In *The Relevance of the Beautiful and Other Essays*. Trans. Nicholas Walker, ed. Robert Bernasconi. Cambridge: Cambridge University Press.

Sahi, Jyoti. 1980. *The Child and the Serpent: Reflections on Popular Indian Symbols*. London: Routledge & Kegan Paul.

Schimmel, Annemarie. 1975. *Mystical Dimensions of Islam*. Chapel Hill: The University of North Carolina Press.

———. 1979. *A Dance of Sparks: Imagery of Fire in Ghalib's Poetry*. New Delhi: Ghalib Academy.

———. 1979. "The Ritual of Rebirth." *Parabola* 4 no. 2: 88-89.

———. 1982. *As Through a Veil: Mystical Poetry in Islam*. New York: Columbia University Press.

———. 1997. *Nightingales Under the Snow*. 2nd Edition. New York: Khaniqahi Nimatullahi Publications.

Schuon, Frithjof. 1969. *Spiritual Perspectives and Human Facts*. Trans. Macleod Matheson. London: Perennial Books.

———. 1976. *Islam and the Perennial Philosophy*. Trans. J. Peter Hobson. Westerham: World of Islam Festival Publishing Company.

———. 1984. *The Transcendent Unity of Religions*. Wheaton, Ill.: Theosophical Publishing House.

———. 1994. *Understanding Islam*. Bloomington: World Wisdom Books.

———. 1995. *Stations of Wisdom*. Bloomington: World Wisdom Books.

———. 1995a. *The Transfiguration of Man*. Bloomington: World Wisdom Books.

http://www.frithjof-schuon.com/interview.htm (24 October 2003).

Sharma, Satya Pal. http://www.spiritualworld.org/hinduism/index.htm (2 August 2003).

Singer, Milton. 1966. "The Radha-Krishna *Bhajanas* of Madras City." In Milton Singer, ed., *Krishna: Myths, Rites, and Attitudes*. Chicago: University of Chicago Press, 90-138.

Singer, Milton, ed. 1966. *Krishna: Myths, Rites, and Attitudes*. Chicago: University of Chicago Press.

Sivaraman, Krishna, ed. 1995. *Hindu Spirituality: Vedas Through Vedanta*. New Delhi: Motilal Banarsidas.

Smith, Huston. 1984. "Introduction." In Frithjof Schuon, *The Transcendent Unity of Religions.* Wheaton, Ill.: Theosophical Publishing House.

———. 1985. *Forgotten Truth: The Primordial Tradition.* New York: Harper Torchbooks.

———. 2001. "Nasr's Defense of the Perennial Philosophy." In *The Philosophy of Seyyed Hossein Nasr.* Ed. Lewis Edwin Hahn, et al. The Library of Living Philosophers, XXVII. Chicago: Southern Illinois University, 139-158.

Stein, Achva Benzinbergn. 1993. "Thoughts Occasioned by the Old Testament." In Mark Francis and Randolph T. Hester Jr., eds., *The Meaning of Gardens: Idea, Place, and Action.* Cambridge, Mass.: MIT Press, 38-45.

Stokes, Jim. "The Story of Joseph in the Five Different Traditions." http://bahai-library.com/articles/stokes.joseph1.html (19 February 2004).

Turner, Colin. 2002. "Layla and Majnun: The Classic Love Story of Persian Literature." http://www.traveltajikstan.com/books/layla_majnun (28 March 2002).

Vivekananda, Swami. 2001. *Bhakti-Yoga: The Yoga of Love and Devotion.* Kolkata: Advaita Ashrama.

———. 2001a. *Jnana Yoga: The Yoga of Knowledge.* Kolkata: Advaita Ashrama.

———. 2002. *Raja Yoga: Conquering the Internal Nature.* Kolkata: Advaita Ashrama.

"What is an Avatar."
http://www.avatara.org/essay.html (21 July 1999).

Wilber, Ken. 1996. *Eye to Eye: The Quest for the New Paradigm.* Boston: Shambala.

Wilson, C.E. 1974. "The Common Ideals of Sufi and Western Poetry." *Islamica* Vol. 1.

Yatiswarananda, Swami. 1989. *Meditation and Spiritual Life.* Bangalore: Sri Ramakrishna Ashrama.

Zahed Sheikholeslami. *Classical Persian Music.* Translated and abridged by N. Fotouhi, in "Mahnameh," *The Monthly Publication of the Iranian Association of Boston,* Issue No. 82/December 1997. http://www.iranonline.com/IAB/interest.htm (22 September 2003).